Does Mass Communication Change Public Opinion After All?

Does Mass

Change Public

After All?

A New Approach

Communication

Opinion

To Effects Analysis

James B. Lemert

Nelson-Hall nh Chicago

Library of Congress Cataloging in Publication Data

Lemert, James B   1935–
  Does mass communication change public opinion after all?

  Includes bibliographical references and index.
  1. Public opinion polls.   2.   Attitude change.
3.   Mass media—Psychological aspects.   4.   Mass media—
Social aspects—United States.   5.   Mass media—Political
aspects—United States.   I.   Title.
HM261.L49   303.3′8   80–23826
ISBN 0–88229–474–1   (cloth)
ISBN 0–88229–764–3   (paper)

Copyright © 1981 by James B. Lemert

Manufactured in the United States of America

10   9   8   7   6   5   4   3   2   1

KH
12-14-82

For Rosalie and Dad

Contents

Preface

This book is meant for audiences in several social sciences, including political science, mass communication research, and sociology.

Because the book addresses basic problems with the public opinion research done by each of these disciplines, it runs the risk of giving the impression that "acquaintance with" has been mistaken for mastery of all these fields. Let me assure you that it has been truly chastening to discover, in the course of preparing this book, that many of the ideas herein had already appeared in print,[1] in a discipline outside my own, many years before I began writing.

If nothing else, though, my belated discovery that somebody else had already said it—and often had said it better—made it clear to me that the risks of arrogance must be taken. The literature of public opinion in each field often revealed that I was not alone in my blissful ignorance.

So one purpose of this book is to shorten the length of time it takes for the diffusion of information and ideas from one discipline to others. But if that were my only purpose, this book would have been written and organized quite differently. It is very likely that all of us have missed the impact of the mass media on public opinion because we have misconstrued the nature of the public opinion process. Thus, this book takes a rather different approach to conceptualizing public opinion, and the result is a rather different agenda of research projects. Chapters 3 through 9 especially, present agendas of research ideas.

First impressions of this book may be misleading, especially to someone who simply samples it. I ask the reader to bear with me through all ten chapters. I hope the experience will be nearly as rewarding to the reader as the writing was for me.

Let me thank several people who, in diverse ways, helped with the preparation of this book. John Orbell introduced me to the political science literature. I hope his colleagues will forgive him. Michael Robinson read and criticized drafts of Chapters 1, 2, and 6. Erwin Atwood and Keith R. Sanders led me to crystallize some of the ideas in this book for a roundtable discussion in Chicago, and the feedback from that discussion was helpful.

A number of my former students helped sharpen some of the ideas in this book, and I'm afraid if I tried to list them all I'd surely leave some out. But some students did studies with me, and their names will be reported at appropriate locations. Work on this book began during a sabbatical year, an investment I hope the University of Oregon will figure has paid off. My wife, Rosalie, has served as typist, nag, solace-giver, and intellectual stimulant. Often all at the same time. She knows that I can't thank her enough.

1

The Need for a New Model of How the Media Change Public Opinion

The mass media can, and probably do, change public opinion in the United States. But usually they don't do it in the way we think they have to. Common sense, the polls, and the accumulated mental habits of decades of social research all have led us to single out individual attitude change as both the necessary and the sufficient means of creating change in public opinion on an issue.

Mass media change the outcome of public opinion processes in a number of other ways, however—sometimes as much by what they don't do as by what they do. This book will explore a number of these other ways. Unfortunately, the evidence about these other ways often will be an amalgam of anecdotes and a few more carefully gathered research findings. This evidence is necessary at this time because theorists and mass media researchers often have neglected to study these media effects, have speculated about them without gathering evidence, or have investigated them in ways that seemed to foredoom finding very much. One purpose of this book will be to suggest some more productive areas of study.

As for the attitude-changing effects of mass media, an enormous collection of research findings is available, and we shall use it. But as we shall see later, even highly uniform and widespread changes in people's attitudes toward an issue are neither sufficient nor necessary to create a corresponding change in public opinion.

THE SIMPLE REDUCTIONIST MODEL

Ever since the brilliant work of Lazarsfeld and others at Columbia University in the 1940s, mass communication researchers have been living with an implicit, unarticulated set of assumptions about the relationship between the effects of the media on attitudes and on public opinion. These assumptions stimulated the gathering of a great deal of valuable evidence about media attitude effects, but they also tended toward a simple reductionist position that public opinion is a more-or-less straightforward sum of everybody's attitudes.

For our purposes, we can formulate at least three crucial corollaries of this simple reductionist view of the media and public opinion: First, if mass communication does produce massive attitude change toward an issue, that change is *sufficient* to have produced a change in public opinion. Second—and this is by no means the same as the first—if mass communication has *not* produced attitude change among its audience, public opinion change cannot have occurred. (In other words, attitude change is *necessary* for public opinion change.) Third, the attitudes of all members of media audiences count the same—that is, they are equally important in affecting the outcome of a public opinion process.

This simple reductionist approach, while never formally articulated, became the dominant tradition in mass media research. Other trends also contributed to this tradition. The developing social sciences consciously attempted to copy the data-gathering and testing methods used in the physical and biological sciences.

In the 1940s social psychology successfully applied these methods to the study of individual attitudes and attitude change, but the cost was high. Social psychologist Milton Rokeach suggests, for example, that the much more rapid progress made in the development of attitude measures helped lead the field away from other social psychological concepts, for which convenient measurement devices were slower in developing.[1] For our purposes, then, the early development of social psychology rested largely on the development of convenient operational definitions of attitudes and thereby influenced the direction taken by public opinion researchers.

In the late 1940s and early 1950s, political scientists borrowed from social psychology and produced a series of important survey analyses of individual citizens' attitudes and voting behavior.[2] In the mid-1950s, communication research began to develop as a separate academic discipline influenced heavily by the concepts and foci of social psychology and of one of its own applied fields, speech. In those years, most active speech communication scholars had a background in rhetoric, so they tended to concern themselves with how and whether a communication (often by a source with varying "ethos" or credibility) could change audience attitudes.

The developing mass media research tradition, then, sought to explain media effects on public opinion by means of attitude change. Even today, the single most frequently cited review of the evidence about media effects is Joseph Klapper's *The Effects of Mass Communication,* published in 1960. Klapper's book well represents the implicit, simple reductionist assumptions of the time. In his influential summary, Klapper concluded that "regardless of whether the effect in question be social or individual, the media are more likely to reinforce than to change."[3] In mentioning social and individual effects separately, Klapper's summary was fairly unusual for its time, but the research findings he reviewed concerned only individual-level effects. Therefore, it is hard to see how a summary generalization about the book could have mentioned social-level effects, without qualification or explanation, unless some simple reductionist assumptions had been made.

For our purposes, we will treat any kind of reductionism as the attempt to explain and reconstruct social-level phenomena from individual-level data. The limits of reductionism remain an unsolved and controversial problem today among social scientists—controversial, that is, on those rare occasions when reductionism is still discussed as a problem.[4] Political scientists Campbell, Converse, Miller, and Stokes concede that reconstructing collective events from individual acts has not met with much success.[5] Historian Arnold Toynbee put it a little more strongly, saying that our "ignorance" of how to relate collective and individual phenomena has characterized all scholarly efforts since Aristotle.[6]

A major key to relating individual and social levels appears to be, as Ernest Nagel and others put it, the development of "suitable correspondence rules" linking individual and collective concepts.[7] Most often, media researchers have embedded simple reductionist assumptions in their problem selection and analysis and have transmitted their assumptions to their students without even articulating them. We are entitled to the suspicion that, while many social scientists would have been a little uncomfortable with their simple reductionist "correspondence rules" if they had been required to make them explicit, the obvious successes of research in this tradition have rarely made it seem necessary to articulate and then to examine these rules. The three corollaries listed earlier—that attitude change is sufficient and necessary for public opinion change and that everybody's attitudes count the same—in effect are three such correspondence rules.

The reductionist effort to relate individual and social levels is not necessarily questioned here. In the field of public opinion, at least, this book will try to suggest some possible correspondence rules for converting individual attitude effects into public opinion effects. It will become obvious as we proceed that much more work remains to be done on these new "rules." But, as this book will show, rejecting simple reductionism is not at all incompatible with empirical research. In fact, using the approach to generate hypotheses is one of my chief aims.

In addition to the mental habits of media researchers, the simultaneous (but not entirely coincidental) development of the polling business helped promote a simple reductionist model of public opinion. For commercial reasons, preelection polls became a "loss leader" for pollsters in the 1940s. Today, polls have such a long record of generally successful prediction of elections that they form a key part of quite profitable businesses specializing in political campaigns. The model of public opinion implicit in polls is a simple reductionist one that now also goes well beyond election results to nonelectoral issues and trends: Public Opinion is treated as a set of percentages projected to a population.

A generation of social scientists now has grown to professional maturity without ever seeing a modern critic of polls focus on much besides the quality and representativeness of poll projections; the underlying model itself has not been seriously questioned since the late 1940s.[8] In his 1967 presidential address to the American Association for Public Opinion Research, Leo Bogart hinted at such criticism, but the book he later published as an expansion of these remarks seemed to back away from such a complaint: ". . . our understanding of public opinion is inseparable today . . . from the findings of public opinion surveys. . . ."[9]

Never mind, for the moment, that polls are vulnerable whenever we try to apply them to nonelectoral political life. Never mind also that their election predictions are notoriously vulnerable to changes in historical conditions. It is possible to accept poll results (1) as an indicator of public opinion under certain conditions and (2) as an indicator of population attitudes—*without in either case accepting the underlying simple reductionist model of public opinion.* We shall see how these things can be done in Chapters 2 and 9.

At the same time that new media research traditions and polling techniques were being developed and legitimized, the ranks of competent critics of the underlying simple reductionist model were thinned by age, career changes, and loss of confidence created by their inability to supply an alternative research strategy. Probably the last major criticism of the underlying public opinion model was provided in 1947 by Blumer, who felt forced to concede that he was hard pressed to suggest research techniques for the older model of public opinion he felt was realistic.[10] As long ago as 1937, Allport was flaying the "fictions" and "blind alleys" embedded in the older approach to public opinion that was then prevalent among journalists and scholars.[11]

In retrospect, then, we shouldn't have been surprised that the approach the polls embodied should have been regarded as a welcome, operationally viable alternative to the vague "group mind" tradition preceding it. Significantly, however, the single methodological suggestion Blumer *was* able to make was used two decades later by two political scientists, Warren Miller and Donald Stokes. The results of their study, and a succeeding one, can be interpreted as supporting some of the arguments made by Blumer.[12] But there was no sign that the political scientists involved had heard or read Blumer's argument.

Symptoms of the Model's Inadequacy

It would be both misleading and unfair to ignore several recent signs of dissatisfaction with what the prevailing research tradition has delivered to us.

Nimmo notes that the prevailing media effects tradition assumes that attitude change is necessary to produce voting change. He argues that, since researchers find that the media are unlikely to change attitudes, their results do not adequately account for those voting changes that do occur during a campaign. He believes that elections are won by breaking through the "weak perceptual barriers" of relatively uninvolved and uninformed voting blocs and getting them to view the alternative candidate as a better representative of their own basic values than the candidate of their own party.[13] Nimmo argues that the resulting "image" campaigns, which rely heavily on superficial television exposure of candidates and feedback from polls, have the effect of altering voting behavior *without* altering attitudes. It is often difficult to see how Nimmo's "perceptual" effects of mass communications would differ from an attitude effect, but that is beside the point.

My purpose here is to show that social scientists are beginning to reflect dissatisfaction with the ability of the traditional media effects approach to account for the social impact of mass media.

Blumler and McLeod explicitly criticized what they termed the " 'limited effects' model" of mass media impact, a model they attribute to Lazarsfeld et al.[14] Their panel study of 1970 voter turnout in Leeds, Great Britain, suggests that mass communication both increased and decreased turnout among young voters.

Another symptom of dissatisfaction is provided by the developing research field concerned with the "agenda-setting" function of the media. Like Nimmo, agenda-setting researchers seem to start by accepting the premise that the media aren't likely to change attitudes; but then they look for some other things that the media do change. In their original agenda-setting study, McCombs and Shaw found the issues given prominence by the media in the 1968 presidential campaign also were the issues that uncommitted voters thought were the most important in that campaign.[15] Shortly thereafter, McLeod, Becker, and Byrnes disputed some of these findings,[16] but this relatively new line of research has shown no signs of ending with the earlier findings cited here.

A dramatic rediscovery among media researchers has been the "new" interest area of "political communication." In the early 1970s, both the Association of Education in Journalism and the International Communication Association formed political communication interest groups in their organizations. What these researchers seem to have most in common is the desire to look for additional political effects to add to the list of attitude effects produced by the mass media. Political communication researchers who are members of these two organizations have produced a noticeable increase in references to Walter Lippmann's ideas about how the media construct "fictions,"—that is, constructed versions of political events, issues, and personalities.[17] These representatives of reality are said to be the stimuli to which political actors respond (see Chapter 3).

Political scientists also appear to have an increasing interest in the mass media. Patterson and McClure have examined whether television could change voters' minds.[18] Until recently, those few political scientists who were concentrating on studies of mass communication published their results in journals outside of political science, such as *Public Opinion Quarterly*. Now, however, several major political science journals seem actively to be seeking media-oriented research papers. Recently, for example, Miller, Goldenberg and Erbring matched newspaper content differences with survey response differences in an effort to test newspaper effects on trust/efficacy feelings.[19]

It seems fair to say that the signs of dissatisfaction cited so far probably reflect unhappiness with the failure of the simple reductionist research strategy to test all the media effects it should have tested; the dissatisfaction does not seem to have been with the underlying assumptions themselves. For example, Blumler and McLeod, in disputing what they (and others) term the "limited effects" model of media impact, seem not to be disputing the underlying simple reductionist model itself. Their concern seems to be whether researchers have prematurely closed the book on the list of media effects, and they want to add some effects to the list. And, in a tightly reasoned and elegant attack on the "limited effects model" Chaffee and Choe recently showed that previous researchers had prematurely excluded the possibility that the mass media can help important numbers of people to make up their minds about who to vote for, during the campaign itself. (One of the findings regularly reported had been that almost everybody makes up their mind about their candidate either long before the fall campaign starts or on a last-minute whim.) What Blumler-McLeod and Chaffee-Choe apparently have in common is a challenge to the list of effects allowed by Klapper, but implicit agreement with Klapper about what to do with that list, once determined.[20]

Even the uses and gratifications approach illustrates the same point. A principal concern seems to have been to *locate* people who will be most susceptible to attitude change. These persons then are segregated and studied separately. Presumably the reason previous research failed to find strong media effects was that these "susceptibles" were mixed together with people who were using the mass media for other purposes. Again, it is the statements about media effects on individuals that are challenged, not the model underlying both new and old statements.

Similarly, a renewed interest in the way the media may help provide political socialization[21] *adds* evidence about an "extra" effect (i.e., attitude formation) to what we think we already know. But it does not change the way we translate individual-level effects into social ones. In Chapter 4, the reader will encounter some additional results suggesting that the mass media *can* have dramatic attitude formation/change effects. But in the case of this book, it is not *necessary* that the media have these effects. And, again, it is not even sufficient for public opinion change that such effects be produced (see Chapter 5).

However, a few stirrings of restlessness may concern the underlying simple reductionist model itself, though it is sometimes hard to tell.

In his recent presidential address to the American Political Science Association, Wahlke asserted that political behavior research had, among its other failings, consistently ignored level-of-analysis concerns. However, the remedies suggested concerned the other failings and, if anything, might worsen reductionist difficulties by concentrating on using bio-physiological concepts.[22]

Political communications researcher Maxwell E. McCombs wrote that traditional effects studies "typically . . . fragmented the on-going process of communication. . . . What has passed for . . . theory has been, in reality, a loose collection of orientations toward data and a few empirical generalizations."[23] Unfortunately, the examples of promising new approaches cited were on the "let's add this one to the list" type.

British political scientist Colin Seymour-Ure has explicitly criticized our narrow focus on individual attitude change and has added a number of elite effects to the list. More importantly, he argues that a number of social-level effects have been ignored. In this connection, he lists individual-level and social-level effects.[24] His list even attempts to take both levels into account at the same time (for example, media effects on the relationship between individuals and bureaucracy).

But I hesitate for at least two reasons to say for certain that he is trying to do more than add to a list which may be incomplete, but which itself is unchallenged. First, despite the fact that the list of effects has been broken down into individual-individual, individual-political system, individual-group, group-group, and group-system categories, each effect has been treated as if it were a single effect. There appears to have been *no effort to construct new "correspondence rules" for the same effect at two different levels of analysis.* In that sense, Seymour-Ure's approach might be regarded as still accepting a simple reductionist model. Second, most of the individual-level anecdotes he plugs into his list concern well-known political figures such as Richard Nixon and Edmund Muskie. Little attention is paid to effects on more ordinary members of the political system, so we are left to wonder how he would relate these individual effects to higher levels of analysis.

However, one relatively new approach may, in some of its applications and interpretations, represent an important departure from simple reductionism in the social sciences: "coorientation" research.

It would be misleading to say that a single data-gathering and conceptual approach characterizes coorientation research. But in very general terms, the coorientation school feels that mass media researchers, in their preoccupation with individual audience members' reactions to communications, have ignored higher-level units of analysis. These important higher-level units are created by comparing the *joint* attitudes and perceptions of two or more individuals who are *co*orienting themselves toward each other and toward some attitude object. For example, does each perceive accurately how the other feels about the object? Does each think the other agrees with him or her? If the answer to both questions is yes, does each know that the other knows he knows, and so on? It is possible to generate an enormous set of higher-level units in this way. The process creates variables that cannot be reconstituted from data provided by the individual respondent alone. Probably it will be a number of years before we can evaluate the usefulness of this approach.

So far, at least, the coorientation approach has been used somewhat more often for analysis of two-person groups than for analysis of the linkage between public opinion and decision-makers.[25] The latter analysis will be a major focus of this book.

Scheff and McLeod and Chaffee have pointed out some of the major conceptual and analytical problems involved in comparing the orientations of large aggregates of people (i.e., "public opinion") with those of an individual decision-maker.[26] Let me add some criticisms. For one thing, which people are compared with the decision-maker? Everybody—or what amounts to the same thing—a sample survey of everybody? Just the people who have expressed their attitudes to the decision-maker—in that sense, the only ones who have tried to *co*orient with him? For another thing, how do you determine the "dominant" orientation of this aggregate? The majority view? The plurality, if not a majority? On and on go the problems in coorientation research—problems that may have been settled much more often under pressure of having to define concepts operationally than in light of theoretical considerations. We will return briefly to consideration of the coorientation approach in Chapter 8.

Coorientation researchers and I have had to face many of the same conceptual problems in our separate approaches to the study of public opinion. In Chapter 2, I offer some of my own answers to some of these conceptual problems.

2

Components of the
Public Opinion Model

*Our knowledge of the microscopic aspects of public opinion must
remain of little avail until the relation of these bits of information
to the operation of the political system in the large can be shown.*
V. O. Key, Jr.

This chapter defines some components that are basic to an analysis of the role of the mass media in the public opinion process.
Some ideas presented here are not new, having appeared in one
form or another in widely scattered and often unappreciated works.

I have tried to resist the temptation to dwell on aspects of the
public opinion process that are not of any particular use in developing the role of mass media. At times, though, it will be necessary to
consider basic problems with what we think we know about certain
nonmedia aspects of the public opinion processes.

Almost of necessity, this chapter runs the risk of disjointedness.
It is composed of a series of definitions, each with a defense and
an explanation. So perhaps a brief overview will be in order before
we begin.

Public opinion will be given a definition that seems unusual at
first glance. The most obvious objections to this definition will be

considered and countered, and an attempt will be made to show that the definition does indeed encompass the kinds of things we usually think of as public opinion, while also having some unique advantages.

Then a distinction will be made between two public opinion situations; they will be termed the *influence framework* and the *election framework*.

Attitudes will be distinguished from public opinion; then attitudes toward issues will be distinguished from attitudes toward political participation. A series of attitude effects will be presented, with special emphasis on a concept called attitude object change.

Two other key elements—participation and power—will also be introduced and defined, with the suggestion that changes in participation and power can easily produce changes in public opinion.

PUBLIC OPINION

Public opinion is a perception imposed by the perceiver on information about citizen attitudes toward a publicly debated issue, personality, candidate, practice, or outcome.

A perception? Is public opinion a subjective phenomenon, then? Yes, it is, in the sense that the perceiver uses a more or less subjective process (1) to try to construct an impression of the current state of public opinion or (2) to try to anticipate a public reaction to a move then being considered. As Turner put it:

> Assessments of public opinion are continuously being made. . . . Since public opinion in an objective sense is a myth, an important aspect of public decision-making consists of accepting or repudiating the various assessments of opinion.[1]

But if the process of perceiving public opinion is indeed subjective, aren't we forced into an impossible research situation, with as many different versions of public opinion as there are people perceiving "it"?

While the process of perceiving public opinion may be subjective, it does not follow that it is idiosyncratic. A large number of political forces act to modify, "correct," or at least set limits to discrepancies among versions of public opinion that may be held by key decision-makers. Not least of these forces is pressure from the news media on decision-makers to define their current perception of public opinion on a controversial issue. And when relatively standardized national poll results are printed and broadcast, they will usually comprise part of the information about attitudes that is taken into account by decision-makers in forming their perceptions. Furthermore, serious misjudgments of public opinion may cost the decision-maker dearly.

In a valuable and neglected study of letter-writing to President Franklin D. Roosevelt, Sussmann reported many cases in which FDR's perception of public opinion on an issue did not coincide with perceptions held by members of Congress. In many cases, FDR pressured recalcitrant legislators by stimulating letter-writing to them by their own constituents:

> Reading this mail, the members of Congress became aware that even in their home districts it was the President, rather than they, who was coming to have first claim on the voters' allegiance. . . . Nor could the congressmen any longer claim a monopoly of knowledge of what the folks back home had on their minds. Roosevelt had new ways of assessing public opinion, including the polls and the mail [to FDR].[2]

But at least twice it was FDR, not the legislators, whose perception of public opinion was too idiosyncratic. His two misperceptions resulted in (1) a "colossal blunder . . . from the standpoint of legislative strategy" and (2) one of his two most notable failures to mobilize public support for a policy he wanted.[3]

Perhaps the ultimate "corrective" for an idiosyncratic perception of public opinion is when a major candidate goes down to ignominious defeat because his election strategy was based on that misperception. Converse, Clausen, and Miller interpret Goldwater's landslide defeat in 1964 as resulting largely from a misperception ". . . of that political reality which becomes important in winning votes and elections."[4] Goldwater's campaign decision-makers were misled by waves of enthusiastic mail, and Goldwater failed to move toward the center of the political spectrum in order to attract more votes.

So idiosyncratic assessments of what public opinion is can be very costly, politically, for key decision-makers.

Note that the political pressures exerted toward consistency are most likely to affect key decision-makers, who will often be elected or unelected government officials or legislators, political party officials, lobbyists, journalists, corporation public relations executives and so on. In cases where it seems necessary to gather and assess information about citizen attitudes, then, the penalty for idiosyncratic perceptions usually is greater for those decision-makers who ought to be most aware of public opinion. It is no accident, then, that the several studies of "pluralistic ignorance" almost uniformily show that the typical "man on the street" has perceptions of public opinion that are grossly discrepant from the information gathered by the researchers.[5] Presumably, key decision-makers' perceptions would have been closer to the mark, but to the best of my knowledge none of the "pluralistic ignorance" research has compared decision-makers' perceptions with those held by citizens under less pressure to be "correct."

In any event, though, my emphasis on key decision-makers means that the number of persons whose public opinion perceptions are critical to the political outcome is greatly reduced most of the time. Therefore, the subjectivity problem—the problem of getting inside the head of the perceiver—begins to shrink to more manageable size.

Nevertheless, it *is* possible to ask many people about their public opinion perceptions, such as in the "pluralistic ignorance" studies cited above. And under some conditions it seems *necessary* to do so. Such conditions came together in the November 1978 statewide tax election in Oregon. On the ballot were two competing property tax relief measures. If both passed, a provision in one of them required that the one receiving the greater majority would be the only one adopted. Voters therefore were placed in the position of having to guess what other voters would do. Based on our interviews with voters leaving the polls, it appears that as many as half the votes one of the two measures got came from people who were more afraid of the other measure's getting a majority than in favor of the one they voted for.[6] Since both measures failed, this was another case of "pluralistic ignorance." In such cases, the ballot itself invites voters to base their decisions on their perceptions of what others would do. The 1980 Carter-Reagan-Anderson race may boil down to the same kind of perceptual situation: Do anti-Reagan voters think Anderson has a chance to win?

Except in unusual circumstances, then, only the perceptions of relatively small numbers of key decision-makers matter much when we consider the linkage between public opinion and public policy. But how do we get at public opinion even if "it" is inside fewer heads? The job has already been done—and several times, at that.

▶ Remember Herbert Blumer? In Chapter 1, we saw that his tentative, relatively diffident suggestion about how researchers could study public opinion was later independently used by a succession of political scientists—including Miller and Stokes and, using the same data, Cnudde and McCrone. Neither pair of researchers referred to Blumer or to the specific problem of measuring a concept called public opinion. As part of a larger study, Miller and Stokes had asked more than one-hundred congressmen for their perceptions of constituency opinion on three broad issues and then tried to see how much influence these perceptions had on the way each legislator voted. Roughly similar kinds of studies have been done with state legislators—obviously influenced by Miller and Stokes' example, not Blumer's research suggestions.

▶ A number of coorientational studies have measured perceptions of public opinion and compared these perceptions with attitudes of members of the relevant public (see Grunig and Stamm[7] for a partial summary). In one study, for example, Martin et al. found that daily newspaper editors in Wisconsin wrote headlines for stories about a student demonstration that were more in accord with their perception of reader views than with their own attitudes toward the student protests.[8] Thus far at least, a number of the coorientational studies done by communication researchers have shown some conceptual difficulties in determining how best to define the "real" state of mind of the relevant public. Nevertheless, these studies clearly have attacked the subjectivity problem, with useful results.

▶ Both congressional and coorientational studies asked decision-makers to describe their perceptions, but other means of getting at subjective impressions of public opinion are available. Sussmann's study of letter-writing to FDR was done after Roosevelt's death. She drew large samples of the input—the letters themselves. She investigated the procedure Roosevelt established to have the letters summarized for him. She was able to reconstruct, from these summaries and from interviews with his associates, some of his perceptions. From the same sources, she was able to infer that Roosevelt placed greater reliance on letters as a source of constituent opinion than on polls, which were then relatively new. And in several cases, Roosevelt's speeches and decisions themselves seemed to have been in response to, or in anticipation of, a version of public opinion he had constructed for himself. In short, although asking decision-makers directly for their perceptions has some methodological advantages, it is not the only available technique.

Sussmann's approach is not the only indirect technique, either. Pressures from journalists and from political colleagues often lead decision-makers to articulate their perceptions of public opinion, whether they want to or not. For instance, the public outcry immediately after the firing of Special Prosecutor Archibald Cox in October 1973 led Presidential Assistant Alexander Haig to characterize public reaction as a "firestorm." Among his concessions (to "public opinion"?) following the "firestorm," President Nixon promised the Senate that he would give its leadership the ability to prevent a summary firing of the next special prosecutor.

Some writers, such as Bruce H. Westley, have asserted that terms "such . . . as 'public opinion' . . . have almost no scientific or intellectual standing today."[9] I would agree that the plethora of meanings given in the past to "public opinion" by different theorists and researchers has been less than helpful. But I would suggest that the pragmatism which seemed to bolster simple reductionist research efforts remains an important criterion to assess any conception of "public opinion." Simple reductionism, in my view, has failed several pragmatic tests. It doesn't explain old media effects findings very well and it hasn't generated much productive new research. So I shall be perfectly content to appeal to pragmatism: if productive new research ideas are not generated by my approach, and if my approach doesn't explain old anomalies and contradictions better, then my conception of public opinion will have failed the test. I hope that we shall see.

What we have seen so far is that empirical research *can* be done using the definition I am proposing. Further, many things we commonly regard as public opinion—polls and elections, for example —are *not* ruled out by this definition, as we shall see in the next section.

ELECTION AND INFLUENCE FRAMEWORKS

Perceptions are imposed on information about citizen attitudes within two general situational frameworks: (1) *elections* and (2) a less structured, much more frequent *influence framework.*

As recurrent ritual, elections help maintain the potency of public opinion as a factor to be considered in the political influence framework. Elections also help maintain the visibility and legitimacy of polls as a reflection of public opinion, a matter we shall discuss in more detail later.

But as an everyday political matter, public opinion perceptions occur in the political influence framework, not in the election framework. In the influence framework, decision-makers may receive information about citizen attitudes in a great variety of forms, either *directly* (e.g., from letters, telegrams, phone calls, feedback from crowds) or *indirectly* (e.g., from reports of informants, polls, editorial expressions, letters to the editor, news media definitions of the state of public opinion).

In the election framework, however, there are very few kinds of information: the voting outcomes, the turnout, and (when done) interviews with people who have just voted. Further, unlike the influence framework, there is broad agreement about the legitimacy of these three limited forms of information in the election framework. There still may be disagreement about what an election result means, but there is broad agreement on the information to be interpreted. The influence framework, however, leaves more room for variation because there is less consensus about what forms of information should be considered. In the influence framework decision-makers can (1) select only some of the diverse forms of information about citizen attitudes, rejecting the rich variety of others and/or (2) weight one form of information more heavily than another (polls versus letters from constituents, for example), while attending to both of them, and/or (3) pay more attention to a poll done by Gallup than a poll done by Harris, or more attention to letters written by literate constituents than by less literate ones—and so on.

Greater perceptual variability is possible in the influence framework than in the election framework for another reason, too. In an election, the issues and the options are generally more simplified than in the influence framework, where the matter may not yet have even reached the formal agenda of the political system.[10] Furthermore, because of the much greater legitimacy attached to election outcomes, decision-makers have a much greater tendency not to dispute whether citizens acquiesce in a decision outcome. In the more unstructured influence framework, however, citizen acquiescence will often be a central point of dispute between winners and losers in a policy decision.

Despite all this, it is a mistake to assume that no variations will occur in the way The Voice of the People is heard in elections. Almost invariably, the news media report alternative interpretations of the meaning of election outcomes, some by contending interest-group spokesmen and others by political reporters and presumably nonpartisan pollsters and social scientists. Further, winning candidates often claim the vote "mandated" various policies they espoused. Although a great deal of older evidence suggests that a majority of voters don't usually make choices on the basis of specific policy alternatives, the mandate is an old political game. Even after elections, then, observers often debate What Public Opinion Was Saying, and especially *why*.

A consistent theme in this book will be that social scientists have tended to regard elections (and their surrogate, the polls) as the principal avenue by which public opinion is expressed. As a means of expressing attitudes, voting has therefore also received much more attention than other acts of participation, and our knowledge of how the media affect public opinion has suffered as a result (see Chapter 5). The reason the influence framework should have received far more attention from public opinion analysts was stated well, ironically, by an election specialist:

> In the American institutional context, direct control [by elections, of public policy] is difficult to imagine. The impact of any or many elections is limited by . . . the diverse checks and bal-

ₛ . . . the proliferation of nonelected public authorities
wers of bureaucracies and courts, and the undisciplined p.
system. *However, the very dispersal of power which makes contr*
unlikely also makes influences more probable. In . . . conflicts anᴗ
bargaining . . . some agency is likely to support the vital interests
of any significant number of voters. (Emphasis added.) [11]

The term "influence framework" is used because, at best, public
opinion is only one of many competing influences on decision-
makers. Sometimes several competing influences all may act in
roughly the same direction (e.g., Burstein and Freudenberg[12]). In
such cases, we are talking primarily about "competition" in a vari-
ance-accounted-for sense. But probably more often we are talking
about public opinion (and compatible "forces") competing *against*
several other potential influences. A wide variety of factors other
than public opinion may be aligned with, or opposed to, public
opinion in the influence framework. Some of the other factors include advice from the decision-makers' colleagues, activities of
lobbyists and interest groups, the decision-makers' own ambitions
and policy preferences, advice from staff, and so on.

In our political culture, most decisions tend to be made in the
influence framework while most of the political razzmatazz re-
volves around Election Day. While there may be such a thing as
Influence Day, it doesn't seem to be scheduled far enough in advance to be printed on the calendars we get from our insurance
agents.

The influence framework is *not* equivalent to what we usually
think of as the period between elections. It includes, as well, information about citizen attitudes that may be coming in during an
election campaign. Such information—letters, polls, donations,
bumper stickers, the size and enthusiasm of crowds—is much more
like influence framework information than like election framework
information. In contrast with election results—where everybody
knows the limited types of information to pay attention to—the information coming in during the campaign is much more variable
and there are few ground rules determining which kinds of information about citizen attitudes are important. In short, the influence framework includes both campaign and noncampaign
periods.[13] The judgmental situation is essentially the same.

other thing before we go on to the next section: My dis-
⌐n between influence and election frameworks is not intended
⌐ule out the consideration of previous election results as one
⌐t of information about citizen attitudes in the influence framework. That is, decision-makers may very well refer to previous
elections during their influence framework considerations. And,
of course, they may very well try to anticipate how voters would
react at the next election. The distinction between the two frameworks is based on major differences in the information available
and in the complexity of the perceptual process.

ATTITUDES

An attitude is a state of affect felt by the individual toward what
is, for that individual, a psychological object.

There are nearly as many definitions of this concept as there are
writers in the field. For example, some distinguish between *opinion*
(what the individual says or puts on a questionnaire) and *attitude*
(what the individual *really* feels). We shall not use the vocabulary
of that particular distinction, though it is obvious that attitude measures often get what the respondent wants to give. The term *opinion*
will be reserved for use in the higher-level term *public opinion*.

As defined, the individual's attitude has two components: the
feeling state (affect) and the object of that feeling state. Let's consider each in turn.

We shall follow traditional attitude theory in characterizing the
affective component as having *direction* and *intensity*. Direction
refers to whether the sign of the affect is positive (favorable),
neutral, or negative. Intensity refers to how positive or negative
the affect is. Does the individual like it a lot, or just a little?

What is a psychological object? Anything that the individual con-
siders to be one: a song, the singer of that song (or maybe both the
song and the singer together), a photo, a time of day, a job, a
house, the idea of world peace, a flower, a poet, Edward Kennedy,
all or some politicians, and so on.

In addition to direction and intensity, attitudes have *salience*.
As used here, salience involves *both* the affective and the attitude
object components. A salient attitude is one on which a large number of other attitudes depend and is usually a rather central attitude

in the daily life of the individual. For example, attitudes toward oneself generally will be more salient than attitudes toward many public affairs issues discussed in mass media. A successful attack on a salient attitude probably would require a much greater amount of reorganization among dependent or related attitudes than a successful attack on a peripheral, isolated attitude object. It might be easier to produce change by reducing the connection between the object of the communication and the salient attitude.[14]

People may hold intense attitudes that are not salient, but the reverse probably is not true. One way to distinguish between salient and intense but peripheral attitudes was demonstrated by Stouffer. During the height of media coverage of the U.S.-USSR Cold War, Stouffer asked a national sample of Americans about what was worrying them. Worries about work, home, and family predominated. Less than 1 percent mentioned the communist threat. Even when the questions were more and more explicit about international political affairs, war, and so on, far less than 10 percent spontaneously mentioned the threat of communism. But when given an attitude intensity question that asked respondents to rate how great a danger American communists were to the country, more than 40 percent rated them a very great danger or a great danger.[15] For the less than 10 percent who spontaneously mentioned communism as worrying them, American communism was probably a salient attitude object. But many more people also rated it strongly as a threat, and we can conclude that these people held attitudes about communism that were roughly as intense, but not as salient.

ATTITUDE EFFECTS

Traditionally, attitude research has tended to concentrate on two kinds of changes in affect—*attitude change* and *attitude reinforcement*—and has tended to view them, at least conceptually, as mutually exclusive phenomena. Somewhat less attention has been paid to two changes that involve the attitude object component—*attitude formation* and *attitude object change*.

Types of Attitude Change

In common-sense terms, we generally think of attitude change only as complete *conversion* from one point of view to its opposite.

In research practice, however, attitude change has generally included much more than conversion. Figure 2.1 illustrates the many kinds of attitude change that researchers tend to treat as the same. Suppose a researcher has respondents rate some concept on an evaluative scale, then presents them with a communication about that concept and has them fill out the scale again.

Very often, the methods researchers use to score shifts in affect lump together into a composite attitude change score all the changes listed below the scale in Figure 2.1. It will be important for us to separate them *when we can.* To complicate the scoring of attitude change even more, researchers often count as attitude change only those shifts *toward* the direction advocated by the communication. When this happens, other shifts we might consider as attitude change are either subtracted from the attitude change score or are tallied separately in categories that may confuse attitude change with attitude reinforcement.

In general, where possible, we will specify the type of attitude change under consideration. Otherwise, the term "attitude change" will have to refer to the most general case—*the movement of affect toward a new sign.*

Attitude Reinforcement

The second general kind of affect shift is attitude reinforcement, defined as an increase in the intensity of affect felt toward an object without a change in sign.

Attitude Formation

The third effect mass communication can have is attitude formation. In principle, attitude formation involves both the recognition of an attitude object and the learning of an affective response to it. A good example of this process occurs when a mother tells a child, "That's a no-no!" Both the object and the affect presumably are communicated in that statement. But attitude formation is not limited to children even though we have surprisingly little clear evidence about the process with adults. For many of us, Rep. Peter Rodino was, in January 1973, a "new" attitude object. The ways in which we attached our own affective response probably

Figure 2.1
Five Types of Attitude Change

Good ——:——:——:——:——:——:——: Bad
| extremely | quite | slightly | neither | slightly | quite | extremely |
| +3 | +2 | +1 | 0 | −1 | −2 | −3 |

Type of Attitude Change	Does Sign Change?	Intensity Up?	Intensity Down?	Examples Before/After
Conversion	yes	no	no	+2 to −2
Super conversion	yes	yes	—	+2 to −3; −1 to +3
Ordinary change	yes	—	yes	+1 to 0; −2 to +1
Minor change	no	—	yes	+2 to +1; −3 to −2
Commitment	yes	yes	—	0 to +1

differed, but affect toward him was learned by millions of Americans as the House impeachment inquiry began. The same would be true of Howard Jarvis in 1978, a man known to relatively few Americans prior to the California "tax revolt."

One reason for ambiguities in evidence about adults' attitude formation is that *formation* may be scored and treated as if it were *change*. Attitude scoring tends to confuse commitment effects with attitude formation. (As we'll see later in this book, I've had to combine formation with change in the study of the "bandwagon" effects. But at least I don't claim the effects to be an attitude change.)

Another cluster of reasons for ambiguities resides in the fact that most of the relatively few studies of attitude formation have placed it within the framework of childhood socialization. Emphasis on socialization of young children, in turn, led to a deemphasis of media impact on attitude formation in two ways.

First, the effect of concentrating on the young has been to pit the mass media against powerful agents of socialization—parents, peers, and schools—at an age when these other agents were thought to be at their greatest power in attitude formation. For example, the prevailing consensus among students of political socialization has been that parents are critical in transmitting to their young children the basic political values that are thought to mold and pervade most of the political attitudes developed in later life.[16] There has been general agreement that, as the child enters school and then adolescence, peers and teachers begin to exert influence. Only fairly recently have researchers rediscovered the opportunity to study the role of mass media in socializing adolescents. Even now, slight attention has been paid to socialization processes among mature adults, and researchers who have concentrated on this group have tended to look at the acquisition of skills and habits rather than attitude formation.[17]

Second, attitude formation is not limited to the socialization process. People habitually recognize new attitude objects and attach an affective response to them whether or not they are being prepared for new social roles!

This brings us to the final general class of attitude effects, attitude object change. It is hard, sometimes, to distinguish attitude formation from object change.

Attitude Object Change

In a sense, attitude object change is the substitution of one attitude object for another. In its purest form, when attitude object change occurs, we would expect both the object and its associated affect to be replaced by an entirely new object and *its* associated affect. The importance of attitude object change is that it might therefore lead to changes in the way we react and behave *without any change in the affect felt toward either the old or the new object*.

Conceptually, both attitude formation and one kind of attitude object change involve the recognition of a new attitude object. It is generally more useful to distinguish between them by whether the affective response is new or whether it has been previously associated with the object. If the affect is also new, it is attitude formation; if old, it is object change.

Perhaps our tendency to create euphemisms represents what I mean by object change in a relatively clear and distilled form. We say an unmarried girl is "in trouble," a euphemism that tends to divert attention from her past behavior to her present predicament. The Nixon administration referred to "protective reaction strikes" in an effort to deemphasize the fact that the United States was still dropping bombs on North Vietnamese and Viet Cong targets after it had declared a bombing halt and to emphasize the defensive character of the air strikes. "Public power" is the term now used to refer to what conservatives bitterly attacked as "socialistic ownership of the means of production" during the Tennessee Valley Authority controversy many years ago. During the Cuban missile crisis, the United States imposed a "quarantine" on Russian ships, studiously avoiding the more warlike term "blockade." Advertising is full of euphemisms. Remember Lanolin (sheep grease)? Presumably people would rather buy the former than the latter. Similarly, it makes a difference whether journalists accept "sidewise waffling" or use the term "recession" when referring to a decline in our gross national product.

Some writers feel that what I am calling attitude object change is not the substitution of one object for another so much as it is a change in the attributes to which one reacts regarding a more or less constant attitude object.

These writers feel that the change in the object is only a substitution of a part (or aspect) for the whole, or of one part for another part. For example, in this view the euphemism "public power" substitutes a more favorable aspect (a utility operated for public benefit) for a less favorable one (ownership by the state). Both aspects are part of the whole. In this interpretation, the euphemism merely elevates the visibility and prominence of one aspect over another. Since most attitude objects in politics and in other kinds of social communication are complex and multidimensional, they are indeed susceptible to shifts in the criteria and dimensions used to judge them. As Newcomb, Turner, and Converse put it:

> We may perceive another person as being, among other things, a good conversationalist, a sloppy dresser, and a likely target when we need to borrow money. Although we may have attitudes toward each of these perceived characteristics separately, we also form attitudes toward the person as a whole, for we cognize him as a whole. . . . The fact that we may have such mixed reactions even to an object that we perceive as a whole at one level . . . means that we may express different attitudes when the cognitive context suggests a less inclusive aspect of the object.[18]

We just don't know enough yet about object change to settle the question whether (or when) object or attributes are exchanged. Prevailing attitude measurement techniques are insensitive to object change, because the only change they allow to show is a change in affect, and many object changes can take place *without* a change in expressed affect. Furthermore, even if object change did produce a change in the affect being expressed on attitude scales, it would be scored as "attitude change" because present attitude measurement devices implicitly assume that the object being asked about is a constant, while only affect is a variable. There is little question that students of attitudes and polling have tended to operate on what Bogart calls a "single opinion" model:

The prevailing model underlying our discipline is that of the single opinion. A person holds an opinion, which he communicates to an interviewer. When he is influenced to change his mind, he replaces his former opinion with another one. This model has the virtue of great simplicity, but it makes no sense, because conflicting and contradictory opinions may be held simultaneously and because they constantly jostle each other for dominance.[19]

Another unsettled question remains about object change. Some writers feel that object change is not really distinct from attitude change. In fact, Newcomb, Turner, and Converse feel that object change is really the primary method of producing attitude change.[20] In this view, new information about the object alters the criteria for evaluating it, leading in turn to changes in affect. Object change then would be a necessary way station on the road to attitude change, and thus always would be reflected indirectly by scales measuring changes in affect.

This would be a more convincing argument if it did not imply satisfaction with measurement practices that are not sensitive to object change except through affect change. What happens if the object changes—perhaps as part of a defensive reaction to a message—while the affect shows no sign of change? This result is quite possible without changes in affect. The implication is that traditional attitude measurement practices would be insensitive to these effects, and Guerrero and Hughes have shown that these effects can and do occur.[21] Rokeach also has cited results that, in my view, suggest that the failure to separate attitude object change from affect change will almost certainly lead us astray.[22]

Unless our methods allow object change to be expressed as easily as affect change, we probably never will be able to settle (1) when or whether objects or attributes change and (2) whether object change is just another way of talking about attitude change.

To detect object change, we need to give respondents the chance to tell us more about the objects they are rating. Edelstein has tried to apply such an approach to the study of how people choose their news media. He gave respondents the chance to express media preferences in relation to specific topics they themselves helped provide, and to say what attributes they were using in their choices.[23] A study by Grothe of "attitude change" among American tourists in the Soviet Union illustrates both how useful open-response items can be and how misleading standard fixed-response items can be. The open-response items allowed respondents to specify aspects of the USSR they liked least and most. For these items, it became apparent that they liked their contact with Russian people a lot, but they still did not like the Soviet government and political system. The scale measuring attitude change used a fixed concept—the USSR—and recorded only a slight net improvement in the favorability of attitudes toward the USSR.[24] This result almost certainly masked the extensive object differentiation shown by the open-ended items.

In summary, we don't yet know enough about attitude structure to settle many questions about object change. But unless we begin to try to isolate object change phenomena, we probably never will know enough.

Attitude object change may be an important effect of messages received through the mass media, especially among normally inactive and relatively unsophisticated persons. At the moment, object change seems the best available concept for explaining how certain changes in public opinion processes are produced. The reason for its importance is that most members of the population do not seem spontaneously to have worked out very many relationships among their political attitude objects.[25] Unlike political elites who consciously use the mass media to articulate issues for others, the great majority of our population may be vulnerable to attitude object change. However, I should point out quickly here that many researchers dispute this picture on nonelites. These researchers feel such a picture greatly underestimates the presence of ideology in the population.[26] Nevertheless, I'd suggest a relatively productive way of testing whether there be mass-elite differences in ideology would be through testing for object change differences.

The way elites and the mass media define issues can have important consequences for a population that seems relatively susceptible to messages directing their attention toward certain relations among attitude objects and away from others. For instance, McClosky, Hoffmann, and O'Hara reported that:

> ... followers of each [major U.S.] party, often ignorant of the issues and their consequences, find it difficult to distinguish their beliefs from those of the opposition and have little reason to be concerned with the consistency of their attitudes. ... In short, if we mean by ideology a coherent body of informed social doctrine, it is possessed mainly by the articulate leadership, rarely by the masses.[27]

Attitude object change, then, is one of several possible effects of the way the mass media *define situations* (Chapter 3).

ISSUE ATTITUDES
vs. PARTICIPATION ATTITUDES

To this point in our discussion of attitude effects you have probably been thinking mostly of attitudes toward objects such as political parties, candidates, issue proposals, the media, and so on. And why not? The topic of this book is public opinion, after all, and what could have more to do with public opinion processes than these kinds of attitude objects? If you agree that this is reasonable, you are in good company. In fact, attitude and attitude change studies historically have been preoccupied with this kind of *issue-centered* attitude.[28] However, the distinction between attitudes toward issues and attitudes toward the behavior of political participation is crucial to understanding how the mass media affect public opinion.

For purposes of this book, issue-centered attitudes are what we normally think of as attitudes in public affairs matters. Issue objects concern such general areas as policy proposals, political groups, candidates, government(s), the quality of life, the presidency and/or the current president, the economy, and so on. Attitudes toward behavior, on the other hand, may include such objects as the situation within which the behavior would have to take place, one's sense of adequacy in performing a given act or acts, the consequences of a given act if successfully completed, and so on. Often, attitudes toward *issues* are the focus of political communication in the media; attitudes toward *behavior* tend not to be, *especially when the behavior involved is participation in the influence framework.*

Judging from the history of thought about attitudes and public opinion, it has always been rather easy to ignore the problem of attitudes toward behavior. In fact, early in the history of social psychology, one of the major justifications for focusing on issue attitudes was the presumption that if one knew about attitudes, one knew about behavior. Attitudes were viewed as more or less decisive predispositions toward behavior. Therefore, what little early work was done on attitudes toward behavior tended to be outside the mainstream of social psychology. Rokeach believes that separating issue attitudes from behavioral attitudes has "severely retarded the growth not only of attitude theory but also of attitude-change theory."[29] In my view, this separation also helped for many years to hide the inadequacy of a simple reductionist approach to mass media and public opinion. It did this by directing our attention away from political participation as a means of communicating citizens' issue attitudes to decision-makers.

Nevertheless, it is now extremely difficult to pretend that issue-type attitudes predict behavior. In a major review of attitude-behavior studies, Wicker concluded: "Most socially significant questions involve overt behavior, rather than people's feelings, and the assumption that feelings are directly translated into action has not been demonstrated."[30]

Equally harsh things have been said by a number of other writers, including Schramm, who seems to have concluded that the discrepancy between attitudes and actions has been so great that it is better not to pay as much attention to attitude effects as to other kinds of media effects.[31]

Another sort of reaction does not deemphasize or dismiss the results of attitude studies. It does just the opposite, in perhaps an unintentionally ironic contrast to the way social psychology originally justified its preoccupation with issue attitudes. Instead of saying that we study attitudes because they predict behavior, this school of thought says, in effect, we study attitudes because they do *not* relate to behavior. A slight variant of this view has also been expressed by Chaffee and others in the communication theory literature.[32]

A number of other writers, however, are making and using the distinction between attitudes toward issues and attitudes toward behavior. Rokeach distinguishes between attitudes toward an "object" (his name for issue objects, as I've defined them) and attitudes toward the "situation." The situation generally is a social context that may or may not be regarded as an appropriate opportunity for behavioral expression of issue attitudes. Thus, Rokeach feels issue attitudes and situational attitudes "affect behavior in direct proportion to their perceived importance with respect to each other."[33]

Fishbein also proposes that behavior is a joint function of issue attitudes and situational factors, but his vocabulary and level of analysis differ slightly from those of Rokeach. For Fishbein, behavior is a function of (1) attitude toward behavior, (2) "normative beliefs" (which include what I am calling issue attitudes) and (3) motivation to comply with "normative beliefs."[34]

In a test of Fishbein's approach, Ajzen has reported results which appear to show that there is not much difference between Rokeach's formulation and Fishbein's more fully elaborated approach. The motivations aroused by the social situation appeared to determine whether attitudes toward behavior or "normative beliefs" best predicted behavior.[35]

EFFICACY AS AN ATTITUDE TOWARD PARTICIPATION

A major focus of American political science almost from the outset was a kind of behavior: the act of voting. Ironically, though, it was not until the marriage of social psychological and survey approaches to political science that scales were developed to measure attitudes toward voting and other acts of political participation. Since then, and for thirty years, political scientists have been using a measure they call *political efficacy,* and probably it is still the single most frequently used measure of attitudes toward participation. Political efficacy refers to the individual's feelings that he or she can accomplish things through political participation. Generally, efficacy feelings have been strongly related to the act of voting and to even more active kinds of campaign activities.[36] The relationship has been found so often and in so many different elections that we can probably feel safe in saying that, if two people have exactly the same strength of voting preferences, the one with the greater sense of efficacy will be more likely to vote.

Remember when I said that public opinion was a perception imposed on information about citizen attitudes? Voting is one way the citizen can communicate some information about his or her issue attitudes, but it is hardly the only way. Rarely—and only very recently—has political science extended its interest in efficacy and participation beyond election campaigns to the rest of the influence framework (see Chapter 5). And rarely has its interest in measuring attitudes toward participation gone beyond extremely general attitudes, such as feelings of efficacy, to measures that either incorporate the situation in which participation is to take place or specify the particular act of participation.

In Chapters 5 and 6, we shall look some more at how journalists and political communications influence participation by means of intermediary effects on issue attitudes, attitudes toward participation, or both.

PARTICIPATION

Participation in public opinion processes is the act of expressing issue-related attitudes, either by voting in the election framework or by a great variety of acts in the influence framework.

Most frequently, participation is necessary in order for the attitude to become visible to the decision-maker. But because of the way we have defined public opinion, information about citizen attitudes can come to a decision-maker *without* active *participation* by citizens on one occasion: *when and if the results of a survey are either made public or transmitted privately to some decision-maker.*

In the election framework, the basic form of participation is the act of voting. As mentioned earlier, other activities during the election campaign are not included in the election framework because the processes of imposing a perception on information about the extent and intensity of support are much more like those taking place in the influence framework. Further, voting participation seems to comprise a distinctly different mode of political participation, separable from several other distinct modes.[37]

Voting is probably the easiest and most routinized act of participation. Journalists routinely provide far more help to voting in elections than they do to any form of participation in the influence framework, probably because they feel it admirable and nonpartisan to facilitate voter turnout (see Chapter 6). Compared to many other countries, though, voting turnout is low in U.S. national elections, and even lower for state and local elections.

Even though voting participation is relatively low in the United States, other forms of participation occur even less often. While all their percentages may be too high because of social desirability factors, Verba and Nie estimate that more than five times as many people vote regularly as contact public officials to influence them concerning some issue.[38]

We are only beginning to get some careful evidence on participation outside of election campaigns. One estimate by Verba, Nie, and Kim is that about 20 percent of Americans have at some time contacted public officials, but Milbrath's 1977 book puts the figure at closer to 14 percent.[39] One of the major reasons for our lack of reliable information on such participation has been the fact that political science until recently examined participation primarily during relatively high-stimulus election campaigns. We shall return to this and other points about participation in Chapter 5.

In the late 1960s and early 1970s, evidence about participation outside of campaigns began slowly to accumulate. Verba and Brody reported that active participation regarding the war in Vietnam may have been visible, but it was not extensive. In their survey of 1,499 respondents in the spring of 1967, only eight people —one-half of 1 percent—said they had taken part in a demonstration.[40] This tiny percentage included acts of participation that may have occurred only once during a period of years.

How is it possible to believe that "the streets were filled with demonstrators," then, if they were such a small portion of the population? Even one-half of 1 percent is a lot of people when it is multiplied by the total number of adult Americans: Verba and Brody project it to 750,000 demonstrators. That number would be right up there with even the truly immense civil rights "March on Washington" in the heyday of Martin Luther King. It doesn't take nearly that many demonstrators to send nervous quivers through elected officials. And it would be a good hypothesis that extensive television coverage of demonstrations had the effect of inflating their visibility and extent.

It is rare for a commercial polling organization to ask about participation in the influence framework, but a Gallup poll seems to have been done several weeks after President Nixon's dismissal of Special Prosecutor Archibald Cox. Some 30 percent said they had written or telegraphed a congressman or senator about Watergate. While this isn't a large percentage of all Americans, it would project to 4.2 million American adults.[41] The Gallup survey did not make clear how much of the reported participation (messages to Congress) was in response to the Cox firing. Nevertheless, we do have some supplementary information. Western Union reported that more than 450,000 "Public-Opinion Mailgrams" were sent to Congress, Archibald Cox, and the White House in the period immediately after the firing.[42] Congressmen, according to news reports, reported being "swamped" by the flood of mail and telegraph messages. The White House was impressed enough to call it a "firestorm" and change its Watergate tactics for a time. Compared to the normal volume of public opinion messages, then, it does not take a large percentage of participating Americans to make a considerable impression in the influence framework.

One reason that even smaller amounts of participation often make devastating impressions on decision-makers is that, unlike elections, our political system is not well set up to cope with unstructured, unanticipated, and nonroutinized forms of participation. Thus, high participation incidents in the influence framework *exceed the capacity of decision-makers to cope routinely with the "flood" of information about citizen attitudes.*

POWER

We turn now from attitude and participation to power, a third component of public opinion. We have already seen that the act of participation means that some attitudes are visible to decision-makers while others are not. In this sense, participation gives these holders of visible attitudes more *power* than others. But we won't concentrate on this meaning of power. Instead, I'll mean by power the relative quality of the participation. Since we will often need to refer to the concept of participation quality, it will be convenient to use the label "power."

As Dreyer and Rosenbaum put it, "If opinion is to affect policy, it must make its way through the political system to decision-makers, and the system does not give equal weight to all opinion." They stress two distinct but related processes: (1) methods "by which opinion flows into the governmental structure . . . and affects the political decision-maker's assumptions or perceptions about the state of public opinion" and (2) "the way in which policy is made *within* the government structure and how public opinion is integrated into this policy."[43]

Largely because studies of public opinion and public policy have tended to concentrate primarily on the second process—see, for example, Luttbeg[44]—not enough attention has been paid to the first. And as for power research itself, many writers recently have criticized its almost exclusive preoccupation with whether the powerful succeed in getting decision-makers to do what they want them to do.[45] Power is just as crucial in determining whether issues become subject to debate (and popular participation) and in determining who participates. In my vocabulary, such determinations clearly are related to controlling the forms of information about citizen attitudes that may be available to decision-makers. The term "power," then, will be used merely as a convenient label for some important differences among actual or potential participants.

In the public opinion process, power is the relative ability of political actors (*a*) to block or initiate public discussion of potential issues, (*b*) to influence perceptions of public opinion held by key decision-makers once an issue "goes public," (*c*) to define issues and options under discussion, (*d*) to influence participation by others, and (*e*) to induce decision-makers to adopt a given policy. Abilities *a* through *d*, at least, greatly affect the kinds of incoming information about citizen attitudes. Obviously, though, there is some overlap between *e* and the others. For example, suppose you want decision-makers to keep the present policy by blocking discussion of a potential issue (*a*)? Or you want them to organize certain options out of the debate (*c*)?

Despite the fact that it is not always easy to separate power as control over public opinion information from more traditional senses of power, the effort will be helpful in our analysis of how the media affect public opinion. Both indirectly and directly, the mass media help control the flow of information about citizen attitudes. Indirectly, the media aid and/or interfere with the power of participants to control the flow of such information. And the mass media themselves directly affect the kinds of information reaching decision-makers about citizen attitudes.

Most writers agree that power is an idea whose time for misuse came a long while ago. Nevertheless, we shall try to follow two of the several suggestions made by Bachrach and Baratz: (1) Power is not the possession of political actors, but instead will be used as a convenient label to describe one or more of a number of *relationships* among actors, and (2) these relationships are not fixed; power can change.[46]

Chapter 7 will deal explicitly with how the mass media can alter these relationships, and Chapter 6 will deal indirectly with the same problem.

Journalists themselves benefit from the reputation for power (over public opinion, for example). Despite our tendency to equate power over public opinion with the power to change attitudes, and despite the publication of voluminous evidence that the media don't reliably change issue attitudes, plenty of people still believe in "the power of the media."

As this book attempts to explain, they probably are right, but for the wrong reasons.

OVERVIEW

We've seen that citizens' attitudes toward issues are not the only element in the public opinion process. If we hold constant the way decision-makers perceive public opinion, we are equipped by now to note three general kinds of changes in public opinion outcomes that can be brought about by mass communications: (1) changes in the amount, composition, and intensity of participation, (2) attitude change, attitude formation, and object change, and (3) changes in the relative power of participants.

Each of these three has been left deceptively incomplete. For example, if attitude change on an issue is to result in public opinion change on that issue, the change must ultimately be made visible. But if a person's attitude changes, *he may be less likely to participate and express his "new" attitude* (see Figure 3 in Chapter 5). We need to specify a number of intervening mechanisms before we know how these three kinds of changes can be produced by political communications in the mass media. The following chapters are devoted to this task.

3
Situation Definitions in the Mass Media

In his classic *Public Opinion,* Walter Lippmann wrote that people deal with their environment by constructing "fictions"—artificial representations of reality.[1] In print a few years later, W. I. Thomas coined his famous aphorism, "If men define situations as real, they are real in their consequences."[2] Though the two men obviously were discussing closely related concepts, at first little overlap occurred in the kinds of applications people were making of their ideas. Even now, Thomas's "situation definitions" have tended to be applied to the analysis of individuals in small groups,[3] rather than to the analysis of public opinion. Somewhat more recently, a bridge of sorts was supplied by sociologists such as Blumer and Turner, both of whom stressed a collective process by which social issues are identified and conceptualized.[4]

But the role of the mass media in shaping these collective definitions was largely left between the lines of both Blumer's and Turner's writings. However, Monica B. Morris did adapt Turner's ideas to a study of the way the Women's Liberation movement was given public definition by Los Angeles area newspapers.[5] In her study, it seemed to be taken for granted that the newspaper definitions were equivalent to the collective (public) definition.

Even in Lippmann's writings, the mass media role in helping to construct fictions was strongly implied—especially in his examples—but not explicitly articulated as a generalization. Similarly, political scientist Murray Edelman's work on the power of political symbols to evoke entire systems of interrelated beliefs also strongly implies a media role in defining situations for audiences, but his principal interest appeared to be in governmental sources of these symbols and, of course, in the symbols themselves.[6]

NEWS AND SITUATION DEFINITIONS

The present chapter will be devoted to a discussion of how the mass media—especially the news media—help construct the facts on which people act and react. I'll use the term *situation definitions* to refer to these constructions, though *fictions* would do about as well right now.

It is risky to pretend that we can always separate "facts" and "attitudes," though it is easy to find fairly clear-cut examples suggesting that we can make that separation. For example, Lippmann discussed a 1919 Senate debate in which contending partisan factions each accepted the same version of the facts—that is, that the British had ordered American naval forces into action without consulting the United States. What each side made of these "facts" (which weren't so, by the way) depended on their partisan position. The Republicans used the incident to attack the League of Nations; the Democrats used it to attack the Republicans, blaming them for delaying a declaration of peace and indirectly causing the affront of U.S. independence.[7] McLeod and Chaffee cite a more recent example of the separation of "facts" and "attitudes." Assume that an incumbent "hawk" congressman were running for reelection. Both a hawk voter and a "dove" voter would have cast their votes on the basis of the congressman's Vietnam policy; they agree on these relevant "facts": The war is the voting issue and the congressman is a hawk. But the dove voter would have voted for the challenger and the hawk voter would have voted for the incumbent.[8]

Existing attitudes are not changed in either example, but it is clear that the definition of the situation has organized the political opinion process along one set of cleavage lines and not another. That is one of the major reasons why the situation definition is a useful concept.

Lang and Lang provide an even clearer example of changes in cleavage lines. Hugo Black, then a nominee for the Supreme Court, made a 1937 radio speech conceding that as a youth he had been involved in Ku Klux Klan activities. Before the speech, persons supporting Black's nomination tended to be Democrats, Jews, and Catholics. The effect of Black's concession was not so much to change the overall percentages of people supporting his nomination as it was to change *who* supported the nomination. Now he received far more support than before from Protestant Republicans and far less from Democrats, Jews, and Catholics.[9]

Obviously, in this case the facts about Black changed in many people's minds, and the attributes to which people were reacting underwent a drastic rearrangement. I doubt that anybody would argue that this was not an important public opinion effect. (Mc-Combs and Shaw have proposed that their agenda-setting concept should encompass this kind of attribute change: "Every phase, every attribute of each public issue or whatever object is being described is not described with equal emphasis."[10] Conceptually, however, setting the agenda of public issues differs in some important respects from defining an issue. The former concerns whether something is an issue and how important an issue it is; the latter concerns how things that are thought to be issues are conceptualized and will often involve what I have termed attitude object change.)

As simplifications of reality, situation definitions are an inevitable and inescapable byproduct of journalists' activities. Does the journalist term it a "crisis" or a "problem"? If a crisis, is it the "energy crisis" or the "natural gas crisis"? Did the firing of Archibald Cox as special prosecutor constitute "Mr. Nixon's refusal to comply with a court order"?[11] Did the Cox firing "edge the nation closer" to impeachment?[12] Do we have a "tax revolt" or don't we?

As Shibutani calls rumors "improvised news,"[13] so does the news process produce something like the "levelling" and "sharpening" found in early studies of the rumor process. Every news story inevitably leaves out detail and imposes constructions on reality. Writing the lead of a newspaper story both imposes a construction on events and leaves out details. Writing the headline for that same story generally carries the process even further. In television, finding a theme to unify two- to three-minute news stories would be a clear-cut example of imposing a construction. And in both radio and television headline briefs it seems clear that many details are left out.

A somewhat more subtle process operates with so-called "second-day" stories. Continuing news stories increasingly impose on journalists the need to recapitulate previous events quickly and succinctly, since news values imply that yesterday's news is not nearly as important as today's. Thus, for example, the term "in disgrace" is used as a quick, convenient label for the conditions under which Richard Nixon resigned. There isn't time to go into a lot of detail about these conditions, journalists feel, because today's real story is about litigation in which Nixon is involved currently, or about how his books are selling, or about how much money he made from his interviews with David Frost. A similar process operates when news magazines rewrite the week's news stories, condensing them for the much more limited space that is available.

The process of constructing situation definitions cannot be avoided by either the journalist or the audience. Definitions provided by the media may have the greatest impact when nobody is aware of them. But we can recognize them more easily when any of several things occur:

1. *When there is disagreement about how to define a given situation.* The disagreement may be among various news accounts, among contending interest groups, or between a fairly uniform set of media definitions and the ones offered by an interest group.

An example of a disagreement among news accounts comes from a study by Mann showing that different newspapers came up with different "official" estimates of crowd sizes during some anti-war protest demonstrations.[14] No one has answered the empirical question of how often media disagree on situation definitions, but it is somewhat doubtful that it happens often when they are covering the same event. In any case, even if media definitions often disagreed, the question would remain whether anybody but researchers were aware of it. How often to audiences overlap? How often do audience members compare media accounts?

The abortion issue is an example in which contending sides dispute situation definitions and one side also disputes the prevailing media definition. "Right-to-life" proponents argue that the term *abortion* disguises the issue. They would prefer to have us think of it as *killing little people,* or something of the sort, and they resent the continuous media characterization of the issue as "the abortion issue." From their point of view, this distances the issue from us, making abortion an antiseptic, clinical procedure.

When situation definitions themselves become the object of debate, a good hypothesis would be that polarization of attitudes has already occurred and that the issue will remain an issue for a long time. When less energy is expended to define an issue, chances of resolution are probably greater.

2. *When a news agency runs a correction or retraction of a previous version of the "facts."* Generally, this kind of cue about situation definitions occurs far more often with regard to matters outside than inside the public opinion process because legal sanctions are somewhat less available to persons, companies, and groups involved in political controversies.

3. *When later developments quickly suggest a change in definitions.* For example, suppose a Harris poll leads journalists to define public reaction to a presidential "fireside chat" as supportive, but a few days later a Gallup poll presents figures that suggest another interpretation. A characteristic "corrective" response by journalists would be to write that public reaction to the speech now isn't known for sure. This kind of cue about the existence of situation definitions is fairly likely to occur when journalists prematurely define the current state of public opinion and the issue is regarded as important enough to monitor the several polls' results continuously.

4. *When developments—much later—show that a situation definition that had guided action at some time in the past was*

"wrong." For example, some time after the New Hampshire primary of 1968, we learned that people who voted for McCarthy weren't sending anybody a message about Vietnam. Journalists defined McCarthy's performance as due to Vietnam (and, in successive "second-day" stories, many gradually began calling McCarthy's performance a "victory").[15] It was not until Scammon and Wattenberg's *Real Majority*[16] that many became aware that the "history" they had learned wasn't necessarily so.

Obviously, historical "corrections" show the defining process clearly, but they don't necessarily change the results of what has already happened. Edward J. Epstein's famous historical investigation reducing the total number of Black Panthers allegedly killed by the police may be an example of a redefinition that took place in a short enough time to make a difference. While it took some time for the redefinition to occur, Epstein's piece received relatively early public attention because it appeared in a general circulation magazine[17] and was quickly picked up by journalists. In addition, unlike the fast-moving nomination process in 1968, there was more time for this redefinition to catch up with events.

Classes of Media-Provided Definitions

Broadly speaking, journalists provide situation definitions that can affect public opinion in three areas. The first area is whether or not a potential issue is defined *as* an issue. The second is in proposing the definition of an issue and of the options available to settle it. The third is in defining public opinion itself. We'll take each of these areas in turn.

Is It on the Agenda?

Obviously, the first group of situation definitions falls into the area of agenda-setting research,[18] recently a very popular topic of mass communication research. Most of this research, however, has been preoccupied with comparing how the media rank issues with how the public does. This research hasn't been concerned with issues which *don't* receive media attention. The often unexamined side of the coin is whether media "nonissues" are thus organized out of the public consciousness and left off the public opinion agenda. It may very well be that much stronger evidence of agenda-setting will be found here than by concentrating only on issues which do receive coverage.

Edelman argues that political symbols operate to prevent basic, underlying socioeconomic problems from coming to the surface as issues, even though they are the primary causes of diverse problems that *are* considered issues. For example, he feels that citizen apathy, housing problems, crime, social unrest, unemployment, and even mental illness probably have roots in the economic system. But he feels we are diverted from the underlying cause by treating each aspect as a separate issue and also by thinking of each aspect in terms that beg the question.[19]

Warren Breed's well-known "reverse content analysis" took quite a different approach to the same problem of how issues get excluded from public agendas. He found that the majority of items excluded from local newspapers concerned the very "politicoeconomic" issues that independent sociological researchers said were afflicting the communities they studied.[20] Many discussions of press performance provide a series of anecdotes along the same lines.[21]

Hungerford and Lemert found that Oregon newspapers displaced coverage of Oregon environmental news "up the road a piece"—outside their own circulation areas—as if there weren't similar problems at home.[22] Similarly, Rubin and Sachs found that both electronic and print media in the San Francisco Bay Area had "discovered" environmental issues, but their coverage of issues tended always to be outside the state of California, as if that state didn't have enough of its own.[23]

Hungerford and Lemert called this displacement a kind of "Afghanistanism" in environmental news and cited survey evidence from roughly the same time period showing that Oregonians tended to think of environmental problems as always worse somewhere else in Oregon.

More research of this kind is needed, especially research comparing news media *non*-issues with popular consciousness of issues. As mentioned, agenda-setting researchers characteristically have looked at both media and popular agendas, comparing ranks assigned to issues that *did* get media coverage.

Closely related to *non*-agenda issues is the question of how and whether the mass media help to organize *options* or recommended solutions out of the public opinion process. For example, immediately after Gerald Ford pardoned Richard Nixon, a House Judiciary Committee member called for the committee to investigate whether grounds existed for considering impeachment proceedings against President Ford. The option was never heard about again. And Harris and Gallup polls asked many questions about reactions to the Nixon pardon, but none of their published questions offered respondents this option.

Turning back to the rank ordering of issues that do reach the media agenda, if the media help determine people's issue priorities, we would expect that this would also show up in ways other than those measured so far in agenda-setting research. For example, does the media agenda of regional issues predict the relative amounts of mail received on those issues in a congressional office?

Agenda-setting involves a kind of implicit situation definition. Another, very closely related, kind of implicit situation definition involves what has been called *status conferral.* If appearance in the news confers a kind of importance on the person, group, or movement covered, the conferral results from an implicit message about the subject of the news story. At this writing, the present author and a University of Oregon colleague appear to have had an unwished-for monopoly on published status conferral research.[24]

We turn now to the second group of media situation definitions.

Definition of Issues

It is well known that you can get startlingly different poll results by rephrasing questions. These changes in percentages illustrate the apparent susceptibility of many members of the population to an attitude object change induced by a situation definition implicit in the poll question. For example, a California polling organization asked the "same" question in two different ways in 1968 and got a perfect reversal of percentages concerning academic freedom:

> Professors in state supported institutions should have the freedom to speak and teach the truth as they see it. Do you agree or disagree?
>
> Agree: 52 percent   Disagree: 39 percent

Professors who advocate controversial ideas or speak out against official policy have no place in a state supported college or university. Do you agree or disagree?

      Agree: 52 percent   Disagree: 39 percent

Half the sample was asked the first version of the question and the other half got the second version.

Another example: in late 1978, two national survey organizations asked their samples about banning TV advertising to children. When the question was put in the context of costs and benefits of government regulations, 63 percent *opposed* banning the advertisements. But when the second survey organization put the question in the context of trade-offs people were willing to accept for better nutrition, 60 percent said they were *willing* to stop advertising to children, "even if it meant running the risk of [children's television] program cutbacks."[25]

Philip Converse probably would argue that most of the American population would be susceptible to object change because they lack an organized, linked (and therefore constrained) set of beliefs about what object goes with what other objects. In the late 1950s, he doubted whether more than 10 percent of the American population had worked out an organized set of political beliefs.[26]

As noted in the previous chapter, though, other camps of researchers dispute whether "constraint" marks a sophisticated belief system or an unsophisticated one. Studies of belief structure have become mired in a debate which tells us more about the researchers' primitive (unexamined) assumptions than it tells us about belief structure, according to Bennett.[27] Nevertheless, it is a good bet that nonelites are more open to object change—if they can be reached at all—than are political decision-makers.

In any event, object change may be induced by media situation definitions. As pointed out in the preceding chapter, it is unfortunate that attitude research methodology has largely been insensitive to object change. It is quite possible for object change to occur and not show up as a change in the only place conventional attitude scaling allows it to show—the affective component. Arguments that treat object change as either equivalent to—or a necessary step for—attitude change ignore this fact.

Object change did show up in the Hugo Black surveys mentioned earlier in this chapter. But the reason was that this particular kind of object change was reflected in changes in expressed affect *and* there was a marked rearrangement of groups favoring and opposing the Black nomination. As Lang and Lang put it:

> *When the appointment was first announced* ... divisions (of opinion) ... were a matter of economic status. *After the discussion and the speech,* the socioeconomic division along party lines disappeared. .... The main line of cleavage was religious. [Emphasis in original.][28]

Attitude scales such as the Semantic Differential allow the respondent to express a change only in the affective components. Since this is the case, object change, if it is detected, ordinarily will be mistaken for attitude change. Recently I reanalyzed some Semantic Differential data I gathered with David K. Berlo and Robert Mertz.[29]

We had subjects rate a variety of potential communication sources as part of a large-scale factor-analytic investigation of the dimensions people use in judging sources. During the course of this work, subjects sometimes rated the "same" source under different conditions. Since they received no communications from these sources, and since subjects did all ratings in a short period of time, it seems extremely unlikely that rating differences for the same source could have been due to attitude change.

Table 3.1 provides a representative slice of the results for Nikita Khrushchev, then the premier of the USSR. Large differences appeared in ratings on all scales, but it was apparent that not all the changes in expressed affect went the same way across the four scales. Had we done a before-after study using Khrushchev as a communication source, we might easily have mistaken for attitude/meaning change those rating changes resulting from differing judgment situations. In the normal before-after design, subjects would rate Khrushchev "before" in something like the contextfree "As a Source" situation. In the "after" measurement, however, the Soviet leader would undoubtedly have been rated in something more like the "Soviet Foreign Policy" or the "Modern Art" situation (depending on the topic of the experimental communication).[30]

Table 3.1

Changes in Mean Ratings of Nikita Khrushchev
in Varying Judgment Situations
(N=91)

Judgment Situation

Scale	"As a Source"	"As a Source on (the Topic of) Soviet Foreign Policy"	"As a Source on (the Topic of) Modern Art"
Safe (1) — Dangerous (7)	6.2*	5.2*	4.1*
Strong (1) — Weak (7)	1.7*	1.8*	4.2*
Expert (1) — Ignorant (7)	2.3*	1.4*	5.6*
Reliable (1) — Unreliable (7)	5.3*	4.0*	5.7*

*Differences between source judgment situation on this scale, $p < .011$, F test.

In any event, given the present insensitivity of attitude scaling techniques to object change, it would seem we must be content mostly with anecdotal evidence about the effects of object change. When situation definitions lead to object change, the resultant change can in turn have dramatic effects on participation.

A plausible case can be made that object change took place in the 1969 race between Tom Bradley and Sam Yorty for mayor of Los Angeles, and that the result of the object change was to stimulate massive turnout among persons who otherwise probably would not have voted.

What, then, were the attitude sets that were "exchanged" during this race?

First, a March 1969 Gallup poll reported that some 67 percent of Americans said they would vote for a "well-qualified" black man for president if their political party had nominated him. This poll was taken shortly before Bradley led a large field of candidates in the April primary election, and there is reason to believe that the percentage for Los Angeles would have been several points higher than the percentage of Americans, since both large city and Western respondents exceeded that figure.

In the April primary, Bradley, a black member of the city council and a former Los Angeles police captain, got 42 percent of the vote in the primary, far ahead of Mayor Yorty's 26 percent.

So one attitude set might be termed something like "fair play for qualified blacks." Granted, there undoubtedly was a measure of "social desirability" reflected in that 67 percent figure; some respondents undoubtedly said what they thought interviewers wanted to hear. On the other hand, that percentage represented a substantial gain over percentages recorded in previous years (e.g., 38 percent in 1958). Further, the percentage nationwide since then had increased by 10 percent in July 1978.[31] And in the 1969 survey, far fewer people said they would vote for a well-qualified woman for president. (A "well-qualified woman" had closed some ground by 1978 but still ranked slightly below a black.)

The second attitude set also had something to do with Bradley's race. The Watts and Detroit ghetto riots and the "Black Power" movement probably were early precipitating events in the formation of what Scammon and Wattenberg called the "Social Issue."[32] The Social Issue might more properly be termed the Social Control Issue—a bundle of white fears about race, crime, college protests, hippies, drugs, and the counterculture. In addition to Scammon and Wattenberg, Maullin was among the first in a long line of social scientists to analyze the 1969 Bradley-Yorty election in Social Issue terms.[33]

Yorty had been relatively inactive in the primary race, but as the returns came in, he launched a counterattack that received a great deal of attention from the national and the Los Angeles news media. Yorty said Bradley had finished ahead because of a "Black bloc" vote. Later, a pro-Yorty group ran an ad for Yorty that included a very large picture of Bradley. There was no explicit mention of race in the ad, but the message seemed clear enough. Another group talked about the damage to real estate values if Bradley were elected. There was much talk, as well, of declines in police morale and threats to law and order if Bradley won.

The *Los Angeles Times* repeatedly endorsed Bradley and decried Yorty's tactics. It assigned reporters to investigate Yorty's statements and even printed rebuttals in the same stories with Yorty's charges. But the success of Yorty's situation definition was evident in the *Los Angeles Times* itself. While Yorty rarely if ever raised the race issue on his own after his initial statements, he was continually asked about the race issue by the *Times* and other journalists. While it seemed evident that the *Times* heartily disagreed with Yorty, it was also painfully evident that the newspaper accepted his definition of the situation. Editorials continually referred to Yorty's "racist" campaign. News stories and editorials continually referred to Bradley as a "black councilman." And in the main news story the Sunday preceding the May 27 election, Ralph Bunche was quoted at length about Yorty's "recklessly racist" campaign. The principal relevance of Ralph Bunche —who lived in New York—appeared to have been that he had lived in Los Angeles many years before, was now a United Nations undersecretary with a distinguished career—*and was black.*

The result of all this was a record 74 percent turnout with Yorty getting 53.25 percent of the vote in the May runoff. Bradley got hardly any more votes that he had in the April primary, if we add in the votes Alphonso Bell got in the primary. Bell, a moderate white Republican Congressman, had endorsed Bradley soon after the attacks from Yorty began. In comparison with the primary, very large increases in turnout were shown among middle-class whites, middle-class Jews, and lower-class Mexicans, *all of whom voted heavily against Bradley.*[34]

According to Maullin, the emphasis on race appeared to turn off the Mexicans, who did not want to be identified with a black. The Jewish vote is especially interesting, because probably Jews would be the single most likely cluster of voters to have had *both* "fair play" and Social Issue attitudes. Their own history as an ethnic minority, plus their previous voting history, strongly suggested that they would have expressed "fair play" attitudes under normal conditions. Therefore, we might expect that object change took place most strongly among them.

In 1973, Bradley narrowly won an election in which the turnout was somewhat lower than the record 1969 level. In 1977, he was reelected, with the turnout much lower than in either of the previous two races. It would be interesting to see how the Jewish vote went in 1973 and 1977.

One last note about the Yorty-Bradley elections of 1969 and 1973. In 1973, Yorty waged a campaign that very closely resembled his successful 1969 effort. But this time the *Los Angeles Times* defined the situation as Yorty's "slashing personal attacks" instead of as his "racist" attacks. And, of course, Bradley was promising to keep the streets safe this time, and the campuses were quiet.

Although the *Los Angeles Times* and other local media had stopped defining the contest in racial terms in 1973, there was little evidence of change in the way the national media defined the situation. The wire services and the networks continued to define the election in racial terms, uniformly referring to Bradley as Yorty's black opponent. But national media carried far fewer stories about the election.

In 1977, Bradley swamped a field of eleven other candidates in the April primary, getting a majority and avoiding a runoff. Turnout in the primary was less than 40 percent.

Because situation definitions are unavoidable when the news

media try to report "the facts," it would not be surprising to find that situation definitions can *reduce* participation as well. In either the influence or the election framework, we would expect to find, for example, that issues defined as technical or scientific matters would tend to have less participation concerning them than if they have been politicized. Along these lines, an interesting historical analysis might be made of the kinds of media situation definitions that took place concerning the nuclear power issue and when and why those definitions began to change.

Not politicizing an issue is also one way in which options are defined out of the public opinion process. To illustrate, the nation-wide meat boycott in the spring of 1973 was uniformly defined by journalists (and usually by activists) as a *consumer* issue, not a political one. Estimates indicated that at least a million consumers boycotted meat purchases—especially beef—during April 1973.

As one probably would expect, however, the boycotters had no lasting effect on the price of beef. Had the issue been defined in political terms, it is at least arguable that the long-term effects of a mobilized citizenry might have been greater. (I attended an organizational meeting of meat boycotters in Eugene at the start of the boycott, and it was apparent that at least these organizers resisted the idea of politicizing the issue, perhaps because they weren't sure they would get as universal support if they did.) Had even one third of that participation been directed into the influence framework, it would have made a considerable impression, ranking in size with the "firestorm" following the firing of Archibald Cox.

This discussion of the effects media situation definitions can have on audiences is not meant to ignore the possibility that audience members often come up with their own situation definitions. And, obviously, both media and individual/group constructions can be placed on events. One way of looking at the media influence on audience situation definitions would be to compare the words and terms used by audience members in describing a situation with those used in the media to describe that same situation.

To a limited extent, a study reported in the next chapter will touch on this matter. In that study, we compared who audiences thought were "winners" and "losers" with who the media thought won and lost the 1976 New Hampshire and Massachusetts primaries.

Definitions of "Public Opinion"

Definitions of winners and losers also fit into the third and final major class of media situation definitions. Crotty terms the media an "aggregation" agency—that is, an agency that collects, sorts, transmits, and interprets all sorts of information about citizen attitudes.[35] Beyond the commercial polls, many other forms of information are constructed about public opinion. For instance, certain elections are grouped together by the press and interpreted as all concerning the same issue (for example, the "Watergate elections" of short-term congressmen in spring 1974) and other elections tend to be excluded (for example, the single exception to the "Watergate elections," in which a California Republican won a seat in the House).

The passage of Proposition 13 in California was almost uniformly defined in news media accounts as the start of a "Tax Revolt" by American citizens. Yet analyses by Mitofsky and by Lewis—and by me of voting on Oregon's Measures 6 and 11—suggest strongly that the Tax Revolt definition was far too oversimplified a reading of American public opinion. Nevertheless, that almost certainly remains The Meaning of Those Elections—in both decision-makers' and journalists' minds.[36]

Another instance: Whenever someone calls for a massive strike, demonstration, rally, or related action, you can expect that journalists will try their best to enumerate the number and reactions of persons who struck, the size of the crowd of onlookers, and so on. Often photos or footage of crowds and crowd reactions will appear with the news. Another form of media-provided information that may reach decision-makers is the letters to the editor that get printed. The journalists' classic man-on-the-street interview is another old standby, as are various other forms of reaction stories, such as interviews with leaders of groups thought to be in opposition to a news development.

Journalists collect and relay to decision-makers many other forms of information, including reactions from various domestic or foreign editorial pages to an important event and interviews with other decision-makers about the kind of feedback they've been getting.

Generally, journalists' activities as collectors and definers of information about citizen attitudes are fairly manifest if one only bothers to look and listen. After all, as more or less self-proclaimed surrogates for The People, journalists have a fairly strong vested interest in this kind of information. Occasionally, however, information about citizen attitudes is relayed by journalists to decision-makers in somewhat less obvious ways, such as in private conversations or in the form of questions put to decision-makers in interview situations: "Mr. President, do you really feel that the people support your proposal to _____?"

When the news media provide situation definitions about the citizenry, these definitions can affect the relative power of decision-makers in a number of ways. To illustrate, if someone is defined as having lost public support, other political elites may tend to believe it, whether or not it was originally true.

Another illustration: Under some circumstances elites must act before all the facts are in. Mayor Richard Daley is thought to have brought thousands of troops to Chicago in 1968 partly on the strength of news accounts quoting Jerry Rubin and others to the effect that more than 100,000 demonstrators would "hit" the Democratic Convention, putting LSD in the water supply, and so on. Mayor Daley had to act months beforehand and at best he had incomplete information at hand.[37] (Incidentally, nobody apparently informed Mayor Daley or the reporters that the effects of LSD probably are eliminated when it is put in large bodies of water.) The demonstrators who did show up were badly outnumbered by police and National Guard troops. There is little question that Chicago 1968 hurt the Democratic Party as well as Mayor Daley's chances of getting a seat at the 1972 convention.

CONSEQUENCES OF SITUATION DEFINITIONS

Because situation definitions in the media provide an omnipresent background, it may be easy to forget, in later chapters, that much of what is said concerns the impact of these constructed facts. These facts can have important effects on (1) the amount and makeup of participation, (2) whether or not the public opinion process takes place in the influence or the election framework, (3) power relationships among participants, (4) the kinds of information decision-makers think they have about citizen attitudes, and (5) the kinds of attitude sets that citizens bring to bear on issues in either the influence or the election framework.

Situation definitions probably produce object change far more often among nonelites than they do among the politically sophisticated. Nevertheless, it is a plausible hypothesis that decision-makers and politically astute audience members may often be influenced by the version of the facts they feel they have to act on. In that sense, at least, they too are influenced by situation definitions.[38] After all, if Lyndon Johnson intended not to run again in 1968, why did he wait until after the New Hampshire primary to make his announcement?

Under some conditions, both elites and nonelites can be sucked into a kind of contagious reaction. Summarizing the effects of news media definitions concerning a fictitious "oil shortage crisis" in Germany, Kepplinger and Roth assert that German newspapers helped precipitate a panic and a run on gas stations:

> The decisive prerequisite for the mass media to have an effect is that they create a spark which sets off development. This development, in turn, proceeds according to its own laws. . . . The social effect of the mass media is to be found not in the addition of effects upon individuals, but in the ignition of chain reactions in the social structure: Some people are influenced by the mass media and react to them; other people see them react and follow their example.[39]

But situation definitions also are affected by some of the same variables they affect. Power, for example, means that some people have a great deal more ability than others to determine the kind of situation definitions the news media impose on events. This ability, in fact, is part of their power.

4

Attitude Change
and Attitude Formation

As mentioned in Chapter 1, some scholars have voiced their unhappiness with the simple reductionist approach by saying, in effect, "The media do, too, change attitudes!" Since these scholars appear to have accepted the fundamental assumptions of simple reductionism, it is *necessary* for them to demonstrate attitude-changing effects.

I don't believe that demonstrating attitude change on issues is either necessary or sufficient (see Figure 5.1 in Chapter 5). We would have to make additional assumptions before even widespread attitude change on an issue would be sufficient to provide public opinion change. The same distinction can be made regarding the larger group of scholars who want to add extra effects to a list of media effects; since they start from simple reductionist premises, it seems they must demonstrate that such effects occur before they can talk easily about social effects. The approach in this book is neither confirmed nor disconfirmed by any such evidence of effects.

Nevertheless, the possibility of media-produced attitude change probably will always fascinate us.

This chapter separately reviews the existing literature covering effects on attitudes toward issues and effects on attitudes toward participation. Far more research has been done on issue attitude change than on participation attitude change. The reader probably has read many reviews of these issue attitude results, so my review of this area will be mercifully brief. As for attitudes toward participation, the literature is both scarce and in need of closer examination. The chapter then will turn to the results of an unpublished panel study in an attempt to illustrate some of the opportunities still available even in the issue attitude field, and the chapter will conclude with further study suggestions.

ISSUE ATTITUDES

Earlier, issue attitudes were defined as those whose object concerned (or might be made to concern) substantive matters under dispute in political opinion processes: Is Jimmy Carter doing a good job as president? Should the Palestinians be guaranteed their own homeland? And so on. Typically, all the attitude questions in public opinion polls are about issue attitudes. Poll questions very rarely ask about attitudes toward participation.

When we use the words *attitude* and *opinion* we usually take it for granted that we are referring to feelings *about issues*. So it is no surprise that research about the attitude effects of mass communication is also preoccupied with issue attitudes.

What Carl Hovland Didn't Tell Us

It is well known that audience surveys generally report little evidence of widespread and short-term attitude change that can be attributed to mass communication. And usually surveys don't find much evidence of attitude change that can be attributed to anything else, either.

It is further well known that experiments, on the other hand, seem to imply that mass communication messages *can* change attitudes. If experimental message *A* is associated with more attitude change than experimental message *B,* it seems natural to conclude that the experimental results conflict with survey results.

In his famous article reconciling this apparent conflict, Carl

Hovland covered many of the differences in focus produced by each of the two research methods.[1] For example, surveys had an uncertain focus on communication events and a clear focus on audience differences, while the reverse seemed true of experiments. And the time gap between communication event and effects measurement usually is much greater for surveys than for experiments. And so on, down through a list of many differences.

But Hovland left one important set of points out of his discussion, perhaps because he was concentrating on direct methodological differences, not media sociology.

If surveys get any focus at all on mass communication events, they measure reactions to *existing* mass communication events. When experiments deal with variables that might be under voluntary control of mass communicators, the researcher is forced by experimental methodology to manipulate and compare *different* communications. Now, suppose that all *existing* message choices in an area such as public affairs show very little variation. (There is a good deal of evidence that this is so.[2]) Suppose further that the restricted range of the existing public affairs message tends to fall into a set of choices that, the *experimental* evidence suggests, will be *less* successful in producing attitude change. For example, the experimental evidence clearly suggests that explicitly drawing conclusions for audience members generally is much more successful than leaving the desired conclusions to be drawn by the audience. Norms of objectivity systematically inhibit the drawing of explicit conclusions in the news columns. My purpose here is not to say whether, or to what extent, journalists should be taught to draw conclusions in the news. I just want to suggest that *there may be no contradiction at all* between the results of surveys and the implied results of experiments *if* we assume that journalists traditionally and reliably make the less successful message choice.

Given the results regarding the effects of drawing explicit conclusions, it should be no surprise that it is only in journalism history books (remember Thomas Nast?), some English texts, and a few self-congratulatory books by cartoonists ("And Then I Drew . . .") that satire stands up as a successful *mass* persuasion strategy. Satire doesn't draw the conclusion explicitly, and a large number of studies of written, drawn, spoken, filmed, and televised satire suggested that satire may at times even be counterproductive.

Results in several other experimental areas suggest that messages may have diminished mass attitude-changing effects because of journalistic conventions that reliably produce the less successful message option. I would include here a tendency toward the one-sided editorial, for what we know about editorial page audiences strongly suggests greater success with what Hovland termed the "two-sided" message.

Of course, in many other areas the experimental evidence doesn't yet add up to a clear conclusion about which message choice will be more successful. And, given the general movement away from experimental methodology by mass media researchers, one cannot be too optimistic about our chances of coming up with many more clear-cut choices in the short run.

Long-Term Attitude Change

In an interesting series of reports, political scientist Michael J. Robinson has argued that network television news practices have had important long-term effects on Americans' support for the political system and for candidates such as George Wallace.[3] These effects occur mostly among the television-dependent audience, Robinson believes.

There is little or no dispute about declines in system support, as measured by polls done from the 1960s to the early 1970s: We do have some sort of effect looking for a cause. What is still disputed, though, is whether network television news practices are that cause.

In his published work to date, Robinson has relied on three kinds of evidence for network journalism as contributing cause. In an experimental study, he found that the CBS documentary, "The Selling of the Pentagon," seemed to weaken subjects' confidence in their ability to judge the issues raised by the documentary. This experiment provided a more direct tie to network content than do the other two kinds of evidence. The second kind of evidence relies on those omnipresent survey data sets produced by political researchers at the University of Michigan. Generally speaking, when Robinson holds education and other demographic variables constant, he still finds that people who are dependent on television for the news are more likely to show a sense of malaise that he attributes to network news.

The third support is primarily anecdotal—for example, the start of the decline of public trust in political institutions roughly coincided with the networks' shift to a half-hour evening news format. Robinson feels the extra fifteen minutes allowed television journalism the latitude inadvertently to create the malaise.

The evidence provided so far by Robinson and associates is important, provocative—and insufficient. Certainly the short-term experimental evidence should not be limited to "The Selling of the Pentagon." The effects of the "thematic" biases Robinson attributes to network newscasts ought to be tested experimentally in small-scale, short-run studies. Existing survey data banks should be used to a greater extent. For example, would Robinson extend his predictions concerning malaise directly to efficacy feelings and then to participation? Would we be able to predict, for example, that when no candidate such as Wallace is available on the ballot, path analysis would show that heavy television dependency leads to lower efficacy, which leads in turn to lower participation?

Finally, more survey data should be gathered expressly to test Robinson's hypothesis. As the next chapter on participation emphasizes repeatedly, we have been largely the prisoners of the outlook and survey data archives of the University of Michigan. These data many not have been sufficiently sensitive to mass communication exposure variables to allow the kinds of tests which may be necessary. Robinson's work has been rather too dependent on the 1968 data from those archives.

Recently several researchers have tried to test Robinson's hypothesis, with decidedly mixed results.[4] For example, Becker and Whitney got results largely supporting Robinson for everybody *except* young people low in formal education, while O'Keefe and Mendelsohn got results consistent with the Robinson hypothesis *only* among young people (and the elderly). And, in another study, O'Keefe found no evidence supporting Robinson. Beyond that, though, McLeod and colleagues got results running in the *opposite* direction: after controls for education and political interest, the amount of exposure to televised public affairs coverage was related to *lowered* voting abstentions.

The Langs and others have argued that major panel studies of short-term reactions to election campaigns systematically have underestimated the amount of media-produced attitude change because the surveys started too late.[5] Most of the attitude change, they argued, probably took place long before the campaign started and long before the interviewers contacted respondents. Having already taken place, attitude *change* thus didn't show up, and an entirely too static, pessimistic picture of the effects of mass communicated election campaigns thereby was created.

If this argument holds, the question then arises: When *does* the attitude change occur? Did it occur just before the candidates were formally nominated—that is, during the primaries? Or did it occur before the primary season? (For convenience, I've made a number of simplifying assumptions, one of which is that whatever change occurs happens during the same extended period of time for everybody.)

It seemed to us that the 1976 presidential primary season provided an excellent chance to test the proposition that important changes in preferences can occur in the primary season. Voter attitudes toward the prime contenders in both parties seemed rather unstable, and popular awareness of many of the Democratic contenders seemed unusually low. Later in this chapter, some results of this previously unpublished study will be reported.

ATTITUDES TOWARD PARTICIPATION

Rarely have mass communication researchers tested whether the mass media can change attitudes toward participation, for reasons that are developed at length in the next two chapters. As a type of attitude toward participation, efficacy has been treated as if it were the fixed result of early childhood and adolescent experiences, not susceptible to media impact. Researchers have tended to think of political attitudes as if they always concerned substantive issues, rather than what people could do about issues. And journalists themselves are preoccupied with explaining issues and policies, not with reporting what people can do to influence policy outcomes.

This brief summary of some later arguments has several implications for research on attitude change. Public affairs content rarely directly "attacks" attitudes toward participation (attitude change theorists often use military metaphors). Evidence from issue attitude research suggests that sudden and remarkable change is more likely as subjects have *less* experience in defending the attitude. Therefore, a plausible case can be made that public affairs messages directed at participation attitudes would stand a better than average chance of producing changes in these attitudes.

Perhaps Robinson's argument about long-range changes can be brought in here, as well. Though it is not always clear whether he is referring to issue attitudes or generalized participation attitudes, his experimental data clearly suggest that the manifest content of a CBS television documentary on policy issues had the latent effect of diminishing audience members' confidence in themselves and their participation while having little or no effect on attitudes toward the Pentagon.

Chapters 5 and 6 will develop some important hypotheses about both short-term and long-term media effects on attitudes toward participation.

We turn now to a panel study of attitude change and attitude formation during the volatile 1976 primary season, the "bandwagon" study.

METHOD OF THE BANDWAGON STUDY

Although no single phase of the 1976 primaries bandwagon study is very complex, there were so many phases that the reader is invited to look at Table 4.1 before we proceed.

We can divide the data sets into surveys of Oregon political *elites,* key *journalists,* and several groups of potential *voters.* In addition, we monitored network and print coverage of the New Hampshire and Massachusetts primaries, with most attention paid to NBC and CBS's weekday evenings and the Tuesday late-night election wrap-ups.

In all cases, first-wave interviews were done the week before

Table 4.1

Design of the "Bandwagon" Study

The Two Voter Panels	First Wave (pre-New Hamp.)	Second Wave (Wed.-Sun. after Primary)	Data Source
N=240 (120 each)	102 obtained 98 obtained	93 obtained post-N.H. 79 obtained post-Mass.	Telephone interviews Telephone
The Two Voter Controls N=128 (64 each)		49 obtained post-N.H. 40 obtained post-Mass.	Telephone Telephone
Elites			
110 Democratic Central Committee Members	64 usable returns	61 usable post-N.H. returns	Mail
65 Republican Central Committee Members	28 usable returns	27 usable post-N.H. returns	Mail
Journalists			
21 Political Reporters/ News Editors, representing 16 Oregon broadcast/ print news agencies in Portland, Salem, Eugene	16 obtained	16 obtained post-N.H.	Telephone

the New Hampshire primary. All elite and journalist second-wave interviews were done during the rest of the week following Tuesday's New Hampshire primary. Roughly half the voters were also interviewed after New Hampshire; the other half were interviewed after the following Tuesday's Massachusetts primary. Both voter panels were matched with control groups who were interviewed only after their respective primaries.

Following is a brief summary of voter, elite, and journalist data sets.

Voter Interviews

Each of four groups of potential voters was sampled randomly from the Eugene-Springfield (Oregon) telephone directory. Sex of the designated respondent was determined randomly ahead of time, with the restriction that half in each of the four groups would be the male head of household and half the female head of household.

The four voter groups were the New Hampshire panel, the New Hampshire control group, the Massachusetts panel, and the Massachusetts control group. Each respondent was randomly assigned to one of the four groups. Members of the two panels were interviewed by telephone before the February 24, 1976, New Hampshire primary. Panel members were not told that we would be contacting them again, but we wanted to check for sensitization effects by interviewing control respondents after the New Hampshire primary (to compare against the New Hampshire panelists) or after the Massachusetts primary (to compare against Massachusetts panelists).

Our chief focus will be on the two panels, but in certain instances we wanted the option of increasing the number of cases by combining panel with the appropriate control, if there appeared to be no differences between panel and control. (As it turned out, there were *no* differences between panels and controls on any key dependent variables.)

Almost all the post-primary interviews were done on the Wednesday through Sunday immediately following that election. A few interviews were done immediately after the results were first broadcast Tuesday night and even fewer were done on the

Monday preceding the next primary. Thursdays produced the most interviews, regardless of the primary and regardless of whether respondents were panel or control members.

Despite the time constraints, nine interviewers[6] produced fairly high completion rates for a panel study: 93 of 120 (78 percent) sampled for the New Hampshire panel and 79 of 120 (66 percent) for the Massachusetts panel were interviewed both times. Completion rates for the two control groups were 49 of 64 (77 percent) and 40 of 64 (63 percent), respectively.

Elite Data

All members of the Oregon Democratic and Republican State Central Committees were sent two questionnaires. One was to have been filled out "before February 23" (there was no mention of the New Hampshire primary), and the other, which had been placed in a sealed envelope, was to have been filled out "by February 29." Both questionnaires were to be sent back together, in the same envelope, thus guaranteeing anonymity while providing a before-after match of questionnaires.

Slightly less than half of the 65 Republican Central Committee members returned usable matched sets of questionnaires, while slightly more than half of the 110 Democrats did. Four elite respondents returned only the pre-New Hampshire questionnaire and another 11 returns were not usable for other reasons, such as the fact they were postmarked the day of the Massachusetts primary or later.

The questions appeared to arouse considerable interest among respondents, who often supplied extra marginal comments. Probably this was because the early parts of the questionnaire asked them to "handicap" both parties' nomination races. Each party's state headquarters provided us with its list of central committee members. In a few cases we discovered that these lists were incorrect or outdated, but the questionnaires were sent by first-class mail so that they would be forwarded or returned as undeliverable. (Indeed, one respondent completed both questionnaires while working in the Democratic primary in Manchester, New Hampshire. Only two envelopes were returned as undeliverable.)

There were no telephone reminders or follow-up post cards, because of the anonymity procedure.

Journalist Interviews

During the same time period that interviews were done for the New Hampshire voter panel, telephone interviews were also being completed with a purposive sample of twenty-one key journalists in Portland, Salem (the state capital), and Eugene (the state's second largest city). Of the twenty-one selected, sixteen gave interviews both before and within five days after the New Hampshire primary. Six of the journalists were chief political correspondents for a Portland or Salem newspaper or a Portland television station; the other ten were editors in charge of making news assignments for their television, radio, newspaper, or wire service reporters. Of the entire group of sixteen journalists, the largest number (six) worked for television stations; the next largest group (five) worked for newspapers; three worked for radio stations, and two for the Portland bureaus of the wire services. All were male and all had had considerable experience as working journalists. They constituted well over half the Oregon journalists who served as "gatekeepers" for much of the 1976 political news reaching the citizens of Oregon's three largest population centers.

All but one of these interviews were done by the author.

Unlike the elite and voter surveys, we did not ask the journalists for their own preferred candidates. Journalists were asked to handicap the races, along roughly the same lines as the other two samples, and they were asked a number of questions about which of the candidates they felt would have to be "staffed" (covered by themselves or their own local staff) if all the candidates were to come for the Oregon primary. We thought this line of questioning would give us an idea of whether there would be a kind of newsworthiness bandwagon among journalists.

RESULTS OF THE BANDWAGON STUDY

If a bandwagon effect exists among voters during the primaries, we would expect the following things to happen:

1. Candidate name familiarity would go up, especially for those defined as clear winners and losers;

2. Voters' perceptions of winners and losers would resemble media portrayals;

3. There would be favorable attitude change toward winners

and, among those who didn't know the winning candidates before the primary, formation of favorable attitudes toward winners; and
4. Expressed intent to vote for the winners would increase.

Name Familiarity Effects

Table 4.2 summarizes results on familiarity with candidates' names.[7] When asked to name as many Democratic and Republican candidates as they could, it was clear that many voters had not sorted out many of the Democratic candidates' names before New Hampshire. Clearly, New Hampshire aided Jimmy Carter more than any other candidate in this regard, because Carter ranked about fifth before New Hampshire and climbed to the top among Democratic candidates after New Hampshire. He was also near the top after Massachusetts. George Wallace clearly was much better known than Carter before New Hampshire, and his candidacy in Massachusetts reinstated awareness of him after that primary. Jackson, the declared winner of Massachusetts, was mentioned by panelists as often as Carter after that primary but already was fairly well known to Oregon voters.

Carter showed a 47 percent net increase from before to after New Hampshire. Following him were Shriver (+39 percent), Morris Udall (+28 percent), Birch Bayh (+23 percent), and Fred Harris (+17 percent).

As for the Massachusetts panel, Carter showed a net gain of 39 percent, followed by Udall (+35 percent), Bayh (+31 percent), Jackson (+29 percent), Shriver (+29 percent), Wallace (+21 percent), and Harris (+17 percent). It was also clear that by the time of this primary people were sorting out more of the noncandidates from the others (Kennedy, −18 percent, for example).

We also noted a kind of agenda-setting effect occurring in the crowded Democratic field, especially among persons who were following the primary results through network television. When we asked respondents to name as many of the candidates as they could, we recorded the names in the order mentioned, both before and after each primary. Jimmy Carter's name was the first mentioned far more often after New Hampshire than before it. Overall, only 8 percent of the New Hampshire panelists named Carter first

Table 4.2
Name Familiarity Changes: New Hampshire and Massachusetts Panels*

	New Hampshire (N=93)			Massachusetts (N=79)		
	Before N.H.	After N.H.	p-level, sign test	Before Mass.	After Mass.	p-level, sign test
Ford	83%	95%	.01	90%	97%	.05
Reagan	83%	91%	.10	89%	90%	
Bayh	16%	39%	.001	23%	54%	.001
Bentsen	10%	2%	.05	18%	8%	.05 (decline)*
Brown	—	2%		1%	3%	
Carter	30%	77%	.001	32%	71%	.001
Church	19%	17%		29%	16%	.05 (decline)
Harris	18%	35%	.001	18%	35%	.001
Humphrey	56%	59%		65%	51%	.10 (decline)*
Jackson	33%	42%	.10	42%	71%	.001
Kennedy	32%	33%		42%	24%	.01 (decline)*
McCarthy	3%	2%		3%	3%	
Shapp	3%	4%		3%	13%	.05
Shriver	19%	58%	.001	27%	56%	.001
Udall	20%	48%	.001	18%	53%	.001
Wallace	62%	72%		65%	86%	.001
Noncandidates, e.g. George Romney	13%	12%		15%	5%	.05 (decline)*

*Respondents were asked to name as many Democratic candidates as they could and, separately, as many Republican candidates as they could. It is therefore conceivable that some persons no longer mentioned Humphrey and Kennedy because they had learned the two men were not actively pursuing the nomination at the time. The same might have been the case for Lloyd Bentsen and various noncandidates. Frank Church would appear to have been the only exception to this.

before the primary, but 33 percent did afterwards ($p<.001$, by sign test). But three-fourths of this increase took place among the slightly less than half the panel who said they depended on TV for their campaign news. After Massachusetts ("won" by Jackson) there wasn't a particularly strong tendency for Jackson to be mentioned first more often—*except* for the TV-dependent panelists (overall, not significant; for TV-dependent panelists, $p<.05$, by sign test).

Our audio tapes of the NBC/CBS newscasts show that Carter's name was mentioned far more often than that of any other candidate during the Tuesday through Friday following the New Hampshire primary. During this period, when a contender's name was given, it was Carter's name 40 percent of the time. The rest of the Democratic field shared the remaining 60 percent. Carter's name repetition margin was somewhat reduced during the early-returns stage of the Tuesday evening newscasts because reporters consistently went down the list of candidates, giving vote totals. But as soon as it was clear that Carter's margin was going to hold up, his name repetition increased, approaching 50 percent of all candidate mentions.

This pattern was most clear in contrasting the February 24 early evening and 11:30 P.M. election wrap-up shows: Carter's name was mentioned 28 percent of the time on the early shows, but 43 percent of the time on the late evening shows. Carter's percentage of mentions increased to about 45 percent the next evening, but by Thursday and Friday (depending on the network), reporters were beginning to focus on the approaching Massachusetts primary, and mentions of some other candidates increased. It was apparent that Jackson and Wallace, both of whom had virtually disappeared from the air during the final days before New Hampshire, were being built up before Massachusetts as the latest challengers to Carter's "momentum."

After Massachusetts, once again a much more even distribution of mentions occurred on the early-returns evening newscasts than later that night and on the days following the election. Overall, Carter's name frequency edge continued on network newscasts. Jackson's name was mentioned more than Carter's only on the late Tuesday night wrap-up shows and on the Wednesday evening news, though Jackson did get about 27 percent of the mentions on the Friday and Monday preceding the Carter-Wallace-Jackson-Shapp contest in the next Tuesday's Florida primary.

The only time Birch Bayh received as many as 20 percent of the mentions during the entire two-week period was after Massachusetts, when there were rumors that he would stop campaigning actively, and the next day, when those rumors were confirmed. The best Morris Udall did during the entire two-week period was 20 percent on one late election night special (New Hampshire). Udall's name wasn't mentioned at all on one of every four newscasts during this period. The best George Wallace did was 38 percent of the mentions on the Friday that both networks had turned their attention to Massachusetts, but he did get 33 percent of the mentions on the following Friday—when network reporters were speculating about his chances of stopping Carter in Florida.

Perceptions of Winners and Losers

Oregon journalists were more willing to pick "winners" and "losers" in the New Hampshire primary than were voters. This shouldn't be surprising, since these Oregon journalists were somewhat more attentive to the primary than were most of the rest of the mass media audience in Oregon. (In fact, only about one in every seven voters said they had paid a great deal of attention "so far" to the primaries, while it was sometimes hard to end the journalists' interviews because they often wanted to speculate further about the candidates and their chances.)

Despite this difference in attentiveness, however, there still was considerable similarity between voters and journalists in their perceptions of who had won in New Hampshire. When New Hampshire panel and control members were combined, 57 percent said Carter had won, compared to 69 percent of the journalists. And 71 percent of the voters said Ford had won, compared to 60 percent of the journalists. Journalists tended to add secondary winners—generally Udall and Reagan—far more often than did voters, who generally named one person and stuck with it. Few voters guessed. If they didn't think they knew, they said so.

If we say it was accurate to pick Carter as the New Hampshire winner and Jackson as the Massachusetts winner, accuracy was higher for New Hampshire. Only 42 percent of the post-Massachusetts voters picked Jackson, compared to Carter's 57 percent for the post-New Hampshire voters (data not tabled, $X^2 = 5.04$, 1 df, $p<.05$).

Was this because New Hampshire made more of an impression than Massachusetts did? Certainly the struggle among the states to be the first would suggest that the states think so. Support for this proposition comes from some of the post-Massachusetts results. About half the people interviewed after that primary "correctly" picked Carter as the New Hampshire winner, despite the presumed "interference" caused by the intervening Massachusetts/Vermont primaries. On the other hand, though, Table 4.3 presents results working against this thesis: Losers were more readily identified after Massachusetts than after New Hampshire.

Table 4.3
Ability and Willingness to Pick
"Big Losers So Far"

	After New Hampshire*	After Massachusetts*†
Shriver/Bayh/Harris	29%	47%
No Big Losers So Far	23%	15%
Don't Know	48%	38%
	100% (N=124)	100% (N=107)

*New Hampshire panel and control combined.
†Massachusetts panel and control combined.
$x^2 = 8.07$, 2 df, p .02

Again, transcripts of network telecasts suggest that part of the explanation probably lies with news media situation definitions. CBS's Walter Cronkite declared Carter "the clear winner" after New Hampshire, as did NBC. But on Cronkite's Wednesday evening newscast following Massachusetts, Cronkite led with the statement that Jackson *had joined with Carter* at the head of the pack, well in front of the rest. Similarly, on a weekend news show, NBC's John Hart, in summarizing the Massachusetts result, said that nobody had a bandwagon going for himself and nobody had "momentum."

In contrast, on the "losers' " side of things, news media definitions were much firmer after the second day of primaries than after the first. As Cronkite put it Wednesday evening, "no single primary makes a loser, but it can push a candidate in that direction. One man clearly pushed yesterday was Birch Bayh." He then went on to say that Bayh had also finished well back in New Hampshire. CBS Correspondent Ed Bradley then reported Bayh would "effectively withdraw" tomorrow. Bill Plante followed with the report that Shriver's campaign was "moribund" while Harris's was a "low budget" effort that probably would continue for a while longer.

It will be recalled that only on the days when clear losers were withdrawing did those candidates get their names mentioned very often.

Another, quite separate, finding also could be used to argue that Massachusetts (and the campaign generally) was not overshadowed by New Hampshire. A third of all respondents interviewed after Massachusetts could accurately give both the time and place of the next primary; this compares with only 20 percent of those interviewed after New Hampshire ($p<.02$ by Chi-square test). Furthermore, there was a tendency ($p<.10$) for discussion of the primaries to be more frequent after Massachusetts than after New Hampshire, and for more respondents to stay up to catch the 11:30 P.M. late-night election report after Massachusetts than after New Hampshire ($p<.05$).

Attitude Effects

Table 4.4 presents attitude results for the two voter panels. Since most of the candidates were virtually unknown to the respondents prior to the primaries, in many cases the effects recorded in the table represent what might be termed attitude formation, rather than attitude change.

Gerald Ford and Ronald Reagan represent exceptions, however. Both were well known prior to the primaries. The New Hampshire primary seemed to have improved Ford's standing significantly by means of attitude change, regardless of whether that change was tested by the relatively low-power sign test or by the *t* test.

Table 4.4

Attitude Formation and Change: New Hampshire and Massachusetts Panels

Candidate	New Hampshire (N=93) Direction of Effect* (Frequencies)		p-Level, Sign Test	Massachusetts (N=79) Direction of Effect* (Frequencies)		p-Level, Sign Test
	+	−		+	−	
Ford	33	15	.02	22	18	
Reagan	27	17		25	26	.01
Bayh	8	13		5	18	
Bentsen	3	3		5	2	
Brown	1	0		1	0	
Carter	23	12	.10	16	13	
Church	9	3		6	6	
Harris	10	7		8	12	
Humphrey	17	17		17	15	
Jackson	7	10		21	17	
Kennedy	11	6		8	11	
McCarthy	0	1		0	1	
Shapp	2	1		5	1	
Shriver	8	15		10	12	
Udall	18	6	.05	13	7	
Wallace	14	16		9	17	

*Ratings of candidates were obtained on a five-point scale, ranging from 1 ("very good") to 5 ("very bad"). Cases counted under the "+" direction of effect include both instances where there was movement, from before to after the primary, of affect toward the "very good" end and cases where a "very good" or "good" response was given to a previously unknown candidate. The reverse was true for the count under the "−" sign: the count includes both a movement of affect in the negative direction and apparent formation of unfavorable responses. For the Democratic contenders, formation effects generally outnumbered cases of change. No claim is made that only attitude change effects have been measured.

Jimmy Carter and Morris Udall were relatively unknown prior to the New Hampshire primaries. Interestingly, though more people came to know Carter's identity, Udall did somewhat better than Carter among those who came to know his name. Significantly favorable attitude effects were recorded for Udall by sign test ($p<.05$) but not for Carter. However, when subjected to t tests, New Hampshire changes for Carter reached $p<.05$ and $p<.01$ for Udall.

Again, though, Carter's New Hampshire rating gains occurred primarily among Republicans, while Udall's happened mostly among the Democrats in our voter sample. Roughly the same thing seemed to be happening among Democratic Central Committee members: Udall gained significant ratings support following New Hampshire, while Carter actually lost some ground.[8] (Again, it is well to remember what the networks were saying—that is, that Carter was the clear winner of New Hampshire while Udall was trying to claim he had won support among the liberals, but had not yet clearly done so.)

The only clear ratings effect Massachusetts seemed to have on the voter panel was a negative bandwagon for Birch Bayh. Both Jackson and Carter emerged with slightly more positive than negative ratings changes, though the net improvement for both of them was exceeded slightly by that for Udall. Reagan, Shriver, Kennedy, and Harris all experienced slight losses.

As a candidate, Jackson started out both relatively well known and relatively unpopular among voters. However, if we combine panel and control groups, we find that only 12 percent of voters gave him a favorable rating after New Hampshire, compared to 21 percent after his win in Massachusetts ($p<.10$ by Chi-square test).

Candidate ratings may not be as severe a test of a bandwagon effect as preference questions, to which we turn now.

Preferences

Table 4.5 presents results for two kinds of preference questions that were asked of voters. In the top half of the table are results for changes in the candidates named by voters as the best each

Table 4.5
Changes* in Candidate Preferences, New Hampshire and Massachusetts Panels

	New Hampshire			Massachusetts		
	+	−	p-Level, Sign Test	+	−	p-Level, Sign Test
Best *Republican Candidate*						
Ford	16	5	.05	15	1	.001
Reagan	5	5		1	9	.05
Best *Democratic Candidate*						
Carter	11	0	.001	8	3	
Udall	6	0	.05	6	1	.20
Jackson	0	7	.02	6	3	
"Right Now, I Would *Vote For*":						
Ford	4	3		1	1	
Reagan	3	3		1	2	
Carter	4	0		5	0	
Udall	6	0	.05	4	1	.10
"Right Now, I Would *Vote for*":						
Humphrey	3	3		2	3	
Jackson	0	3		2	1	
Uncommitted	4	14	.05	3	3	

*The direction signs are defined as follows: "+" includes either movement from another candidate to that candidate or a change from no preference to that candidate; "−" includes either movement away from that candidate to another candidate or a change from that candidate to no preference.

party could nominate. In the lower half are changes in voters' own preferences.

We might consider the "best candidate" response to reflect a kind of legitimacy won or lost by various candidates. Among the Republican candidates, Gerald Ford clearly gained legitimacy after both primaries as the best GOP candidate, while Reagan lost some after Massachusetts. While Ford impressed voters concerning his legitimacy, he didn't seem to gain any votes. His gains were among Democrats who were not willing (at least not yet) to say they would vote for him. And he already had most of the Republicans' votes to start with.

As for the Democrats, Carter and Udall both gained legitimacy as Democratic candidates—at least after New Hampshire—while Jackson lost. But only Udall came close to a significant gain in legitimacy after Massachusetts.

When we look at actual voters' choices, we find Udall and Carter in a virtual stand-off through the first two weeks of 1976 primaries. Udall was the *only* candidate to gain significant voting support after New Hampshire, though Carter came close ($p < .10$) after Massachusetts-Vermont. The reason Carter's gains in legitimacy were not fully translated into voting changes was that Carter's gains were principally among Republicans who were already committed to Ford as their voting choice—in the Oregon primary, at least.

Beyond results for voters, we also find changes among Democratic Central Committee members indicating that it was *Udall*— not Carter—who seemed to have benefited most from New Hampshire. Eight of the sixty-one committee members switched from other candidates *to* Udall as their choice while only one switched *from* Udall ($p < .05$, two-tailed sign test). In fact, after New Hampshire, Udall was the first choice of more Democratic Central Committee members than any other candidate. Humphrey, who before New Hampshire was the top choice of Central Committee members, fell to second behind Udall. Nobody else, including Carter, had more than half the numbers Udall got from committee members after New Hampshire. (Carter's support went from five to six.)

Udall's growth in elite support came partly at the expense of

Humphrey, Harris, and Bayh and partly from the already slim ranks of undecided Central Committee members.

Meanwhile, the ranks of undecideds were also rapidly diminishing among voter panel members (Table 4.5), but only for the New Hampshire panel. This is consistent with our earlier finding that people were more sure about winners after New Hampshire than they were after Massachusetts.

A Bandwagon among Journalists?

We didn't ask the Oregon journalists for their own voting preferences. But we did ask them, in effect, to decide which candidates most deserved coverage. (You will recall that network television news concentrated on the *winners* of New Hampshire and Massachusetts, providing close-to-equal coverage of losers *only* when they were withdrawing from the race.) The journalists were restricted to a maximum of three Democrats, and the three candidates named were recorded in the order mentioned.

One of the things shown by these interviews was the consistency in independent judgments by these journalists. Of the sixteen Democratic contenders (including Edward Kennedy), only six candidates were named both before and after New Hampshire. (Jerry Brown was mentioned by one journalist before New Hampshire; otherwise, the same six candidates were mentioned both times. Carter was mentioned most frequently both before and after New Hampshire, but he was mentioned more often—and earlier —after his New Hampshire victory ($p=.04$, two-tailed sign test). Udall was mentioned by only two journalists before New Hampshire and by seven afterward ($p=.062$).

The other four candidates who would have received coverage by these journalists all stayed the same or lost slightly with the New Hampshire result: Jackson, Humphrey, Wallace, and Kennedy.

The increased emphasis on Carter was accompanied by the perception that Carter's chances had improved as a result of New Hampshire. After New Hampshire, eight of the journalists who had not done so before now mentioned Carter as the candidate whose chances were improving ($p=.008$). To a much weaker extent, Udall's fortunes were also seen to be on the rise ($p=.124$).

So we did see a kind of bandwagon among journalists, too. Perhaps unlike voter and elite reactions, however, the journalists' bandwagon more clearly favored Carter than Udall.

Discussion

We seem to have found bandwagons for Morris Udall and Jimmy Carter among voters, a Udall bandwagon among Oregon Democratic Central Committee members, and a kind of bandwagon for Carter among Oregon journalists. Interestingly, the good things that were happening for both Ford and Carter among voters were taking place among voters of the "wrong" party. So a case can be made that Morris Udall was enjoying a more genuine bandwagon success in Oregon than were Carter and Ford.

The contrast between these trends and the national news reports was striking, especially concerning who was the "clear winner" in New Hampshire. There was also something of a contrast with the way New Hampshire affected the judgments of some of the key political news gatekeepers in Oregon concerning Carter.

It may be, of course, either that Oregon voters are unique or that those living in the vicinity of the University of Oregon react in ways that aren't particularly representative of voters elsewhere. Nevertheless, both Sen. Frank Church and write-in Jerry Brown beat Carter in the Oregon primary. (Morris Udall decided not to campaign in Oregon following his demoralizing Wisconsin defeat. While his name remained on the ballot, all Udall campaign activity ground to a virtual stop in Oregon, and Udall supporters looked to Church or Brown.) And in the November election Ford narrowly beat Carter in Oregon despite a very large Democratic edge in registered voters.

Candidates and journalists, it has often been noted, live in an isolated, nearly airtight cocoon, mutually affecting each other during the primaries. A good case can be made that the bandwagon effects they were observing and talking about bore at best an incomplete resemblance to what really was then happening, at least in Oregon. Over the long haul, however, one can argue also that the greater name familiarity given the front runners by journalists might bring the mental pictures in their cocoon closer to those out among the voters, simply because of attrition and the elimination of voters' preferred candidates.[9] After Massachusetts, both the news media accounts and Oregon voters agreed that Birch Bayh was finished, for example.

Suggested Further Studies of Attitude Change

The results of this study clearly are encouraging for anybody who wants to find dramatic attitude effects at the individual level. It shouldn't be too hard to find similar opportunities in the future, especially at lower levels of office and during presidential primaries such as this one, where there were numerous unknown candidates.

However, I would urge upon the researcher the need to monitor media content and audience reactions simultaneously. Often a record of media content will provide crucial circumstantial evidence about the media environment that even panel survey questions cannot provide. In the present study, for example, we found that questions about which network's primary coverage was watched were of little help in explaining various bandwagon effects. Of most use, from the present survey data at least, were questions about whether the respondent depended on print or television for news of the primaries, but even this is a very insensitive measure. By itself, certainly, it would not have linked our name familiarity effects, definitions of winners and losers, and agenda-setting results to media content.

Another thing researchers need to do is simultaneously measure elite and "mass" reactions to campaign events. We already have considerable anecdotal evidence about several kinds of elite bandwagon effects. The present study adds some to that, but it also adds new evidence about a similar kind of effect taking place among mass audience members. Under what conditions will elites show a bandwagon and the "mass" not? If both show a bandwagon, are they always jumping on the *same* bandwagon?

As for other suggestions, there are plenty of opportunities to look at changes in attitudes toward participation in ways that have not been tried yet.

For example, if we treat candidate preferences as *issue* attitudes, maybe televised presidential debates change attitudes toward voting more often than they change the issue attitudes. To date, research on the 1960 and 1976 debates seems to have focused on whether issue attitudes changed. It might be argued that, in the aggregate at least, both the 1960 and 1976 debates elevated voter turnout over what it would have been otherwise. It is well known that the 1960 turnout percentage was a record high since the institution of women's suffrage. But it may also have been the case that the rather low turnout in 1976 would have been even lower had it not been for the debates. A well-publicized Peter Hart poll led many journalists to predict that less than half of eligible Americans would vote in 1976.[10] Actual turnout was estimated at 53.3 percent.[11]

Our preoccupation with issue attitude effects carries over to political campaign advertising, too. For example, in their book *The Unseeing Eye,* political scientists Thomas E. Patterson and Robert D. McClure analyzed media effects on voters' issue information and candidate and policy preferences.[12] While they appeared to have measured several types of attitudes toward participation, such as turnout intention, their book did not seem to make use of these measures in its extensive analysis of media effects on attitudes. A study by Humke et al. suggests that Patterson and McClure might profitably have examined these attitudes toward participation.[13] Using University of Michigan survey archives, Humke's group found that the number of political ads in a newspaper was strongly associated with voter turnout in a series of elections.

5
The Mass Media
and Participation

Except for the polls, ultimately all information about citizen attitudes comes to decision-makers through some form of participation. Therefore, one important way to change that information is to change the amount, intensity, duration, distribution, or makeup of the attitudes expressed—that is, to change participation.

This chapter, and the next one, will both be concerned with when and how the mass media affect political participation.

WHY WE'VE MISSED THE EFFECTS
OF THE MEDIA ON PARTICIPATION

Political scientists and, to a far less important extent, sociologists have nearly monopolized the study of political participation. For reasons I shall discuss shortly, this near-monopoly seems to have had most unhappy effects on our understanding of how the mass media change public opinion. Fairly recently, critics have accused their own colleagues in political science and sociology of not being interested in studying the mass communication media.[1] While this may have been true, there probably is more to it than that.

The Prevailing Consensus

For many years, the prevailing consensus appears to have been that the mass media do not have a truly independent effect on participation. As a result, political researchers tended to lose interest in finding clear-cut chances to test media effects on participation. Several strands of research contributed to this consensus.

1. Based on an essay by Campbell and studies by Glaser and Simon and Stern, it was concluded very early that the introduction of the new medium of television had had no appreciable effect on voter turnout.[2] If the introduction of an entirely new medium didn't seem to make a difference in turnout, it seemed reasonable to infer that specific messages via that (or another) medium probably wouldn't make a difference, either.

2. Landmark studies of the American voter, combined with political socialization theory, emphasized certain demographic factors—such as social class—as the most important predictors of participation. Since such demographic variables were thought to have occurred prior to media exposure, they tended to be assigned causal priority. Thus, while strong relationships often were found between turnout and media exposure, both turnout and exposure were thought to be largely the result of efficacy or other class-related attitudes that had been acquired during socialization. This trend had progressed so far by 1965 that Milbrath's influential book, *Political Participation*, simply treated exposure to the media as a low-level form of participation.[3] In other words, media exposure became part of the dependent variable. Obviously, when conceptualized this way, the mass media will not be considered as a possible explanation of participation.[4] In their revision of the 1965 book, Milbrath and Goel have greatly deemphasized use of the media as a low-level form of participation, but they have not completely eliminated media use as participation. For example, they continue to regard "keeping informed about politics" (presumably partly by following the news) as one form of participation.[5]

3. A steady stream of findings suggested that the media were far more likely to reinforce than to change issue attitudes. While

there is no logical reason why these findings should have been taken as supporting the failure of the media to influence participation, there is plenty of evidence that these findings regarding attitudes toward issues were extended to questions of participation.[6] (Perhaps the tendency to confuse attitude change with participation change is related to the intellectual heritage of the simple reductionist correspondence rules mentioned in Chapter 1.) As we shall see later in this chapter, not only does a failure to change attitudes *not* mean a failure to change participation, but this "failure" may *produce* a change in participation.

The Nature of the Evidence

Almost all the evidence we have about participation has come from studies done during election campaigns, not between elections and in the influence framework. Probably the convenience of elections has had a lot to do with this. Elections take place at identifiable times and locations, and can be anticipated ahead of time, enabling researchers to write grant proposals and otherwise mobilize their resources. Many events in the influence framework cannot be predicted, and unfinanced "fire-alarm" research would be necessary to get into the field fast enough to take advantage of these events.

But researchers have been preoccupied with elections for at least two other reasons. First, elections are glamorous, suspenseful, exciting (especially to political scientists and journalists) struggles for power. They are aimed at rather massive numbers of people and involve concentrated efforts to persuade them. It is no accident, therefore, that national elections—especially presidential ones—receive far more attention than local ones.

The second reason is more subtle. Having low participation, the influence framework tends to be consigned to the province of research in pressure groups and power, not "democratic" politics. In an unspoken way, elections thus became the last refuge of those who wish to defend the fairness of our existing political arrangements: participation was much higher in elections and Everybody's Vote Counts The Same. Ironically, though, one of the side effects of concentrating on the election framework in the past seems to have been to elevate the importance of elections, *as public ritual* (important for the stability of democratic regimes) *and as a constraint on elite action, while downgrading the importance of the substantive outcomes of elections.*

The preoccupation with national elections has had a number of unfortunate effects on the evidence we think we have in hand about the media and participation:

1. Surveys in election campaigns tend to create conditions corresponding to those identified by Carl Hovland in his explanation of why survey method works against finding that the mass media had changed attitudes.[7] In a campaign lasting months, surveys tend to get a clearer focus on audience variables than on mass communication events. Even in panel studies with repeated measurements, the time between communication and participation will be attenuated, *especially if the individual's only act of participation is voting.* It therefore becomes easier in surveys to measure demographic characteristics rather than specific communication events; furthermore, to do a separate content analysis of all political communication content that might be available to all respondents is nearly impossible in a national sample survey and would require considerable extra effort even if the sample had been drawn from a more limited geographical area.

In contrast to elections, when we study the influence framework, it is easy to find anecdotal evidence that a given mass-communicated message stimulated a wave of telegrams and mail. Though it is anecdotal, this evidence is fairly convincing, partly because of the short time gap between the event and the act of participation, partly because of the contrast between the level of participation before and after the event, and partly because of the content of the attitude expressions received. Let's briefly consider two of many possible anecdotes.

First, according to White House sources, a "massive outpouring" of wires, phone calls, and letters followed President Ford's surprise pardon of Richard Nixon in September 1974. These messages usually mentioned the pardon and often stressed that news of the pardon had impelled the citizen to communicate outrage or praise. Other sources claim that of the almost 4,000 letters received in the first week after the pardon, fewer than 500 of these pardon-related letters approved Ford's action.

Second, the 1970 broadcast in Austria and West Germany of the "Holocaust" series on the persecution of Jews by the Nazis brought many thousands of telephone calls. In West Germany, for example, the station in Cologne received five hundred telephone calls during and immediately after the first program in the four-part series. Another 16,000 calls were said to have been received at the regional headquarters of the West German network concerning the entire Holocaust series. Almost invariably, the West German calls mentioned the program and then went on to express attitudes hostile to, or supportive of, the program.[8] Under such conditions the connection to the mass communication event is self-evident. And in Austria, during the first program itself, the calls tended to be anti-Semitic or urged TV officials also to show cruelties perpetrated by other nations, while after the program was completed, the "number of positive reactions gradually increased," according to Peter Diem, a public opinion analyst who monitored responses to the program. According to reports, the first program generated more telephone calls from viewers than any other single program in the history of the Austrian state network.[9]

In January, 1980, the White House announced it was considering calling for a boycott of the Moscow Olympics. Heavy waves of mail and telephone calls followed, almost all of it mentioning the boycott "trial balloon" and 70 percent of the mail and 80 percent of the calls favoring a boycott.[10]

In all of the anecdotes, there was an extremely short time lag between the communication and the participation. Further, the participation itself usually identified the stimulating communication event. These characteristics mark them as rather typical influence framework events.

2. Perhaps partly because campaign participation and attention to campaign news in the media were both thought to be produced by prior third factors, political scientists have had a very strong tendency to assume that greater exposure to politics in the media will always be *positively* associated with political participation.

This assumption wouldn't withstand close scrutiny even in the election framework, let alone the influence framework. Communication researchers Blumler and McLeod reported, for example, that mass communication appeared both to lower and to raise voting turnout among different groups of young British voters. A uniform, direct, positive, and simple relationship between media exposure and participation becomes even more questionable in the influence framework (see Figure 5.3 later in this chapter and see also Chapter 6). One political scientist has argued that the way television journalists cover politics leads to frustration, cynicism, and a loss of efficacy feelings among people who depend on television for their news.[11] It doesn't take much of a jump to speculate that, if all of these effects occur, the chances of participation could be reduced as television exposure increases among these people.

3. The traditional approach to participation has muddled things in another way. Because participation has been studied primarily in election campaigns, political scientists have been allowed to avoid specifying in any detail how participation is produced. Since our society makes it relatively easy to find out how, when, and where to vote, it has not often seemed necessary to worry much about *how* people are *mobilized* to vote.

We know, to be more specific, that precinct canvassing increases turnout; we even know that being contacted by an interviewer for a preelection poll increases turnout. But we're not completely sure why and how these two events increase participation. And we certainly have not identified many of the other factors that might depress or raise turnout, let alone why or how they would do so.

In voting studies it is hard to avoid the impression that *mobilization* and related terms often serve only as convenient literary devices. Salamon and Evera constructed a black "mobilization index" whose meaning was completely dependent on relative turnout for black candidates in Southern states. Obviously, such an index can be tautological and certainly doesn't shed much light on how the mobilization was accomplished.[12] (Judging by the sociological literature, however, it is also possible to avoid being very specific about how participation is produced in the influence framework.[13])

4. In retrospect, it is easy enough to say that preoccupation with elections helped delay for many years the awareness that political participation is not all of one piece. W. S. Robinson warned as long ago as 1952 that it was a mistake even to combine

just the various forms of campaign and election participation.[14] Nevertheless, the advice went largely unheeded. By 1965, Milbrath's first edition not only assumed that all acts of participation represented the same underlying dimension; it went one step further and argued that political participation had a cumulative, hierarchical structure: People who worked in a campaign also performed all the "easier" acts below that in the hierarchy, and so on. Milbrath's conception was by no means alone.[15]

Now we know that political participation is not all of one piece. Milbrath and Goel now talk of five different types of participation.[16] Verba and Nie found that political participation included four somewhat different factors: (1) voting, (2) campaigning, (3) "communal" activity, and (4) "particularized" activity.[17] Only the first two would show up in data gathered in election campaigns; the last two clusters appear clearly to be noncampaign influence framework activities. Studying participation in election settings, then, artifactually compressed the range of available responses and most certainly delayed awareness that political participation is multidimensional.

So what if participation is multidimensional? The importance of all this for us is that *the ways the mass media cover politics may very well affect the different dimensions of participation quite differently.* Though Verba and Nie's study of participation gave scant attention to the mass media, the one analysis they did make suggests that the number of outside mass media that penetrate the local community *affects communal and campaign participation in different ways.*[18] Based principally on their analysis of variables other than mass communication, Verba and Nie concluded that "What leads one citizen to engage in one type of activity may differ from what leads him to another."[19]

Other data also support the need to evaluate participation effects separately. Though they unfortunately combined their only mass media variable with another communication variable, Sallach et al. found that this combined communication variable predicted some kinds of participation better than other kinds. The amount of attention paid to civic-political matters was much more strongly related to campaigning and trying to influence others' beliefs than it was to either voting turnout or belonging to political groups.[20]

5. Concentrating on elections may have interfered with the asking of important questions about efficacy, participation, and the mass media.

If we assume—as researchers generally do—that efficacy "causes" both participation and attention to campaign news coverage, it still does not follow that efficacy feelings are fixed, unchanging, and unaffected by the way journalists cover politics. Some strands of research already suggest that efficacy is not a fixed characteristic. For instance, the proportions of people with feelings of political efficacy declined between 1960 and 1968.

In order to explain further how concentrating on elections interferes with testing relations among media coverage, efficacy, and participation, it is necessary to touch briefly on two different lines of thought about how efficacy feelings can change.

First, Dahl hypothesizes that efficacy and participation mutually reinforce each other in a circular process.[21] On the negative side, failure to participate contributes to a loss of efficacy, which in turn decreases the chance of participation the next time, and so on. But in an election, the society (and the mass media) makes it fairly easy for a person to vote. *It is harder to find ways to participate in the influence framework.* In effect, Chapter 6 argues that *this participation discrepancy* between election and influence frameworks *is partly the result of news media practices.* Thus it seems possible that concentrating on elections obscures mutual interactions among mass media, efficacy, and participation.

Second, Michael Robinson argues that the practices of network television journalists gradually are having two effects on persons who are dependent on television rather than print news. These network news practices are simultaneously delegitimizing America's political institutions and producing a loss of something like efficacy among these television news-dependent individuals.[22] Most of the examples of network "bias" he cites concern classic between-election influence framework news events—the Vietnam war, Watergate, and so on. If Lang and Lang[23] are correct that most long-term shifts in attitude occur between elections, it would not be surprising to find that election studies would probably not capture Robinson's malaise effects, and almost certainly would not relate them to the mass media in any event.

In either case, then, the effect of concentrating only on participation in the election framework would be to miss or grossly underemphasize any mass media impact on efficacy and participation.

The Data-Gathering Techniques

Even when participation has been studied in the influence framework, certain habits of gathering data have also tended unnecessarily to attenuate possible media effects. Conventional data gathering, for instance, starts by drawing a sample of people who have not necessarily participated, and then sorts participants out of the total sample.

While this approach is admirably suited to accomplishing certain things, it does have the following consequences:

1. The result often is a tiny sample of people who participated, leaving so few in subgroups that it is difficult to do many analyses that suggest themselves.

2. The usual time lag occurs between interview and relevant mass communication events.

3. The extremely low numbers of resultant cases, and the general mental set behind the survey, make it extremely unlikely that questions will be asked about specific events that stimulated participation. Instead, respondents tend to be asked whether they have engaged in a particular type of participation, and *grouped by type of participation, not by events that stimulated the participation*.[24]

It may be inconvenient to study participation by means other than the standard general sample survey, but it is certainly not impossible. Instead of drawing a general sample, we can sample populations of participants *rapidly* after an event such as the Archibald Cox firing. In a way, this kind of "fire-alarm" research has been done,[25] and several times, at that. Many researchers have studied the attitudes of participants in protests—antipornography crusaders, civil rights marchers, and so on. But mass communication has not figured centrally in the analysis of results—or even in the questions asked—despite the fact that the samples were large enough to break down in many different ways.

Besides "fire-alarm" samples of participants, another technique also is available as an alternative to general sample surveys. We could do more intensive analyses of the messages sent to decision-makers by participants. To take a tiny piece of this research, we already have a fairly large number of studies of people who write letters to the editor. Almost invariably, intensive analysis has centered on the demographic characteristics of letter-writers rather than on the messages themselves. The author and Jerome Larkin have tried to show how productive such an approach might be.[26]

A good example of the limiting effects of the general sample survey approach *and* associated data-gathering habits may be found in one of the few studies that have thus far applied path analytic techniques to see whether mass media affect participation.

Johnson concluded that socialization by the family led to interest (or lack of it) in politics for high school students, and then to political participation (or lack of it).[27] Two media variables were not found to be elements in this causal chain. Once again, however, neither the media variables nor the participation measures seem to have been specific to a political event or events. We know the media measures were not specific; the article does not identify any of the participation measures used. But if participation measures were specific to an event, we would expect a weakened correlation with the generalized media measures due to incomparability of measurement situations. And if participation were also general—the more likely situation—the usual reasons for attenuated correlations would obtain. The more prominent media variable in Johnson's analysis—the relative availability of television—reflected characteristics of counties rather than of individuals sampled, even though it is obvious that the students could have been asked directly about their access to television. While it is an admirable new approach, path analysis is stuck with making sense out of what gets put into it, and in this case the usual insensitive media variables were put into it.

(Results from a second path analytic study—by Blumler and McLeod—suggest that Johnson's pattern may be only one of three causal paths.[28] In their analysis of voter turnout in Britain, they found one pattern in which mass communication helped stimulate turnout and one in which, as in Johnson's results, family upbringing led to efficacy, interest, and turnout. They also reported a third pattern: Unfavorable reactions to the campaign, as seen on TV, can lead to a relatively informed decision *not* to vote.

Again, it is a mistake to assume that more media exposure necessarily enhances the prospects of participation.)

MASS COMMUNICATION PARTICIPATION EFFECTS:
A RESEARCH AGENDA

Before we begin, it is worthwhile restating some points made earlier. It is decidedly easier to vote than to participate in the influence framework. The mass media, and the American political culture, greatly encourage participation in the voting ritual—it's just good citizenship—while remaining strangely silent about political participation in any other form.

It therefore seems probable that greater feelings of efficacy are required for participation in the influence framework than would be the case for voting.

Efficacy feelings have been regarded as a very general attitude toward oneself and toward the opportunities for participation. But just as it is probably a mistake to treat all acts of participation as if they reflected different amounts of the same underlying variable, it is also probably a mistake to treat efficacy as if it exhausted all possible meanings for what I've termed "attitudes toward participation." Some attitudes toward participation are more specific to an act and a situation than is efficacy. They *may* also be more susceptible to change, in the short run, than is efficacy. Nevertheless, since almost all the research on participation attitudes has used efficacy or very similar measures, we will have to make what use we can of the efficacy concept.

We are ready now to begin developing some ideas about how the mass media may affect participation. I should stress that these ideas generally have indirect support in a scattered literature as well as some anecdotal support, but at the moment, they have the status of plausible hypotheses that can (and should) be tested.

Three Types of Available Participants

It will be useful to distinguish among three ideal types of media audience members who are available for participation in election and influence frameworks. They are:

1. Persons with relevant issue attitudes, sufficient participation skills, and feelings of efficacy,

2. Persons with relevant issue attitudes, lower participation skills, and/or lower efficacy, and

3. Persons lacking relevant issue attitudes, lacking efficacy, and perhaps lacking participation skills. The effect of mass communication on participation would follow a different sequence of events for each of these three types of potential participants.

Three Sequences of Participation Effects

People of the first type already have issue attitudes that may be brought to bear in reacting to portrayals of an issue or controversy in the mass media. They already have the skills and confidence to participate if they want to. Therefore, we would expect that effects on issue attitudes would mediate between mass communication and participation, as illustrated in Figure 5.1.

Figure 5.1
Participation Effects
Sequence 1

Mass Media Stimuli →	Effect on Individual's → Issue Attitudes	Effect on Individual's Likelihood of Participation (See Fig. 3)

At this point it is possible to spell out, in more detail, why two of the three simple reductionist correspondence rules discussed at the outset of this book seem defective. These rules were (1) if attitude change occurs, public opinion change has occurred and (2) if mass communication fails to produce attitude change, it has failed to change public opinion. (It will be recalled that "attitude change" meant attitude change on issues.)

Sequence 1. The Sequence 1 person—the person with issue attitudes and with both skills and efficacy—should fit the simple reductionist model to a T. Simple reductionism implicitly assumes an audience where (a) everybody has an issue attitude already (which needs to be changed, if mass communication is to make a difference) and (b) it is either irrelevant whether there is participation, or, more likely, everybody's attitudes somehow will be made known. Since the Sequence 1 person seems to have been one on which the simple reductionist model was based, we can now examine the extent to which this model's assumptions stand up under conditions favorable to that model.

Figure 5.2
Possible Media Effects on Issue Attitudes,
With Predicted Effect on Participation

Attitude Effect	Effect on Likelihood of Participation by Individuals with Participation Skills*
Attitude Change	
Super Conversion	Increase
Conversion	No Change
Ordinary Change	Decrease
Minor Change	Decrease
Commitment	Increase, but intensity probably insufficient
Attitude Reinforcement	Increase
Attitude Object Change	
Now associated with salient/high-intensity affect object	Increase
Now associated with low-affect object	Decrease

*Applies to sequence 1 individuals, who have skills, efficacy feelings, and issue attitudes.

Figure 5.2 provides a list of attitude effects, as defined in Chapter 2. These attitude effects are then linked to effects on the likelihood of participation. The predicted effects on participation are derived from fairly extensive research literature that leads to this conclusion about issue attitudes and participation: *The stronger the affect attached to the relevant issue attitude, the greater the chance the Sequence 1 individual will participate.*

A great deal of evidence indicates that the issue attitudes of participants, compared to those of nonparticipants, tend to be more salient, intense, or both. Here is a brief sampling of this evidence, selected primarily for diversity. Verba and Brody reported that people who participated in activities concerning the Vietnam war tended to have more intense issue positions than did the general populace.[29] Verba and Nie reported a variety of findings that participants' attitudes were more intense than nonparticipants' attitudes on the same topics.[30] Analyzing six presidential and six congressional elections, Perry reported the now-familiar finding that persons who were undecided at the time of the interview were much *less* likely to vote than people who had already made up their minds.[31] And among a group of persons associated with a school sponsored by the Christian Anti-Communist Crusade, the most active participants in outside election campaigns had even more conservative attitudes than did the other persons in the school.[32] Leaders and the most active members of environmental groups were more likely than the rest to feel that environmental quality should have absolute priority over economic considerations.[33] (Of course, I should give the usual warning that these are correlational findings. They don't *prove* that issue intensity causes participation, but they are consistent with the belief that it does.)

This first sequence seems to fit Berelson, Lazarsfeld, and McPhee's simple model of media effects during a political campaign.[34] According to their interpretation, the mass media serve progressively to increase information, interest, and the intensity of voter loyalties as the campaign proceeds and as attention to the media increases. Through the process of reinforcing loyalties, the intention to vote is "implemented" and acted on by persons who have been exposed to the campaign. Issue attitude reinforcement, then, would by definition represent an increase in intensity; the greater the intensity (for persons with efficacy and skills), the greater the chance of participation.

While the relation between intensity and participation has much support, this evidence doesn't come close to the level of acceptance that still is accorded this proposition: *The mass media are far more likely to reinforce than to change (issue) attitudes, but if a message does change an attitude, the change most likely will be a slight one.*

In other words, don't expect a conversion. The cumulative weight of the research evidence leads to the conclusion that, among persons with already established issue attitudes, any change produced will be ordinary change or minor change, *each of which involves a loss of intensity.* So if the changed attitude is felt less intensely, we would predict a *decline* in the likelihood of participation by these Sequence 1 people.

Simple reductionist correspondence rule 1 was that attitude change means a change in public opinion. But if ordinary and minor change occur, these changed attitudes are likely to become "invisible" to decision-makers, except under rather unusual circumstances.[35] By itself, then, *attitude change is not sufficient* for public opinion change on an issue—even for Sequence 1 people.

Correspondence rule 2 was that if attitude change did not occur, public opinion change could not have occurred. You will recall that, to a simple reductionist, saying that the mass media "only" reinforce attitudes is about equivalent to saying that the media are impotent and ineffectual. Even scholars disturbed by the failure of the simple reductionist approach to account for "extra" effects tend to accept the equivalence of reinforcement and impotence—otherwise, why try to find "extra" effects?

But if mass communication messages serve ordinarily to reinforce (i.e., *intensify*) issue attitudes, it is conceivable that hordes of formerly inactive citizens would suddenly be impelled to express their attitudes, thus producing a variety of possible changes in the information received about citizen attitudes.[36] A case in point probably was the 1960 Kennedy-Nixon election—in particular, the effects of the televised "Great Debates." A number of studies all led to the conclusion that the debates reinforced the wavering loyalties of Democratic voters, while not particularly weakening or strengthening Nixon loyalists.[37] *Hardly anybody's issue attitudes* (Kennedy-Nixon preferences) *were changed, but the election result was changed* because of reinforcement. The debates legitimized Kennedy in the minds of people who would have liked to have voted for a Democratic candidate, anyway. Turnout by Democrats was unusually heavy, helping to produce the largest election turnout in many decades.

In a well-known article, Festinger said he could find only three studies that tested whether *changed* attitudes resulted in behavior, and their results called into question the common belief that the change was related to subsequent behavior.[38] Festinger concluded:

> . . . it seems clear that we cannot glibly assume a relationship between attitude change and behavior. Indeed, it seems that the absence of research in this area is a glaring omission and that the whole problem needs thinking through.[39]

Ten years and sixteen more studies later, Seibold reached essentially the same conclusion.[40]

If my analysis is correct, what is really more surprising is that we should have *expected* there to be a clear relationship between attitude change and behavior. Recall that attitude change, as operationalized, often confounds (1) commitment with (2) minor and ordinary change with (3) conversion with (4) super conversion. *Each* of these, theoretically (see Figure 5.2), *leads to a different behavioral outcome* when political participation is the behavior involved.

Some better evidence on attitude change as it relates to participation is now appearing. While the different types of attitude change are not always entirely clearly separated, this evidence does support my view that certain kinds of attitude change lead to withdrawal from participation.

In an analysis of the South African general election of 1970, Lever collected data on turnout and voter preferences. This election was notable because it was the first in a quarter century in which the United party was able to make significant gains at the expense of the ruling National party. Abstentions by a number of dissatisfied National party voters may have been the principal reason for the outcome of the election and were "of far greater importance in determining the outcome of the election than shifts of allegiance from party to party."[41] Unfortunately, Lever did not define what he meant by "dissatisfied" party loyalists, so we can't take these results any further.

Hahn took advantage of a panel study to differentiate between types of attitude change.[42] His attitude change groups didn't correspond with mine, but Hahn's results support the view that those attitude changes that result in weakened intensity do lead to withdrawal. He measured changes in attitudes toward fluoridation in the panel and was able to relate these changes to turnout in two elections in which fluoridation was one of the measures on the ballot. "Converts"—people who apparently changed from pro to con or con to pro—were significantly more likely to have voted on the fluoridation issue in *both* elections than people Hahn terms "ambivalents." Both converts and ambivalents were about equally likely to have voted on other issues in the elections—it was only on the fluoridation measure that they differed. Obviously, converts roughly correspond to my conversion type. Ambivalents seem to be a mixture of people who had commitment effects—which should have mildly increased their chance of voting—and people who had experienced minor change, which should have drastically reduced their participation. So the expected differences in turnout could very well have occurred despite a certain fuzziness in Hahn's categories.

Holm, Kraus, and Bochner did a three-stage panel study of reactions to the 1973 Ervin Committee hearings. They reported that, while the percentage of pro-Nixon people declined only slightly, the pro-Nixon people "were . . . withdrawing" from discussing the Watergate affair with others.[43] According to their data, these discussions were overwhelmingly negative toward Nixon. So we can speculate and say that the remaining pro-Nixon people probably were unwilling to be committed to an overt defense of Nixon and were attempting, by avoidance, to hang onto their weakening pro-Nixon attitudes. Unfortunately, these researchers seemed more interested in using interpersonal discussions to explain attitude change, rather than attitude change to explain participation in discussions, so we can't push their results much further.

Nevertheless, we can piece together some anecdotal support from other sources for the proposition that minor and/or ordinary change were producing withdrawal. In another panel study of reactions to the televised Ervin hearings, Michael Robinson concluded, "Opinions about Nixon's guilt stayed relatively stable during the hearings but *affections* toward him . . . diminished. . . ."[44] In other words, the people who thought him "not guilty" at the start still believed that way, but they had experienced something like a *minor change* in their affect. Gallup Poll readings during Ervin Committee hearings suggest a kind of *ordinary change* when the attitude object is the Republican party and not Nixon.[45] From January 1973 until just after the close of the hearings, the number of persons saying they were Republicans declined, but the Democrats did not gain; the number of persons saying they were "Independents" increased by precisely the amount that Republicans decreased. This would correspond to a weak change of sign, from Republican to something like "don't know"—ordinary change, in other words.

If we assume, then, that both minor change and ordinary change were at work during this period, were there other declines in participation by Nixon loyalists besides withdrawal from discussions? Yes. During this period, the Republican party reported unusual trouble in fund raising. Attendance at their dinners plunged, and donations dried up temporarily. During the spring and early summer of 1974, in a series of highly publicized special congressional elections, a number of seats in normally safe Republican districts were lost to Democrats. Turnout by Republicans in these elections was abnormally low.[46] During this time period, Republicans also reported trouble in recruiting qualified candidates.

So whether a changed attitude will be expressed by persons with participation skills seems to depend on what type of change it is. Attitude reinforcement appears to be a far more potent media effect than simple reductionist theory allows it to be. As for attitude object change (Figure 5.2), the reader is reminded of the anecdotal support provided in Chapter 3 for the hypothesis that participation can be reduced or increased by object change, depending on the affect attached to the "new" object.

Figure 5.2 can be regarded as a set of propositions that badly need to be tested further by the kind of panel and experimental research which recognizes distinctions between types of attitude effects. However, the evidence is already sufficient to reject both of the first two correspondence rules: Attitude change is neither necessary nor sufficient for a change in public opinion.

We can already say this without having to use the second and third groups of potential participants and sequences that are less made-to-order for simple reductionism.

Sequence 2. Now we turn to the second ideal type. These persons already have issue attitudes that might be brought to bear in reacting to a situation, but they have weaker feelings of efficacy and may lack requisite participation skills. Because voting in elections demands lower-level skills, because of the emphasis on "civic duty," and because of the turnout help provided by media and campaign organizations, these persons often can be brought to the point of voting. These persons bear a closer resemblance to Sequence 1 individuals in the election framework than they do in the influence framework, and the sequence of effects therefore might more closely resemble Sequence 1 in the election framework than in the influence framework. Verba and Nie estimate that about 21 percent of eligible Americans are "voters only," [47] an estimate that seems, if anything, a shade low.

Figure 5.3 still applies, but issue attitude effects alone are not sufficient to predict the likelihood of participation. With these individuals, it is also necessary to have favorable movement in attitudes toward participation. This movement might be reinforcement, if the individual began with a mildly favorable attitude toward participation, or it might have to be some sort of change, if feelings were initially negative.

One reason for separating media effects on participation into different sequence types is the increasing evidence that issue attitudes interact with attitudes toward behavior to predict behavior.

In a number of studies in the social psychological literature, behavior was predicted better by taking into account both issue attitudes and attitudes toward the behavior. [48] An experiment by Weinstein is especially interesting because it involved predicting whether subjects would sign a political petition. He found that improved predictions resulted from an index that combined the student's attitude toward signing a petition with his/her attitude toward the subject of the petition. [49] Putting it in my terms, a fa-

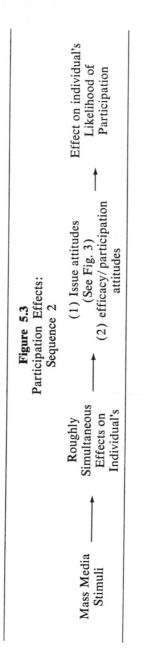

Figure 5.3
Participation Effects:
Sequence 2

Mass Media
Stimuli

→

Roughly
Simultaneous
Effects on
Individual's

→

(1) Issue attitudes
(See Fig. 3)
(2) efficacy/participation
attitudes

→

Effect on individual's
Likelihood of
Participation

vorable attitude toward participation and an intense (and favorable) issue attitude seemed to predict signing better than did either attitude alone.

Both the sociological and the political science literature contain support for the view that issue affect and efficacy feelings together improve predictions about whether a person will participate. For example, a study after the 1967 riots in Newark suggests that an individual's mistrust of the local government, when combined with feelings of political efficacy, increased the likelihood of his riot participation.[50] By itself, mistrust didn't predict riot participation very well. (I'm interpreting "mistrust" as roughly corresponding to the issue attitude component which, when combined with efficacy, predicts behavior fairly well.) In another study Aberbach found that persons who distrusted government were much more likely to vote when they felt they had the ability to understand and affect government.[51] Similarly, Zurcher and Monts found that high efficacy, when combined with low trust, predicted the "mobilization potential" of citizens.[52]

So if the mass media are to increase the chances of participation by Sequence 2 people, they would probably have to intensify issue attitudes while also strengthening positive attitudes toward participating. We know that one effect of the use of media in election campaigns is to intensify party, issue, and candidate predispositions. On the assumption that this continues to take place, one new way to look at media coverage of political campaigns would be to compare the amount of help journalists give potential voters —registration deadline announcements, lists of polling places, and so on—in two otherwise similar localities and then look for corresponding differences in turnout.

If the speculations in the last few pages are correct, there are many more ways of *reducing* than increasing the likelihood of participation among Sequence 2 individuals. Either weakened issue affect or a weaker/more negative attitude toward participation would appear to do it. In this connection, the next chapter will suggest that traditional journalistic practices discourage participation in the influence framework. Later in this chapter, we will also examine some other hypotheses about how journalists' practices often inhibit participation.

Sequence 3. As for the Sequence 3 individual, a very tentative and speculative sequence is presented in Figure 5.4. Such a sequence appears consistent with research findings, but the evidence is scant. Because one problem with Sequence 3 individuals is that they have learned to avoid public affairs content in the mass media, they may not attend often and long enough to get past the "efficacy" stage, a stage that might take several years to attain. Once past that stage, the best that can be hoped for is that the individual would be brought to the point of entering Sequence 2.

One of the best-known research articles about the mass media is Herbert Hyman and Paul Sheatsley's "Why Information Campaigns Fail." They estimated that about a third of the adult population is a "hard core of chronic 'know-nothings.' "[53] There maybe little reason to suppose that this percentage has declined much since the 1940s,[54] but there is reason to quarrel with the term "know-nothings." Obviously, it does not follow that such persons know nothing about home repairs, childbearing, or any number of other things that they may regard as being of more direct and immediate use to them. The key words here are *direct and immediate use;* if a person lacks political efficacy feelings, he or she would probably see little point in following public affairs, since the information could not be used. If they do not follow public affairs, Sequence 3 individuals would lack the background information (and maybe the skills) to comprehend political references easily, even if they were exposed to public affairs content by accident. In fact, encountering by accident such terms as "the Oval Office" in public affairs news would do nothing except further discourage efficacy feelings (also see Paletz et al. for other examples of journalistic practices that might discourage efficacy[55]).

The argument for a distinctly different third sequence could have been made much more conveniently and directly if there weren't so many gaps in the evidence concerning efficacy feelings. So we must string bits and pieces together.

One of the key elements in my argument is that efficacy is not necessarily a fixed personality characteristic. Efficacy can be enhanced or reduced, depending on the individual's experiences. There is some scattered support for this proposition. Eldersveld demonstrated remarkably little interest in these findings, but he

Figure 5.4
Participation Effects: Sequence 3

	Effect on Efficacy	Effect on Interest	Is There Issue Information Gain and Attitude Formation?	Does Sequence 2 Start?
	Positive →	Positive →	Some, If Interest → Continues	Yes
Mass Communication Stimuli	Negative → or No Effect	Negative → or No Effect	[SEQUENCE STOPS].	

did report in passing that previously apathetic persons contacted by campaign canvassers had higher efficacy about voting than did otherwise comparable apathetics who weren't contacted.[56] Based on the strength of his conclusions about other differences (turnout, etc.) between the two groups, one would have thought Eldersveld would have made more of this result. In fact, the result was not tabled, nor was a significance test reported. However, one can approximate what the numbers must have been, on a best-case and a worst-case basis, and in either case, efficacy differences between the two groups appear significant at $p < .05$ or better. In another study, Barnes found that persons with low education seemed to gain both efficacy feelings and political information *if* they participated.[57] Other research—and even more speculation—supporting the point that efficacy may not be fixed has been summarized by Milbrath and Goel.[58]

A closely related point has to do with how people acquire efficacy feelings. Customarily, it has been thought that efficacy was derived largely through parental upbringing, including the social class environment of the child, and to a lesser extent through education experiences. Children from high-status homes brought with them to school advantages in verbal and other skills which were confirmed and reinforced in school. Taken to its extreme, the conventional view sounds like a kind of predestination, with the unfolding of the rest of the individual's political life determined by these earlier experiences. But the Barnes study cited above suggests that, even when handicapped by lack of education, people could arrive at both efficacy and increased political knowledge through the act of participation itself. Barnes suggests two independent paths to efficacy and information: (1) through family background and upbringing, and (2) for those lacking background advantages, through participation. This second path is perfectly consistent with Dahl's speculations about what happens when people don't participate: failure to participate itself further depresses efficacy feelings,[59] so the next time around participation is even less likely, and so on.

Based on a large-scale survey of 1976 nonvoters, Hadley found that one in every five nonvoters possessed both the social class background and the political skills to participate, *but had ex-*

tremely low efficacy feelings.[60] His results imply that this group of nonvoters had had experiences as adults which had produced feelings of political impotence. Obviously, Eldersveld's results suggest strongly that being contacted by canvassers raised efficacy feelings among his test group of apathetics. Lemert and Larkin's study of writers of letters to the editor provides evidence which cannot be interpreted as clearly as can the Eldersveld results. Lemert and Larkin found that writers whose most recent letter had just been rejected by the local newspaper had much lower feelings of efficacy than writers whose letters had just been published.[61] While these "rejected" writers' knowledge of political influence strategies was about the same as that held by the "accepted" writers, it was true that the "rejected" writers were older and had lower educational attainments than the "accepted" writers. So it cannot be said unambiguously that it was recent experience, not demographics, which produced the lower efficacy feelings. But Lemert and Larkin's findings are certainly consistent with Eldersveld's.

Let us suppose that efficacy is not a fixed personality characteristic and that it can be changed somewhat by relatively short-term experiences. But are low-efficacy people normally *available* for any such short-term experiences? And could mass communication be considered as having the "vividness" equivalent to being contacted personally by canvassers, even if the low-efficacy people exposed themselves to political content in the media?

The answers to the first question and the second question are the same: probably not.

Low-efficacy people have learned to avoid public affairs content in the mass media (as noted before, the relationship is so strong that some political scientists even have included mass communication media public affairs exposure as part of their *efficacy* measure[62]). Furthermore, when low-efficacy people are asked about the media they rely on for their public affairs news, they are much more likely to show a decided preference for the low-effort medium of television. A reanalysis of data from the Lemert-Larkin study (Table 5.1) shows this very strong relationship when efficacy is used to predict a choice between newspapers and television on Roper-type use and believability questions.[63] So *if* the Sequence

3 people were to be exposed accidentally to political news, it would most likely be through the medium (television) that, Michael Robinson argues, is *least* likely to provide positive experiences concerning politics.

Table 5.1
Efficacy As a Predictor of Reliance
on Newspapers or Television for News of Public Affairs
Use**

Efficacy Score*	TV		Newspapers	
Low	52.9%	47.1%	100%	(N=34)
Medium	47.8%	52.2%	100%	(N=46)
High	18.7%	81.3%	100%	(N=32)
	41.1%	58.9%	100%	(N=112)
	$X^2 = 9.321$, 2 df, p .01.			

	Believability***			
	TV		Newspapers	
	74.1%	25.9%	100%	(N=27)
	42.4%	57.6%	100%	(N=33)
	28.6%	71.4%	100%	(N=21)
	49.4%	50.6%	100%	(N=81)
	$X^2 = 10.981$, 2 df, p .01.			

*Total scored across three items: (1) "I don't think public officials care very much what people like me think," (2) "Voting is the only way people like me can have any say about how the government runs things," and (3) "Sometimes politics and government seem so complicated that a person like me can't really understand what's going on."
**Respondents were asked to choose the single medium they used "for news of what's going on in the world today." Radio, magazine, and other responses excluded from table.
***Respondents were asked to choose the single medium they would find most believable in the case of conflicting reports about a news story. Radio and magazine responses excluded from table.

The second question concerns the "vividness" of mass-communicated experiences. To state the obvious, the experience is vicarious. Perhaps CBS's "60 Minutes" would provide more involving experiences than would a newspaper or magazine article about public affairs, but in any case, contact by a canvasser (or pollster) would generally seem to be a more vivid experience for more low-efficacy people.

These points suggest to me that, even under ideal conditions, moving people from Sequence 3 to Sequence 2 would take a very long period of time if mass communication is the mechanism by which the movement is produced. Initially, exposure to political communications would be rare and accidental. Even under ideal conditions, the process could take many months or years. Perhaps the rate of accidental exposure to politics would be higher in television than in newspapers, but if Robinson is correct, the experiences themselves might be more positive in newspapers.

There are other steps in the chain of events proposed in Sequence 3. Muller adds results suggesting that, however efficacy is achieved, it leads to the acquisition of political information and skills and, eventually, to confidence that one can influence government decisions.[64] Kenneth M. Jackson found that knowledge of ways to influence political outcomes was correlated both with efficacy and with a measure of political information.[65] Research I am presently conducting at Oregon suggests the same thing.[66]

But what about the step in the chain of events involving the creation of interest in politics? Atkin, Galloway, and Nayman concluded that: (1) exposure to public affairs content probably leads to knowledge, which in turn leads to further exposure, and (2) interest in public affairs probably leads to exposure, which in turn leads to more interest.[67] Both chains of events appear to be mutually reinforcing. And Genova found, as we would expect, that interest in an area of knowledge predicts information about it.[68] We are pretty sure efficacy predicts interest.[69] And we have quite a lot of evidence that interest predicts participation.

We also know that "chronic know-nothings" are capable of acquiring information when they see some point to it. Tichenor et al. found that the "knowledge gap" tended to disappear when a public issue of direct concern to "know-nothings" arose.[70] The way I read Tichenor's results, each of these issues involved a threat to "know-nothings'" jobs. Significantly, however, they didn't seem to use the media to inform themselselves about these salient issues. They usually heard about them from other people—most often from fellow workers, probably. They have *learned* not to use the mass media to keep track of things for them. It would take a very long time, presumably, for these persons to be exposed to enough political/public affairs content in the media to attain efficacy and interest. And, of course, journalists would probably have to do something differently to make further exposure rewarding enough for these people to attend to such content deliberately the next time.

As for newspapers (and television and radio as well), the next chapter argues that, if journalists covering politics were to change their craft practices concerning mobilizing information, there is at least a plausible chance that Sequence 3 would occur over a long period of time. Unfortunately, however, the evidence suggests that a change in these craft practices is rather unlikely.

While he seemed not to be concerned with the role of media in creating the feeling, Bachrach suggests that disinterest and lack of participation may be a reasonable response to a political environment that presents, at best, limited opportunities for effective participation.[71]

Thus far, my argument implies that a major segment of the population does not follow public affairs because of present media practices. What about the roles of the schools and the family in "teaching" some people that they cannot (or should not) cope with politics? Clearly, the mass media would not be alone in discouraging interest and participation by some persons. However, researchers have much more evidence about these other agencies than about the mass media, and attention should be redirected to the mass media as a contributing factor in encouraging and discouraging participation. It is for this reason that discussion of all three sequences appears to be preoccupied with the media.

Another assumption needs to be made explicit again before we go on—namely, that efficacy feelings are not considered to be irrevocably present or absent as a result of early socialization experiences. Nevertheless, we are probably talking about potential changes in efficacy taking place very gradually, especially for Sequence 3 individuals.

A Participation Research Agenda

Some of the most important unanswered questions about the media and participation have already been implied in various parts of this chapter. While our concern is principally with the mass media, we cannot avoid placing some other research items on the agenda. Therefore, hypotheses and/or problem statements will be presented below under three categories: (1) studies of participation that could be done in mainstream political science, (2) studies that should appeal to several social science disciplines—a "mixed" category, and (3) studies that deal explicitly with the mass media and participation.

Studies for Mainstream Political Science

Some signs indicate that political scientists' enthusiasm for behavioral research is diminishing. While at times this book reads as if I wished political scientists had never gotten into survey research, my argument instead is with the kinds of surveys pursued in political science and the conceptualizations they embody. Since political science historically has dominated investigations of participation, it would be a waste of scarce resources for this field gradually to abandon the study of political participation. However, much of this new research requires that *new* data be gathered —the limitations of existing data archives in political science may prevent using them to study some of the following hypotheses.

Participants' efficacy feelings will be stronger and more stable if they have participated in the influence framework than if they have voted. (Influence framework participation is more difficult and places heavier demands on participants' skills and willingness to try.)

As a motive for participating, a sense of "citizen duty" will be cited more often by voters than by influence framework participants.

Influence framework participants will be overwhelmingly more likely to give policy-related reasons for their act of participation than will voters, despite evidence that policy-based voting is on the increase.

Verba and Nie's "communal" type of participation can be broken down by factor analysis into two subtypes if enough cases of communal participation are entered into the analysis. These subtypes are likely to be (1) influence framework participants and (2) the kind of "communal-supportive" participants that gave Verba and Nie's factor its name. The problem with their approach was that they drew a general sample and then sorted out the different types of participants from that. As mentioned earlier, this data approach leads to too few cases of influence framework participation.

Communal-supportive participants will differ from influence framework participants on a number of demographic and attitudinal variables, just as Verba and Nie found that their original four types of participation distinguished people on a number of other such variables.

Studies for Any of Several Disciplines

Any of several social sciences should be interested in this group of hypotheses. Sociology and especially social psychology are wrestling with the problem of how, when, and whether attitudes predict behavior. Political participation is only one kind of behavior, but it is an important one.

Figure 5.2 listed a number of hypotheses concerning the interaction between issue attitudes and behavior. It is not necessary for a study to demonstrate that mass communication produced any of the listed attitude effects. Presumably we could start with a high-efficacy panel study design, locate various types of attitude change or other attitude effects, and then predict the behavioral effects for persons with participation skills and efficacy feelings. At this stage of inquiry it would not be necessary to establish that any set of communications produced these attitude effects. If the predictions hold up, mass media researchers and others could compare mass communications with other possible causal agents, and we would then be operating in the third category of participation studies—those dealing explicitly with the mass media and participation.

An even more ambitious set of studies would test whether Sequence 3 operates as suggested, and whether it would feed people into Sequence 2, and so on. The problem here, however, is locating (or creating) relatively short-term stimuli that could activate Sequence 2 and relatively longer-term stimuli that could activate Sequence 3. As the next chapter suggests, it may be difficult to get journalists to produce these stimuli.

Studies for Mass Communication Research

A healthy recent trend at one of the major research centers doing election studies has been the effort to combine survey and media content data by collecting newspaper and television coverage of gubernatorial and congressional elections at selected time periods.[72] It is especially useful to gather media content data for widely separated and relatively local elections, because these elections tend to expand the obtained diversity of media content. This greater diversity (greater than a national campaign would have) has the potential for creating a mass communication *variable* that really is a variable—that is, it covers a greater range of values. Otherwise, we are compelled merely to compare exposure to a more-or-less constant communication.

Already there is an extensive literature on participation in local elections. Nevertheless, neither political scientists nor sociologists have been very active in using mass communication content variables to explain the participation outcomes of these elections.

Probably the single largest effort to use communication variables to study local elections was made by Richard F. Carter and associates—a massive undertaking that culminated in 1966 with a series of monographs.[73] The analysis combined survey data, public school tax and bond election results, and an effort to construct a number of communication variables. (School bond and tax elections have two big advantages for researchers interested in using communication variables to explain the outcomes. Thousands of them occur in a relatively short period of time, allowing comparative analysis, and relatively little spillover of mass communication content occurs from one district to another.)

Work done by Carter, and by others before him, definitely suggests that both the amount and the makeup of participation can determine whether school financial measures pass. And many believe that this work has firmly established that mass communication affects participation. For example, the likelihood of higher turnout and of defeat increases when people show up at a school board meeting and complain about the schools' programs. On the assumption that the complaints received news coverage, we might conclude that what was really measured was a mass communication variable. An earlier study by Kenny[74] reported that when school supporters sent leaflets to certain voters, participation went up and the chances of approval went down. Again, making certain assumptions—for example, that opponents got hold of a copy and raised the issue of antidemocratic campaigning, either in the news or in their media advertising—we can argue that this also shows mass media influence on participation.

But few of the more obvious media variables that were explicitly incorporated in these studies showed much of a relationship to participation, while many nonmedia variables did.[75] Despite the existence of a great deal of impressive circumstantial evidence provided about the media-participation relationship by Carter and associates, I would suggest that school tax and bond measures remain an unsettled opportunity for more definitive tests of the media-participation relationship. Researchers will need to operationalize the mass communication variables in ways other than those used by the Carter group. For example, instead of asking school personnel by questionnaire about news coverage in their communities, somewhat more attention should be paid to monitoring media content itself and creating media variables from this content.

Another group of potentially productive media studies would follow leads created by research discussed in the preceding section on studies suitable for various disciplines. We noted then that these studies did not require a focus on the mass media, but could be extended to the media if it appeared productive.

Far more attention should be paid to testing whether and when the mass media produce *lowered* participation. To repeat a point made earlier, it is a mistake to assume that more communication exposure always means more participation. Barbic reported that, in Yugoslavia, those who listened/watched broadcast media *moderately* participated more heavily than did those who either listened/watched very heavily or hardly at all.[76] Among other things, this study illustrated that, regardless of whether media consumption is thought to promote or to inhibit participation, the relationship was not a linear one and would be underemphasized by standard correlational techniques.

An old saying goes something like this: "Making love is incompatible with the act of reading a newspaper." Barbic's findings and Lazarsfeld and Merton's speculations about the media "narcotizing" audiences[77] come from roughly the same school of thought as this saying. To the extent that available leisure time is absorbed by the media, less time is available for acts of participation.

But there may be more to it than that. What about specific mass communication content, rather than a gross measure such as time spent with the media? In an interesting case study, Paletz et al. argue that the way journalists cover local government discourages participation by members of disadvantaged population groups.[78] Assuming that we can find examples of at least a few journalists covering local government in a different way, it ought to be possible to do a comparative study of local government coverage and participation in either or both decision frameworks, and then to obtain data about how widespread the practices outlined by Paletz are.

If Michael Robinson is correct about the effects of network television on people's cynicism and sense of impotence, we ought to be able to extend his findings to participation. To my knowledge, his work has stopped short of its logical next step—effects on participation. For example, he has examined attitude scale items and reported votes for George Wallace in 1968, but he has not taken that next step. If television news dependence predicts these attitude and voting choice responses after social class has been controlled, it also ought to predict *withdrawal from participation* by these people, especially (but not entirely) in the absence of candidates such as Wallace.

Figure 5.2 contains a set of hypothetical relations between media *issue* attitude effects and participation. However, there is another set of relevant attitudes—attitudes toward participation—and it is with this set that Sequences 2 and 3 are explicitly concerned. It is interesting how little research evidence exists on whether (and how) mass communication might affect participation attitudes.[79]

Chapter 6 suggests that rarely is media content directed toward this attitude set, *especially* when we look at public opinion controversies. Chapter 6 also suggests that quite dramatic increases in influence framework participation follow on those rare occasions when mass communication provides messages with direct implications for participation attitudes. I call the information in such messages *mobilizing information*. One way to read the massed results of attitude change research is that attitude change is much more likely when it is directed at "novel" targets—for example, participation attitudes—rather than the issue attitudes that have already been the subject of many messages and accordingly are well defended by persons who normally attend to public affairs news.

6
Journalists, Participation, and Mobilizing Information

Interestate 5 bisects Oregon from California to Washington and is probably the state's major freeway by any criterion: length, traffic volume, linkage between major population centers, and so on. Midway in the populous Willamette Valley, the city of Albany lies athwart I-5, about twenty-five miles south of Salem, the state's capital. Everyone who travels I-5 through Albany passes through and under the smoke from a large kraft paper mill that looms beside the highway.

The nearly continuous smoke and aroma of this mill are a favorite topic of complaint and discussion among tourists and motorists in cars, truck stops, restaurants, and gas stations. While the mill is easily the most visible landmark for many miles, it has no signs or identifying insignia of any kind. Therefore, these conversations usually include references to "that plant" or the query "What is it?" "That stinkpot at Albany," is the way Ira Keller, a principal owner of the mill, once jokingly referred to it.[1]

If passersby knew the name of the mill[2]—and the mill is almost never mentioned by name in Oregon news media despite many references to it—they might feel able to complain to it, or about it. In effect, those who already know the identity of the mill are able to act in the political process, while those who do not know its identity are likely to be discouraged from acting on their attitudes toward the mill.

The name and location of the mill constitute one kind of *mobilizing information* (MI). I use the term to refer to information that helps people act on attitudes they already have. If you hold attitudes in opposition to those of another person, and if you have relevant MI and he or she does not, *you* will probably be the more politically effective.

Obviously, interest groups, lobbyists, and others with political savvy don't need to depend on external, *public* sources of MI. They have already acquired much of this information. But other people, despite the fact that they already have intense attitudes they would like to express, may lack access to MI. As a public source of information about political issues, the mass media are a crucial source of MI for "outsiders." If the mass media fail to provide MI in political debates, then, it would seem that those who already know how to operate are advantaged. *Participation by politically inexperienced citizens is inhibited when MI is missing in mass media coverage of public affairs.* Members of Common Cause and other citizen's lobbies may get political MI from headquarters. Members of interest groups may get MI from their organizations. But the citizen who is not associated with these groups or with "activist" friends is almost totally dependent on the mass media for MI.

Later, we shall consider some dramatic examples of how MI stimulated participation when the mass media provided MI. But the concept of MI falls into one of those strange lacunae in the development of our field of the mass media and public opinion, and needs to be described in more detail before we proceed. Despite its importance to understanding how the media influence public opinion outcomes, MI is a relatively new concept, and our thinking about it is still changing. Nevertheless, I'd like to offer some tentative conclusions about our research on MI in this chapter.

Thus far, we have identified three general types of MI in the mass media. These types appear to cut across conventional groupings of media content, such as advertising, news, and entertainment. Because of my focus in this book on political communication and the public opinion process, this chapter concentrates on MI in news and public affairs content, with occasional references to political advertising. But let's attend to these other content areas briefly. Then we'll look at the three types of MI.

MI AND TYPES OF MEDIA CONTENT

In advertising, mobilizing information is a basic stock in trade. The hours of business and address of a business routinely appear in ads. So does information about brand names, styles, and prices. All these pieces of information are intended to enable the individual to act—to buy the product advertised. While advertisers intend their MI to mobilize behavior, this may or may not be true in other content areas. In a film or televised detective drama, MI will sometimes be present in the form of the *modus operandi* of the criminal, and occasionally the detective will point out how the *modus operandi* could have been "improved." Johnny Carson's off-hand comments about places where he likes to eat (or doesn't) might mobilize some audience members. Actresses performing glamorous roles may provide beauty and clothing tips in either advertising or drama.

In news and other editorial content, MI includes many things that might be outside the political opinion process: recipes, garden tips, TV listings, and so on. Political MI in the news might include such things as the names of people and organizations promoting a point of view, with enough accompanying information to enable persons to contact them. It might include meeting times and places of critical legislative hearings, or the names of key legislators whose votes could decide an issue, with enough accompanying information to enable persons to contact them.

In the context of its smoke discharges, the identity and location of the Albany kraft paper mill would be political MI. Depending on the nature of the news item, information that might mobilize consumer action may or may not be political MI. For example, during the Vietnam war, the information that Dow Chemical Company made napalm for the Defense Department led to efforts to boycott its consumer products. Similarly, members of the environmentalist movement have occasionally tried to boycott specific products that allegedly hurt the environment. Ordinarily, however, we would not consider as *political* MI information that might be useful in consumer decisions.

In principle, if it should turn out that political MI doesn't appear often in the mass media, it should have very potent effects when it does appear. This is because political MI would be directed toward an attitude object that would seldom be the "target" of political mass communications: the act of participation. Research strongly suggests that there is a better chance of achieving dramatic attitude changing effects when the topic of the communication is new to a recipient, because he or she has had little or no previous need to develop defenses for any previous attitudes toward the topic.[3]

But even if only a tiny portion of the audience participated as a result of political MI, we already noted previously that increased participation in the influence framework can make a marked impression on decision-makers. This is because, unlike citizen feedback in elections, our political machinery is not well equipped to analyze, digest, and place in perspective a large number of telegrams, letters, and telephone calls.

Thus a tiny percentage of participants, spread over the nation, can create the "firestorm" of participation that followed the Archibald Cox firing.

And the networks can be quietly frightened by the 55,000 phone calls, 15,000 letters, and 1,624 telegrams arriving within four days after former Vice President Agnew's famous Des Moines speech attacking network "bias." Most of these communications strongly agreed with Agnew, and the networks were not much consoled by the results of polls they shortly commissioned.[4]

A study by Lowry found that, by the summer following the Agnew speech, network journalists had drastically cut down on "inferential" statements about the Nixon administration and markedly increased the proportion of "report" statements.[5] Report statements are verifiably factual—for example, the White House is located at 1600 Pennsylvania Avenue. Inferential statements interpret events and often involve opinions, conjecture, conclusions, beliefs, generalizations, and predictions—all of them things Agnew was complaining about.

Network officials protested Agnew's attack loudly, but Lowry's results suggest that, for a time at least, they had reversed Theodore Roosevelt's maxim about speaking softly and carrying a big stick. In fairness, more than a perception of public opinion was involved here. The government's legal potential for damaging television is great, even though the threat has rarely been carried out.

Types of MI

Three types of mobilizing information cut across topics and groupings of content. Each type is listed below, along with a few of the major subtypes. The examples of subtypes, however, emphasize news and editorial content, not other kinds of media content.

1. *Locational* MI usually provides information about both time and place for activity: "advance" stories about forthcoming meetings, many obituaries, most pleas for charitable help, almost all TV-radio program listings, almost all of the currently fashionable clip-it-out-and-send-it-to-us newspaper questionnaires, almost all voter registration and polling-place announcements, and so on.

2. *Identificational* MI usually involves both names *and* enough locational MI to enable persons to recognize and/or contact the person, groups, or entity thus identified. Examples include: individuals' names and addresses; names and phone numbers; names and positions in relatively stable, easily locatable organizations (for example, John Jones, professor of political science at Yale University); physical descriptions and automobiles of unnamed persons being sought by the police; consumer brand names (without much locational MI); company names (usually with at least minimal locational MI).

3. *Tactical* MI makes available explicit and implicit behavioral models. Examples of subtypes include: recipes, gardening and beauty tips, successful and unsuccessful *modus operandi* in crimes, and tactics used in successful and unsuccessful strikes, political movements, and terrorist activities.

Some specific cases have elements of all three types, and some examples within a type have much more detail than others. For consumer action, the identificational subtype may not require locational help (a brand name may be enough to enable a choice). But for most other actions, including political action, it is apparent that some locational help is needed in most of the identificational subtypes. It is usually not enough to know the name of a political actor. We must be able to contact him. Elites may already know how to write to their congressional representives, for example, but many persons would feel at a loss in knowing how to address their letters, even if they knew the name of their representative.

Mobilizing Messages

It is important to distinguish between mobilizing information and mobilizing messages. A mobilizing message may or may not contain MI and has the apparent intent of mobilizing support for a policy position that is not really elaborated in the message. Instead of trying to change attitudes toward a policy position, a "pure" mobilizing message would be directed only at attitudes toward participation; agreement on the issue is generally assumed. A good example of such a message appears in Figure 6.1—a call for a march and rally against the Southeast Asian war. Note how little of the content is concerned with the merits of ending the war. This is because the circular was distributed on various Oregon campuses, and agreement with the policy stand is assumed.

Since pure mobilizing messages assume issue agreement, they are much more likely to appear in communications from special interest groups to their followers than in the mass media. And because the mass media know relatively little about the policy preferences of their anonymous and heterogeneous audiences, we can probably assume that these general media would be less likely than specialized media to carry pure mobilizing messages. In the general media, even advertisements, commentary, and editorials—which presumably could even take a *one-sided* approach in making their case—would still need to make a policy case before attempting to mobilize activity. (As defined in communication and social psychology, a one-sided message presents only arguments in favor of a point of view, ignoring potentially strong arguments against it.) A pure mobilizing message is less one-sided than it is

Figure 6.1

A mobilizing message, distributed in leaflet form on the University of Oregon Campus in Eugene, November 1972. In the fine print are instructions about the march route in Portland, Oregon, and how to get transportation from Portland to Eugene.

123

no-sided; it doesn't really make any case for the preferred alternative.

Special interest groups already think they know what policies their memberships prefer. Therefore, in the short run, at least, leaders of the group may try harder to achieve mobilization effects than to reinforce the issue attitudes of their followers. Look at Figure 6.2, the Ringelmann Chart for gauging smoke pollution. Consider the *issue attitudes* that are *implied, but not stated* regarding (1) air pollution, (2) which villains to look for, and (3) current enforcement of county sanitary codes. This chart appeared in a specialized magazine for ecologists,[6] so probably editors of the magazine are correct in their assessment of the attitudes of their readership.

THE SST DEBACLE

A good example of what can happen when a mobilizing message reaches the wrong people was provided in the American Super-Sonic Transport controversy during the spring of 1971. Because renewed SST funding was in serious trouble in the Senate, backers of the SST ran a series of ads across the country. These ads urged people to write to their legislators and demand they keep America in the SST race with the USSR and the British-French Concorde.

In Oregon, a group called the Oregon Committee for an American SST ran spot announcements on TV and a full-page ad in most of the state's newspapers. The newspaper ads contained a pro-SST coupon, which was to be clipped out, signed, and sent to Oregon's two senators and four representatives. The coupon included the addresses of all six. The ads ran after the House had narrowly defeated SST funding and about a week before Senate action was scheduled.

The ads did stimulate participation, but they "backfired," according to aides of the senators and representatives.[7] An aide to former Rep. John Dellenback, whose district included the environmentally politicized University of Oregon at Eugene, said, "I can't recall when an ad campaign produced an effect so opposite to the one intended." The ad was run in Eugene. All told, the

Pollution Detection Chart

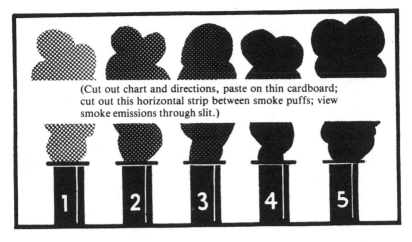

(Cut out chart and directions, paste on thin cardboard; cut out this horizontal strip between smoke puffs; view smoke emissions through slit.)

How to spot those overstepping the limits of permitted pollution. The Ringelmann Chart will help you to determine to what extent the offender is fouling your environment. It has been in use for nearly three-quarters of a century and is considered by many scientists to be one of the best indicators of the severity of air pollution. In fact, the U.S. Bureau of Mines has adopted it as the basic scale for measuring smoke darkness.

Directions for using the Ringelmann Chart

1. Find out what Ringelmann ratings industries may have under your county's sanitary code.
2. Stand about 100 feet from source of smoke or at a location with a clear view of the stack and background.
3. Make sure the sun is at your back. Holding the chart at arm's length, aim it at the smoke stack.
4. Readings should be made by looking at right angles to the smoke plume. Concentrate on the densest part of the plume at a point about two feet above the top of the stack.
5. Make observations for five minutes at a time. The more observations, the better. Change your location and compare readings.
6. Note time of day, wind direction, name of plant and exactly which stack is emitting the smoke.

Figure 6.2

The Ringlemann Chart was printed originally in shaded colors, which allowed persons using it to match smoke emissions with whatever gradations of pollution the chart indicated.

letters in Dellenback's district ran about 85 percent against SST funding.

Walter Evans, an administrative assistant to Sen. Mark Hatfield, said, "The interesting thing is the heavy volume of letters that say they're against it because of the ad. . . ." Hatfield, who had not voted on SST funding at the previous session, voted against it this time. After the ad, his mail ran slightly under two to one against the SST.

Senator Bob Packwood's mail ran eight to five against the SST. "There were a lot of coupons in the mail," an aide said, "but almost as many people scratched out the words 'vote for funding' as left them in."

One of the problems with running the ad in Eugene and the rest of Oregon is that relatively few residents have jobs in industries that would directly benefit from SST funding. And by using the general mass media, those who would oppose the SST were not screened out from exposure to the mobilizing message. Finally, the ads were not pure mobilizing messages. They attempted to make the case for the SST (as they would almost certainly have had to do in the general mass media), but a number of people were apparently annoyed by the Cold War terms in which the ad briefly argued the issue. Many writers also complained about an accidentally and slightly defaced image of the American flag on the coupon itself.[8]

MOBILIZING MESSAGES IN THE GENERAL MASS MEDIA

Are there any situations in which the general mass media can assume that their diverse audience would have a sufficiently uniform and universal attitude to permit a mobilizing message? Certain generally shared attitudes do come to mind. One culturally shared attitude is that voting is every qualified citizen's right and duty. Therefore, news media that are trying to be of service to their audiences may go to fairly unusual lengths to provide mobilizing messages for voters (Figure 6.3). Note also that this mobilizing message, while it assumes readers share the attitude that voting is desirable, does not imply anything about who or what to vote for. In this sense, *it is nonpartisan,* even though it assumes something about audience attitudes.

WHERE DO I VOTE?

YOUR VOTERS PAMPHLET HAS THE ANSWER
READ ITS MAILING LABEL CAREFULLY

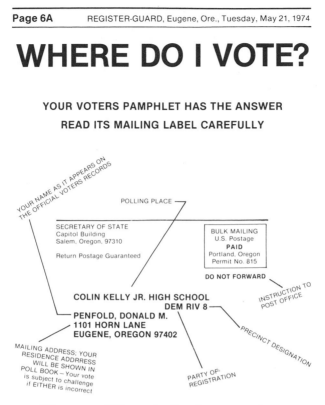

Pamphlet label precise

Voters planning on a trip to the polls next Tuesday for the primary election can look on their Voter's Pamphlet for precise information on where they cast their ballots. The mailing label of the pamphlet tells each voter his precinct number and his polling place. The example here shows how the mailing label provides essential voting information.

Figure 6.3

A newspaper reproduction of an Oregon Voter's Pamphlet mailing label with instructions about how to use the information on the label. The Voter's Pamphlet is mailed to all registered voters before each statewide election and contains information about candidates and ballot measures.

127

A similar shared attitude might be projected onto its audience by a mass media agency: If it is every qualified citizen's right and duty to vote, it is also a right (and duty?) to be counted in a poll on questions affecting him or her. Thus, in recent years we have seen the rise of the radio-television call-in poll and the magazine-newspaper clip-it-out-and-send-it-to-us poll.

In Oregon, at least two groups have even tried to combine media.[9] Poll questions are printed in the newspaper, and a television special is produced to discuss the issues asked about in the poll. It is probably no accident that the poll question format resembles an election ballot. Therefore, the fact that the paper prints it may imply a favorable media stance toward the "right" to be polled, but it is nonpartisan in the same way as mobilizing messages about voting.

In a similarly nonpartisan vein, journalists might feel able to project onto their audiences a desire to be informed of government and other meetings they might wish to attend. Thus we have the traditional meeting "advance" story, which in pure form contains little except the name of the organization, the place and time of meeting, and perhaps an agenda. This journalistic device precedes the meeting (hence the term *advance*) and does not, in the eyes of journalists, construe an endorsement of the purpose of the organization or its agenda.

Hungerford and Lemert reported that meeting advances were by far the dominant context in which MI appeared in news of the environment.[10] In a study of a set of metropolitan and largely "prestige" newspapers, Lemert, Mitzman, Seither, Cook, and O'Neil reported that nearly every meeting advance contained MI —a rate exceeding that of any other item in their study.[11] (Should a group's purposes or membership fall sufficiently outside the bounds of "good taste" or 'community standards," it might have trouble getting advance stories for its meetings. However, if an advance is done, it will almost always have MI in it.)

In other situations, too, journalists may project consensual attitudes onto their audiences, in effect perceiving that "public opinion" clears the way for mobilizing messages. Presumably, even a heterogeneous audience wants to be safe and comfortable. When something occurs that threatens its safety, we would expect mobilizing messages in the media *if* the threat is seen as an immediate one (for example, a tornado), and has been legitimized by governmental authority (a weather bureau warning). Radio and television will carry mobilizing messages under these circumstances. But when the threat is more subtle—for example, a government report says the community's water supply is not adequately treated, and correction would require unfavorable publicity, a lot of money, and a political decision to spend that money—the local news media might be reluctant even to provide news coverage, let alone MI.[12]

The cities of Eugene-Springfield (Oregon) are located in a chronic air inversion area that, when conditions are right, traps air pollution for days. Late each summer, grass seed farmers north of Eugene burn their fields in order to prepare them for the following growing season. In the past, the smoke has frequently settled over the Eugene-Springfield area, and pressure from area legislators resulted, for a time, in increasingly strict regulations concerning grass field burning.

Figure 6.4 provides a good example of a mobilizing message under conditions in which it can be assumed that almost all of the audience shares an attitude—the smoke is irritating, unhealthy for some, and of no immediate financial benefit to the residents of the city. In both 1969 ("Black Tuesday") and 1974, the *Eugene Register-Guard* ran the names, addresses, and telephone numbers of local legislators, environmental agencies, and state political figures. One week after the front page shown in Figure 6.4 appeared, the Lane County legislators had received a total of 625 telephone calls, letters, and petitions. Most of the legislators believed that the feedback was largely in response to the mobilizing message in the newspaper.[13] Telephone callers frequently began their conversations by saying that they had never before contacted anyone in government, but they had decided to call this time, since the number was given.

More than one thousand calls were received at a special number immediately following the *Register-Guard*'s listing of the Lane Regional Air Pollution Authority's "tape-a-complaint" number.[14] Three local radio stations also broadcast the number of the complaint line. This number was *not* listed in the telephone directory,

Good Evening

Eugene Register-Guard

LANE COUNTY'S HOME NEWSPAPER

Partly clear
Weather details, Page 2A

107th Year, Number 316   2 SECTIONS   EUGENE, OREGON, WEDNESDAY, SEPTEMBER 4, 1974   52 PAGES   15 Cents

Smoke obscures a now-dormant past polluter

This 'view' of Eugene greeted motorists on Ferry Street Bridge during smoke's peak at about 5 p.m.
Lost somewhere in the muce are traffic signs, Eugene's skyline and — perhaps most unfortunately — the summer sky

(Register-Guard photo by Wayne Eastburn)

'Black Tuesday' returns

By ED KENYON
Of the Register-Guard

Another "Black Tuesday" that laid a heavy pall of smoke over much of the Emerald Empire brought renewed outcries today from public officials and average citizens alike to "do something" about field burning.

Public reaction to the smoke siege brought immediate comparisons with "Black Tuesday" on Aug. 12, 1969, when Gov. Tom McCall came to Eugene and immediately ordered a halt to field burning.

Tuesday's smoke pall resulted from the burning of an estimated 9,000 acres.

The Dept. of Environmental Quality authorized the burning, starting at 12:30 p.m., then ordered a halt by 3 p.m. when it became obvious weather conditions were adverse.

SMOKY CONDITIONS, according to the National Weather Service, started in the Eugene about 2:30 p.m. and reached a peak at 5:10 p.m., when visibility was reduced to about 1½ miles.

Eugene Mayor Les Anderson said a result of the latest Black Tuesday probably will be "a strengthened resolve on the part of Eugene not to allow an extension of the field burning deadline."

Anderson urged Eugene-area residents to let state representatives know they don't want the Jan. 1, 1975, cutoff date for open field burning extended.

Along that line, the Lane County Medical Society adopted a resolution at its Tuesday night meeting putting

doctors "absolutely against" any extension of the field burning deadline.

The resolution will be carried to a state medical society meeting next week with a request for its adoption, a county medical society spokesman said.

Among other reaction from public officials, Sen. George Wingard, R-Eugene, called for an even more immediate action of firing the Dept. of Environmental Quality's field burning coordinator.

Wingard said he had telegraphed DEQ Director Kessler Cannon asking that "if as obvious the present field burning coordinator lacks the concern for the health and welfare of the citizens of Oregon that the present law demands."

In a conversation with coordinator Douglas Brunnick, Wingard said Brunnick's "greatest concern seemed to be whether or not the fields would all be burned this year."

Brunnick replied today that "Everything is life or a risk" including weather forecasting.

Assuming the responsibility of deciding when to allow burning is part of they job, Brunnick said. He has called the dates on field burning for the Dept. of Environmental Quality for the past three years.

DEQ officials, meeting today in Portland, appeared unaware of the smoke crisis in the Eugene-Springfield area, and the subject wasn't discussed.

In response to questions from a Register-Guard reporter, DEQ Chairman B. A. McPhillips of McMinnville said he had received no information on the situation from the DEQ staff.

The Lane Regional Air Pollution Authority reported more than 600 calls from citizens at its offices in a period of about six hours Tuesday night, but the count was admittedly low, an authority spokesman said, because an answering device ran but 90 minutes after the flood of calls began.

The spokesman, David Gemma, said most callers wanted to know why field burning was being allowed and what officials were going to do about it.

GEMMA SAID callers were told that they should contact the DEQ because field burning is under the jurisdiction of that state agency.

Lane authority Chairman Nancy Hayward said today she is as frustrated as anyone about the situation as is firing off a letter to the DEQ.

Mrs. Hayward said her letter would point out that this is the second "mistake" in allowing field burning of the past month. She said she has evidence showing that the last mistake was made on the basis of meteorological information that was "impossible to misinterpret."

Mrs. Hayward forecast "an active campaign" against extension of the field burning deadline as the major consequence of the latest smoke incident.

However, a used grass grower spokesman contended Wednesday that the incident was not the fault of farmers.

"Maybe we (the seed industry) ought to set up our own weather bureau if we can't depend on the U.S. Weather Bureau," commented Oregon Seed Council Spokesman Scott Lamb.
Related story, Page 1E.

Where to call or write ...

Whom should you breathe fire on for all the smoke that is hanging over the valley?

There is no simple complaint department. But there are several ways to make your views known.

You can call the Oregon Dept. of Environmental Quality in Portland at 1-229-5630. The DEQ determines when burning is allowed.

Or you can have your entire complaint tape-recorded by calling a special number at Lane Regional Air Pollution Authority in Eugene. The number is 343-6351.

Here's a list of legislators and others where you can make your opinions known.

Lane County Legislative Delegation

Sen. Edward Fadeley
280 Sunset Dr.
Eugene, Ore.
343-4909

Sen. Elizabeth (Betty) Browne
4824 Laurel Butte Dr.
Oakridge, Ore.
782-3315

Sen. George Wingard
2323 Fairmount Blvd.
Eugene, Ore.
344-4424

Rep. Wayne Whitehead
93 N. Polk St.
Eugene, Ore.
688-5967

Rep. Larry Perry
2372 Spring Blvd.
Eugene, Ore.
686-8256

Rep. Mary Burrows
3105 Firwood Way
Eugene, Ore.
343-6371

Rep. Nancie Fadeley
280 Sunset Dr.
Eugene, Ore.
343-4969

Rep. David Stults
2040 Highway 99S
Junction City, Ore.
998-3951

Rep. Richard Eymann
Mohawk Star. Rte. Box 54
Springfield, Ore.
803-2298

Members of State Environmental Quality Commission

B. A. McPhillips (Chairman)
P.O. Box 577
McMinnville, Ore. 97128
472-7495

Dr. Morris Crothers
1547 Court St. NE.
Salem, Ore. 97301
363-3393

Grace Phinney
1100 NW 36th St.
Corvallis, Ore. 97330
753-3675

Jacklyn Hallock
2445 NW Irving St.
Portland, Ore. 97210
224-1711

Ronald Somers
106 E. Fourth St.
The Dalles, Ore. 97058
296-6290

Others

Jason Boe
(Oregon Senate President)
2028 Hawthorne
Reedsport, Ore.
271-2474

Gov. Tom McCall
State Capitol
Salem, Ore.
378-3111

Young hijacker releases pilot, then gives up

BOSTON (AP) — A young black man demanding variously from $10,000 to $500,000 ransom for the poor surrendered today after holding an Eastern Air lines pilot hostage aboard a jetliner at Logan International Airport, authorities reported.

The man was identified as Marshal Collins III, 20, of Providence, R.I. FBI Special Agent James O. Newpher said he was charged with air piracy and would be arraigned later in the day.

Collins surrendered, Newpher said, after talking by radio with a black FBI agent for several hours.

Newpher said Collins was armed with a straight razor and a route mail, as well as an ax or hatchet he found on the DC9 jetliner. He said the pilot, Capt. L.E. Whitaker of New York City, suffered minor cuts from the razor and nail and a head wound from the side of the hatchet.

ENTERING LOS ANGELES SMOG FIELD USA POPULATION 91,100 Drive carefully

An apt designation

Ford selects Bush as envoy to Peking

WASHINGTON (AP) — President Ford today named Republican National Chairman George Bush as U.S. envoy to China, nominated former Sen. John Sherman Cooper to be first U.S. ambassador to East Germany and ordered White House commerce aide Kenneth Rush as ambassador to France.

Moving to place his imprint on top diplomatic and political ranks, Ford also recommended that Mary Louise Smith, now GOP co-chairman, succeed Bush as party chief.

A White House spokesman, after making those announcements, also told newsmen that White House chief Alexander Haig Jr. wants to return to active military duty and that the President and Haig are exploring a number of options, including supreme commander of NATO.

While Press Secretary Jerald F. terHorst said Ford had made no deci-

sion, it was clear that Haig would be leaving the White House soon, where he was the top aide during the last year of Richard Nixon's Watergate-shattered presidency.

Bush will carry the rank of ambassador to the Peking post now held by veteran diplomat David K. I. Bruce, but has official title as chief of the U.S. liaison office, since there is no U.S. embassy in China.

INSIDE TODAY

(Register-Guard phone: 485-1234)

Omlid blasts Horton for 'political rantings' over jail

By MIKE STAHLBERG
Of the Register-Guard

Lane County Board of Commissioners Chairman Kenneth Omlid Wednesday blasted District Attorney Pat Horton for his "political rantings" on the city-county jail issue.

Omlid said Horton's criticism of the county board's handling of the jail situation is politically motivated. He said Horton is trying to help Archie Weinstein, one of Omlid's opponents in the November election, get elected.

"Mr. Horton can have only one motive in mind when he makes such blatant misrepresentations about lack of concern or action about our corrections problem," Omlid said.

"REGARDLESS of what Mr. Horton's motives are for sounding off publicly, he is trying to replace me as one of the three county commissioners," Mr. Weinstein, his methods are causing a total disservice to the public and most certainly is demeaning to the office of district attorney," Omlid said.

The board chairman's reference to

Weinstein being a Horton campaign supporter was an allusion to the fact Weinstein was one of Horton's largest financial backers, contributing $1,440 in the 1972 campaign.

Horton, contacted for comment on Omlid's statements, denied that his position was politically motivated.

"I'll take a back seat to no one in my sincerity for jail reform," said Horton. "This issue doesn't change with political broadsides by Mr. Omlid. The issue is we've got a horrible problem. It's the county's responsibility. What is the county going to do about it?"

The DA last week said the county should stop work on a million-dollar new office building and use the money to build a new jail instead.

The former two county commissioners (Frank Elliott and Nancy Hayward) had earlier criticized Horton's suggestion regarding the jail and the public service building on the grounds that some grounds as Omlid used — that a new jail is needed but that stopping

the office building won't get the jail built any faster.

Omlid said Horton "ran out our corrections facilities and programs planning back for years."

He said Horton is "well aware" of the fact planning and study for reopening the jail situation has been going on.

And Omlid said the DA should also know that "to stop the (facilities once) features of the public service facility now would not gain one minute on the construction schedule of a corrections facility."

"Omlid said it's 'my personal conviction' Horton's statements are politically motivated, and that the DA wants to see 'new faces' on the board.

"I ASSUME that since he had great support from Mr. Weinstein, that's the person he would like to see help," he said.

In response to the Weinstein issue, Horton said "I have not publicly endorsed a candidate for county commissioner, and I will not."

and the number could not have been obtained from information unless requested very specifically.[15]

DIFFERENCE BETWEEN MOBILIZING MESSAGES AND MI

All the preceding examples of mobilizing messages had mobilizing information in them. But it is a serious mistake to confuse MI with a mobilizing message. A mobilizing message clearly is intended to energize participation on behalf of some policy preference or attitude that is embedded in the message itself. That is not true of MI. The content of mobilizing information is just that —information—and the use to which it is put depends on many things that are not in the MI itself.

A name and location—say, Western Kraft of Albany—may appear in a business news item about improved earnings per share, or it may appear in a critical environmental news story. The *context* of MI must be separated from the *content* of MI. Figure 6.5 illustrates one way to look at the difference between mobilizing messages (one kind of context) and MI. The column urges people to write their senators about President Ford's controversial nomination of Stanley Hathaway as Secretary of the Interior. It is clearly a mobilizing message. *But it lacks the relevant MI* (in this case, names and addresses of the two Oregon senators).

During the late 1960s, speeches and pamphlets on ending the war also were often long on the rhetoric of mobilization and short on MI. For reasons about which we'll speculate more later, newspaper editorial writers also seem especially prone to calling for citizen action while neglecting to provide the tools for action.

In brief, a mobilizing message may or may not contain MI.

Figure 6.4

"Black Tuesday" refers to a previous field-burning incident. On the left side of the page, under "Where to call or write . . ." is a mobilizing message starting with the words, "Whom should you breathe fire on for all the smoke that is hanging over the valley?" The message then provides names, addresses, and telephone numbers of legislators, the governor, and the State Environmental Quality Commissioners and the special number of the Lane Regional Air Pollution Authority. See text.

Environmental protection requires vigilance

By MARCY WILLOW

Vigilance. If I were to pick a one-word theme for Earth Day, "vigilance" would be it. Seems like every time we turn around, another wild river has been dammed, another virgin forest has been logged, another species of our wild brothers and sisters annihilated from existence, another stretch of our dear Earth covered in concrete and pollution.

We've got to be on top of things — ever watchful of industries and government agencies. And we've GOT to speak out. The lure of profits keeps the Earth-exploiters constantly chopping, drilling, polluting, stripping away at our Earth-home; and the enormous pressure they put on government agencies is constant. The only way we can compete with this big money and propaganda is to stay informed and to speak out.

If I've learned anything at all this past year of testifying at public hearings it's that our legislators NEED our input. Many important environmental bills have been defeated this year simply because 1) the legislators knew almost nothing about the issue, and 2) they did not hear from us. The only information they received was from industry lobbyists; and so they voted accordingly.

While we are spending this week learning about the Earth, and celebrating it, back in Washington D.C. the Administration in conniving against it at an alarming rate.

President Ford has just nominated former Wyoming Governor Stanley K. Hathaway to be Secretary of the Interior. During Hathaway's two terms as governor, Wyoming was transformed from a state famous for its wildlife, wilderness, and wide open spaces, to a state notorious for its social ills and lax environmental standards that encouraged the siting of polluting industries within the state. He pushed for strip mining, oil shale development, and nuclear power plants. He has repeatedly endorsed the timber industry's practice of clearcutting on entire forests. Saying "Man cannot live by pure air or water alone." Hathaway encouraged exploitation despite environmental consequences. In 1970 he waged an unsuccessful effort to overturn a ban on killing golden eagles. A wire to President Ford from a coalition of eight environmental groups concluded with this admonition: "To the Secretary of Interior, conservation must be more than a word; it must be a creed to live by. Governor Hathaway's record shows that his creed is just the opposite — development at any price."

His nomination is now in the Senate Interior Committee where hearings will be held in a week or so, and a recommendation on whether to confirm him will then be placed before the full Senate. We must now allow confirmation of this man as Secretary of the Interior. There's only one way we can stop it. WRITE LETTERS — NOW. Write to your Senators urging them to vote against Hathaway's confirmation. Point out his past record on conservation issues. Point out that in deciding whether to confirm Hathaway, the Senate will have a chance to tell President Ford what it thinks of his policies on such issues as strip mining, off-shore leasing, coal leasing, and oil shale development. Ask your Senator how he can entrust Hathaway the responsibility for crucial environmental legislation like the recently enacted strip mining bill.

If you do nothing else for the Earth this week — at least write this one vital letter!

If you can spend a little more time for the Earth this week...

The whales are in trouble...on the verge of extinction. While every other country is abiding by the ten year moratorium on whale killing, Japan and Russia continue to slaughter whales. One whale every fourteen minutes. Japan has even stepped up their kill in order to get what's left while they still can.

We are only just getting to know these huge, intelligent mammals and their role in the web of life. Once the whalers kill the last whale, that's it. Once the whales have been murdered to extinction, they're gone forever and there's no bringing them back. Here are two things you can do: 1) boycott ALL Japanese and Russian goods until they agree to comply with the moratorium; and 2) send money to Greenpeace V. Greenpeace V is a ship, run by volunteers from nine countries, that is going up into the North Atlantic this summer to get between the whales and the Japanese and Russian whalers. Greenpeace needs money for equipment and fuel. Send as much as you can to: Greenpeace V Trust Fund, P.O. Box 33784, Station D, Vancouver, B. C., Canada, V6J 2E2.

If you want to do more or want more information, come down to the Survival Center. You'll see a lot of determined, dedicated, smiling faces. We have a newspaper clipping taped to one of our file cabinets that tells of efforts to rescue a mother and baby whale beached on the Florida coast last month. It says, "...one teenage girl in a bikini kept her arms around the baby whale for three hours until a truck came for the animals. The girl turned blue, the water was so cold. But she said, 'It's my job. I'm going to keep holding this baby.' And she did."

That's the way we feel. It's our job and we're going to keep holdin' on. But we need your help. Start by writing that letter.

Marcy Willow is associated with the ASUO Survival Center

Figure 6.5

A mobilizing message that lacks the mobilizing information. See especially the portion of the column that urges people to WRITE LETTERS—Now! There is some MI provided later in the column, but that MI has nothing to do with the invitation to write the senators who would vote on Hathaway's nomination. Reprinted from the *Oregon Daily Emerald* (student newspaper of the University of Oregon, Eugene), 23 April 1975.

Another important point: It doesn't follow that, when MI appears, it is in a mobilizing message. Very often, MI itself is factual —a name and address, a time and place—and may appear in news and other contexts that are manifestly not mobilizing messages. Nevertheless, the surrounding context in which MI appears is often confused with the MI itself. The failure to separate MI from mobilizing messages (with their partisan overtones) is a major reason for the frequent failure of modern journalists to provide MI.

When MI appears in the news, its appearance need not imply any intent to mobilize activity. When names of local citizens are printed in the newspaper, for example, addresses are almost invariably supplied, without a second thought, by journalists. Or, to take an unfortunate example, a series of news items describing a skyjacking/parachuting by "D. B. Cooper" almost invariably mentioned that the Boeing 727 jet was the only commercial jet from which "Cooper" could have parachuted (from its rear door). Airline pilots felt that this tactical MI in the news helped produce a rash of 727 hijackings and parachutings. Finally, the airlines announced that they were sealing the rear doors of their 727's.

Few journalists believe they should take any responsibility for the 727 skyjackings, but they apparently don't feel the same way about MI in news of political controversies. A similar discrepancy may be found when the *modus operandi* is routinely provided in many crime stories, but its equivalent is not provided in political news. We now turn to reasons why this distinction is drawn.

WHY JOURNALISTS WITHHOLD MI

Three very general craft attitudes account for the presence and absence of mobilizing information in print and electronic news.[16] These craft attitudes lead to the exclusion of MI in precisely those areas where journalists' own statements about their craft say it is most needed. But we are getting ahead of ourselves. Let me first describe the three craft attitudes and the evidence my students and I have gathered concerning each of them.

MI Is "Partisan"

As we saw earlier, it is easy to confuse the context of MI with the content itself. In many cases, journalists feel that reporting

MI in a news story would either be—or, just as important, be seen as—a partisan act of endorsement.

Since positive or noncontroversial items often involve charitable causes or other community services, journalists may feel they can provide MI in them because the context makes the MI content "harmless" or for the good of the community. For example, an Associated Press report went out of its way to provide the name of a rest home at which an elderly couple had gotten married.[17] The couple had sacrificed $90 a month in Social Security income so as not to "live in sin." As a result, offers of financial aid were "pouring in" two days after the first story, according to the manager of the rest home.[18]

Fears of libel action or of pressures from advertisers also can be reduced to the feeling that MI in controversial/negative contexts is both partisan and risky. Therefore, MI will not be provided in these contexts unless the MI can be attributed to someone else—especially somebody with official standing, as Hungerford and Lemert found with environmental news.[19]

Journalists' extreme sensitivity to the context of MI received very strong support in a study by Lemert, Mitzman, Seither, Cook, and O'Neil of content in eleven metropolitan newspapers. This study will hereafter be referred to as the metro newspaper study.[20]

This sensitivity to context means that news of controversial issues—that is, "public opinion" news—is rarely going to have MI in it. The metro newspaper study found that only a tiny percentage of all the items with MI in them could be considered, even by the most generous criteria, to occur in the influence framework. Journalists may be drawn to controversy and conflict-laden news. But providing MI in these contexts is not part of their "vested interest in disaster," as somebody put it once.

Since most news of political controversies appears in the main news pages, it was no surprise to find in the metro content analysis that MI was conspicuously missing from stories produced and edited by staff working on the main news sections.

The author and two of his students, Mary Ann Nelson and Jack Groves, also did a small experiment with some professional journalists to see whether these journalists would edit out MI from controversial context news items and leave the same MI in positive context items. After they had edited the copy, we asked them why they had made the changes. Journalists were initially told only that we were interested in "the editing process." The concept of mobilizing information was not explained to them until after they had completed the editing and explained their editing changes.

Each journalist got a set of stories, each story on a different topic. The set contained a "safe" item—government source and/or positive context—and a "risky" item—nongovernment source and/or negative context. A story on each topic had two versions—a safe one and a risky one—*but the mobilizing information was the same in each version.* Although a total of fifteen experienced professionals completed the editing tasks, six interviews were partially lost because the interviewer inadvertently discarded the edited copy, bringing back only the questionnaires.

Nevertheless, we do have the editing results for the other nine journalists. Seven of the nine showed a clear preference for retaining the MI in the safe story and cutting it out in the risky version. The other two showed no preference one way or the other. So a sign test for this tiny sample of journalists reaches $p=.016$, two-tailed. These were all veteran newsmen—six editors and three reporters on several dailies in southern and coastal Oregon.

Since the questionnaires were retained for the other six journalists, we do have a somewhat more diverse sample of data regarding why all fifteen cut out the MI when they did so. The other six included male and female reporters for both wire services and Portland's two dailies. Their range of experience in Portland was from a few months to sixteen years, but even the least experienced had had several years of professional experience elsewhere.

Table 6.1 presents a summary of the reasons given for removing MI. Though the twenty-six "partisanship" reasons were by far the most frequently offered, even this total may represent an underestimate of journalists' uneasiness with MI in "risky" contexts. It may be an underestimate because some journalists may not have been altogether above dissembling. Under "Other Reasons," for example, three said they didn't believe in stories that weren't "self-contained." Presumably by this they meant that the MI in question could lead the reader to be *interested* enough to pursue questions further after reading the story.

Table 6.1
Reasons Given by Fifteen Professional
Journalists for Removing
MI from Test Stories

Reason	Frequency (multiple responses allowed)
"Partisanship" reasons (Total: 26)	
Lack confidence in this source	6
Wouldn't use without a statement from the other side	5
Not our job to report this; not company policy	5
False publicity; looks like an ad	4
Biased; reporter makes too many assumptions	3
Might have been OK if government had said this	3
"Dull Detail" Reasons (Total: 9)	
Wouldn't use it without a local angle	5
Unnecessary; readers can find out if interested	4
Other Reasons (Total: 3)	
Makes story incomplete; don't want any "loose ends"	3

The experiment was designed to elicit uneasiness about partisanship, so it should not be surprising to find this predominant in reasons given. Nevertheless, MI was described as "dull detail" nine times.

MI Is "Dull Detail"

Newspapers and wire services still rely heavily on a news format called the inverted pyramid. As perfected by the wire services, the inverted pyramid organizes information with the facts deemed most important at the top of the story in a summary "lead" paragraph and the remaining information in descending order of importance.

In practice in inverted pyramid stories, *a summary of facts comes to be regarded as more important than the facts themselves.* The latter are merely details that may or may not be presented lower in the story, depending on space requirements and the newsworthiness of the details. Rarely will the wire services provide such MI as a person's address, because they know the newspapers they service won't be interested unless the address is of someone in their circulation area. Thus John Jones of 1515 State Street, Chicago, will almost always be summarized as John Jones of Chicago, if Jones is mentioned at all.

The inverted pyramid was expressly invented to allow editors to chop it off from the bottom to fit available space. By a kind of logical extension, such details as addresses become completely expendable.

The metro newspaper study found that about a third of the MI difference between local and nonlocal items clearly was attributable to more addresses and similar details in the local items. For example, forty of forty-one local meeting advances had enough time-and-place detail to qualify as MI, and only three of six bureau-wire-syndicate advances had sufficient MI.

However, part of the difference between local and nonlocal items seemed due to the tendency of local items to be in positive contexts more often. But after both context and "detail" were controlled, a strong difference between local and nonlocal items remained in the main news section but *disappeared* in other sections of the newspaper. This suggests that the remaining difference is limited to public affairs journalists. We'll return to this point later, when we get to the third reason MI is not provided in public affairs content.

Returning to MI as dull detail, we saw that this news value developed as a byproduct of the inverted pyramid. Ironically, though this news value developed for newspapers, it may have been carried to its extreme in broadcast news and in news magazines, neither of which follows the inverted pyramid format. A number of my students and I have studied what happens to printed MI when the story containing it gets on the air.[21]

In a comparison of newspaper and local television news over a two-week period, a dozen local news stories provided MI when they were in the newspaper but lost the MI when they were written for a thirty-minute local broadcast. Only seven of nineteen newspaper stories still contained MI when broadcast. Interviews with local TV news editors suggested that the two most frequent reasons offered for elimination of the MI were both of the "dull detail" type: (1) it would take too much time to prepare the graphics and (2) we don't have the air time to provide the details in a way that would enable the audience to retain them.

Another study compared the same newspaper against another local channel's hour-long newscast over a one-week period. In this case, only ten of twenty-three newspaper items still retained the MI when they hit the air.

A third study compared a sample of 234 local items in a newspaper against 190 local items on an all-news radio station. The printed items were three times as likely as the broadcast ones to contain MI, despite the fact that the all-news radio station broadcast twenty-four hours a day and presumably had more than enough time for detail if they wanted to use it.

So MI often appears to be removed because it isn't worth the effort. Nevertheless, neither detail nor context seems to account completely for the absence of MI. What else do we need to complete the explanation?

Public Affairs Journalists Are Issue-Centered

You will recall that the MI discrepancy between local and non-local items disappeared outside the main news pages after we controlled for context and detail. This suggests that something about public affairs news and/or public affairs journalists inhibits the presentation of MI, over and above context and detail.

A number of indicators suggest that public affairs journalists play at least as great a role as the nature of the news they cover. We'll present more of the evidence shortly, but first let me describe what we mean by saying that public affairs journalists are "issue-centered."

Issue-centeredness implies a greater concern with describing and analyzing public issues than with what people can do about these issues. There are at least two subtypes of issue-centeredness.

The first is a kind of elitist concern with a special target audience that already knows plenty about politics. Editorial writers sometimes say, for example, that the real audience for a given editorial was the governor (or some other decision-maker they are trying to influence). Therefore, it would be a waste of time— and perhaps counterproductive—to bother with MI and other basic background material.

The second subtype is a kind of mistaking words for deeds: an absent-minded impracticality that confuses informing or educating the mass media audience about issues with informing them about how to do something with the attitudes and information they have acquired. To this kind of writer, the audience is always out there, waiting to make up its mind. Therefore, it needs to get the latest word on what somebody is saying about an issue. The presumption apparently is that audience members will always need additional issue information because they will never quite have made up their minds. A symptom of this kind of issue-centeredness might be the fact that public affairs journalists rarely ask questions that are directed at getting anything other than issue positions or defenses of past practices and future policies. It is clear that expressive goals (such as the desire to write well) motivate many people to pursue journalism, and it would not be surprising to find that desire leading to a focus on issue content.

Besides the disappearance of the MI gap outside the main news section, what are some other indicators of issue-centeredness?

The metro newspaper study found that by far the lowest MI rate occurred on the editorial pages, especially in editorials, where only about 7 percent of the editorials had MI in them. A subsequent study of another group of newspapers by Ralph Thrift produced almost exactly the same low MI rate in editorials.[22] The number of editorials in Thrift's study was 1,445, far larger than in the metro newspaper study, and the twenty-four West Coast daily newspapers varied considerably in size.

Even though editorials supposedly confer freedom from the restrictions against partisanship that inhibit news writers, in the metro newspaper study even the news stories in the main news pages were three times as likely to have MI as were the editorials. And significantly, editorials on controversial topics seemed to have the same MI rate as those on noncontroversial subjects. Thus, context didn't seem to depress the MI rate in editorials—nor did lack of space. Two of the four editorials with MI were quite short —less than two hundred words.

As a follow-up to the metro newspaper study, Jackman Wilson in 1976 interviewed editorial writers for the *Portland Oregonian* and the *Eugene Register-Guard,* two of the three largest dailies in the state.[23] Wilson took some of each writer's own editorials to him and asked why an address or some other kind of MI was missing in obvious spots.

The interviews, though admittedly with a small sample, certainly confirm the existence (if not necessarily the extent) of elitist issue-centeredness. A May 6, 1976, *Register-Guard* editorial didn't give locational MI about Sen. Mark Hatfield, its writer said, because the editorial that mentioned Hatfield was intended to influence the Senator directly on a timber clear-cutting bill.[24] A May 3, 1976, *Oregonian* editorial on illegal aliens, its writer said, omitted MI because it, too, was directed at tightened enforcement of the law by U.S. immigration officials, not at generating widespread hostility toward aliens.[25] This writer, too, said his editorials often were directed only at specific decision-makers: "Lots of times we'll try to influence the governor or some legislator with one of our editorials." He also said MI was *not* excluded from his paper's editorials because of space limitations:

> No, I don't think it's a space consideration, I think it's good writing. You can't be on a perpetual crusade. ... This notion of getting everyone excited and moving on an issue, I think that's dream stuff.

The implicit elitism in these explanations supports the existence of elitist issue-centeredness in some editorial writers. Obviously, though, the *extent* of this type of issue-centeredness is not determined through anecdotes.

A number of studies of the interaction of political columnists with their Washington sources suggest strongly that political actors and decision-makers are the principal audience for these columnists.[26] To the extent that this is so, the following finding also provides some support for the elitist explanation. In the metro content study, not a single one of the eighteen syndicated political columns carried MI, compared with ten of twenty-five other syndicated columns. (The problem with this evidence, however, is that it doesn't eliminate context as a competing explanation.)

Three sets of additional evidence support issue-centeredness as an important factor behind the removal of MI, but leave open the question whether elitism or impracticality has produced that issue-centeredness.

The first set has already been mentioned: When context and detail are controlled, bureau and wire reports (many of them coming from Washington) still contain MI less often than local stories in the metro study, but only in the main news sections. The residual discrepancy between bureau/wire and local items disappears outside the pages written and edited by public affairs journalists.

Table 6.2

Metro Newspaper Study: MI Rate
by Apparent Source* of Item,[a]
Controlling for Context and
after Removal of Detail[b]

Items in Controversial/Negative
Contexts Only
Source

Percent of Items	Government (N=370)	Business (N=53)	Staff[d] (N=35)	Other (N=122)
With MI (N=103)	13.0%	37.7%	22.8%	22.1%
Lacking MI (N=477)	87.0%	62.3%	77.2%	77.9%

$X^2 = 22.43$, 3 *df, p* .001.

All Items Except
Controversial/Negative[c]
Source

Percent of Items	Government (N=157)	Business (N=200)	Staff[d] (N=102)	Other (N=335)
With MI (N=326)	30.6%	59.5%	43.1%	34.3%
Lacking MI (N=468)	69.4%	40.5%	56.9%	65.7%

$X^2 = 41.62$, 3 *df, p* .001.

[a]Letters to the editor and items whose source could not be classified are excluded.
[b]Meeting advances and addresses were excluded by not counting them as MI.
[c]More than 700 of these 794 items were in positive contexts.
[d]Staff items included investigative reports, advice columns, editorials, and certain feature items without an apparent news "peg."

The second set of evidence was not reported in any detail in the metro study and thus is provided here in Table 6.2. When government is the apparent source of an item, the MI rate declined rapidly. Well over half of the government-source items are in controversial/negative contexts but we can hold context constant. And when we further refine the test by removing detail (addresses and meeting advances) from the table, the relationship continues to stand (Table 6.2).

Finally, though, the relationship in Table 6.2 *disappears outside* the main news section. Just as was true for the nonlocal versus local news comparison, the lower MI rate for government items again holds only in the public affairs sections of these newspapers. This suggests again that we must allow for the issue-centeredness explanation, and we cannot dismiss this result as purely due to the reluctance of government sources to provide MI.

The third set of evidence for issue-centeredness comes from a study of letters to the editor by Lemert and Larkin.[27] More than half the letters with MI in them were rejected by the editor during the study period, a significantly higher rejection rate than that for letters without MI. Further, an interview with the editor made it clear that a number of implicit and nonpublic policies systematically worked against the printing of letters to the editor with MI. These policies were essentially issue-centered: "The way we conceptualize the Mailbag is as a forum discussion, as opposed to a 'bulletin board,' " the editor said.

So far, we probably have teased out more support for the elitist type of issue-centeredness. What about the impractical, mistaking-words-for-deeds kind of issue-centeredness?

It seems plausible that letters to the editor often are written for expressive reasons—almost by definition! Perhaps the need to express one's policy views produces an impractical obsession with the words, at the expense of considering what action(s) one wishes to follow those words. While it was true that the editor prevented most of the MI from being printed in Lemert and Larkin's study of letters to the editor, it was also true that most of the letters submitted did not contain MI. Further, interviews with the writers themselves showed them extremely confident of the ability of their words to persuade their readers. And, in comparison with a sample of nonwriters, they rejected mobilization as the chief purpose of their letters. On the other hand, writers also were more likely than nonwriters to reject an item which was meant to tap the impractical, expressive purpose. Clearly, the writers themselves were issue-centered. But as was the case with the editor, the question of the cause of the issue-centeredness was unresolved. Resolving this question is possible using roughly the design employed by Lemert and Larkin. But improvements are necessary in item(s) meant to tap "expressive" motives and at least one item will have to be added to tap writers' elitism.

An interesting study by Roxana H. Cook suggests also that persons preparing "Free Speech Messages" for San Francisco Bay area television and radio stations were perfectly capable of providing MI in their messages when left to their own devices.[28] The Free Speech Messages might be an electronic equivalent of letters to the editor. Cook's findings would argue against the "expressive needs" explanation of issue-centeredness, to some extent. Slightly more than half of all the FSMs had MI in them, a rate significantly higher than the rate for the same stations' editorials during the study period.

What other evidence might there be, then, more clearly supporting the impractical, mistaking-words-for-deeds kind of issue-centeredness?

The metro newspaper study turned up several examples in which an editorial issued a Clarion Call for Action, but somehow left out the MI necessary for that action. An editorial in the *Seattle Times,* for example, concluded that citizens should "force" public officials to consider adopting a new higher-education financing plan, but it lacked all MI: e.g., what officials, how "force"? An editorial in the *St. Louis Post-Dispatch* urged citizens to attend some public hearings but didn't tell when the hearings would be (or how to find out). An editorial in the *Idaho States-man* had the headline, "Prompt Action Needed," but it gave no MI and the required "prompt action" was left unspecified. If we assume that elitism would not have produced such embarrassing examples, we can suppose they show the impractical, expressive side of journalists.

A similar kind of example occurs when a newspaper editorial endorses a candidate who is not on the ballot, urging voters to write in the candidate. With embarrassing frequency, the editorials fail to mention the several steps that are required *successfully* to write in the candidate. In Oregon, for example, one must (1) avoid using the punch ballot for that office, (2) specify *exactly* the office the write-in is for and (3) write in the complete name of the candidate, without any spelling errors. Otherwise, the ballot is spoiled. Oregon history has many examples of newspaper-backed write-in campaigns which failed in part because the editorials failed to provide the tactical MI, and large numbers of spoiled write-ins were recorded. It is hard to imagine that the editorial writers *intended* to cripple their endorsed candidate's write-in campaign. A more reasonable explanation would seem to lie in the area of mistaking words for deeds.

We saw in Figure 6.5 that a mobilizing message could urge newspaper readers to write their senators but neglect to give the necessary MI. Clearly, in this case, calls for action were mistaken for action itself.

A comparison of MI rates for printed commercial versus political ads showed commercial ads to be nearly six times as likely as political ads to contain MI.[29] Since the backers of candidates and propositions would have little or no reason to withhold MI if it occurred to them to use it, one could argue that at least part of the discrepancy was due to the fact that it never occurred to them. (Probably they assumed that the act of voting didn't require additional MI, and rare were the attempts to mobilize campaign participation.)

A study of British antinuclear protest groups strongly underlines the value-expressive motives of participants. More than 85 percent disagreed with the statement that protests and demonstrations which fail to achieve their ends were a waste of effort. And 80 percent felt their Labour Party should "put principles before power," with only 14 percent disagreeing.[30] The author, Frank Parkin, repeatedly emphasizes the "expressive style" of the participants, a style which values "gestures" more than practical results. To the extent that this "expressive style" also describes activism in the United States, it could help explain both the low MI rate in letters to the editor and part of the failure of public affairs content to have MI in American newspapers.

Unlike the partisanship and detail explanations, it is hard to find a content variable that can operationalize and directly test issue-centeredness. Nevertheless, at least two studies cited here provide fairly strong indirect support for issue-centeredness. But these results, and the anecdotal support cited here, don't help us determine for sure which subtype of issue-centeredness is more important. Many more interviews and some directed observations of journalists seem essential here.

In the meantime, let me add a tantalizing anecdote that also can be interpreted in many ways. In the case that follows, it appears that the editorial writer knowingly provided MI, but we are left to speculate about the reasons why similar MI was not provided in later editorials. Certainly it wasn't an accident.

John L. Hulteng called my attention to this dramatic example of an editorial that not only included MI, but went on to urge citizens to participate in very specific terms. That editorial, "Showdown in Tallahassee," appeared in the *St. Petersburg* (Florida) *Times*. It is reprinted in Figure 6.6.

The St. Petersburg paper, which has received a number of favorable comments recently on its innovative approaches, had the misfortune to let a typographical error slip into one of the three telephone numbers listed in the editorial. Editorial page staffer Donald K. Coe explained in a letter what happened after the editorial was printed:

> The bill referred to in the editorial was passed, although it collided with a House version later and the final product was a compromise version. The three state senators whose phone numbers were listed voted for the bill. I do not know how many calls the three received, but they were called. Sen. Robert Graham, one of the bill's sponsors, said newspaper editorial help was invaluable in passing the measure because at the beginning of the legislative session it didn't have a snowball's chance in hell. Our Tallahassee reporters thought the phone number idea was a good one and urged us to use it again.
>
> However, because one number was typoed, the editor of editorials decided not to repeat the technique. Perhaps sometime in the future. Sorry, I can't recall that we even tried to find out [whose number it was] or his reaction. Ours was that we felt somewhat red faced.[31]

With the coming of video display terminals to the newsroom, one

"The policy of our paper is very simple — merely to tell the truth."
- Paul Poynter, publisher, 1912-1950

18-A   **Monday, March 20, 1972**

Showdown In Tallahassee . . .

Richard Deeb (904) 224-6358.
John Ware (904) 224-7231.
Harold Wilson (904) 224-7819.

How those state senators from Pinellas County vote this afternoon might determine the fate of land and water use in Florida for years to come.

Voters should call them at the above numbers before 2 p.m. today. All three should be urged to approve Senate bill 629, the land and water management act, AS PRESENTED to the Ways and Means Committee. They should be urged to remove an amendment to the bill tacked on by Ways and Means changing it from an action measure to another study.

Co-sponsored by Sen. Henry Sayler, R-Pinellas, Robert Graham, D-Miami Lakes, and others, the un-amended bill seeks to protect Florida's land and Florida's water from selfish interests whose concern for the dollar exceeds their concern for protecting state resources for its residents and future generations.

About 20 senators favor the action bill; 20 favor yet another time-wasting study. Deeb is among the latter. Ware and Wilson are among eight fence-sitters.

The un-amended version of SB 629 will help Florida plan its future rationally and realistically. The amendment should be knocked off and the bill passed today.

Figure 6.6
A rare case of an editorial providing MI. Obviously, the editorial writer knew what he was doing when he led with the names and telephone numbers of the three key state senators. See text.

146

wonders whether the fear of telephone number misprints will continue. The reporter (and computer storage) make the chances of a typographical error very slight.

Summary: Why and Where MI Is Withheld

The joint effects of (1) partisanship fears, (2) the treatment of MI as dull detail, and (3) public affairs journalists' apparent issue-centeredness create circumstances in which MI is least available where it may be most needed:

- In news of controversial political issues
- When government is involved in the controversy
- In the main news and editorial pages, where most of the public affairs items are concentrated
- In the influence framework, located
- Out of town where people can't look up some MI because they lack access to nonlocal telephone books.

BUT DOES MI MAKE A DIFFERENCE?

Implicit in this chapter has been the assumption that mobilizing information can be a potent, short-run agent for activating participation. So far, anecdotal evidence in support of this assumption has been scattered here and there through the early part of this chapter. This section adds some more evidence.

In his synthesis of results of the war bond campaign, Cartwright concluded that war bond sales greatly increased when campaign messages specified the desired behavior for the audience.[32] It seems clear that Cartwright's principle relates closely to MI and mobilizing messages. If we regard "buy war bonds" messages as mobilizing messages, it is not surprising that they had limited effect until MI was included in them.

> Examination of a number of campaigns of mass persuasion will reveal that quite commonly the course of action being encouraged is described in relatively general terms. It is rare that the proposed action is described in concrete detail or given a precise location in time. ... The fact seems well documented that, unless a proposed action is defined quite specifically, it is probable that it will not actually be carried out in behavior, even though it has been accepted as desirable.[33]

We've already seen that MI is a basic tool in advertisements. Lazarsfeld and Merton argue that advertising is usually more successful than propaganda in achieving its goals because advertising "canalizes" existing attitudes, directing them toward one brand rather than another, while propaganda tends to run directly against existing attitudes.[34] Though the point is never stated directly, we can probably assume that they were also somewhat aware that directing communications toward brand purchases implies MI, while issue-centered propaganda does not.

Neither Cartwright nor Lazarsfeld and Merton presented much detailed evidence. The evidence that remains is entirely anecdotal. Let me cite some of it in hopes that, some years from now, we will have much more carefully gathered evidence to consider.

Going to the Well at WDIO-TV

After news of asbestos contamination in the water of Lake Superior hit the news media, many residents of Duluth, Minnesota, feared their drinking water had been contaminated by waste from Reserve Mining Company's Silver Bay plant. After scientists confirmed the presence of asbestos in municipal water, "officials at WDIO Television (Duluth) invited residents of the city to bring containers to a well at their studios to get uncontaminated water. The response was overwhelming. Bob O'Brien, a photographer-producer, estimates that ten thousand persons take home more than forty-five thousand gallons of water each month from the station."[35] The population of the entire Duluth area is about one-hundred and fifty thousand persons.

The Run on Horsemeat

During the national meat boycott in spring 1973, the news media ran a feature story about Mrs. Ed Rooney of Portland, Oregon, who for three years secretly had been feeding horsemeat to her husband, a Portland high school coach. He thought he had been eating beef. Mrs. Rooney said the horsemeat was considerably cheaper, and it was a way of making do. The feature mentioned, in passing, that she had bought the horsemeat at the J & H Horsemeat market, then the only market in the state with a license to dispense horsemeat for human consumption. The store was cleaned out of horsemeat by long lines of customers the next day. And when it opened again at 9:00 A.M. the following Monday, "block long lines . . . ran five-deep at the counter," and some thirty-seven hundred pounds of horsemeat had disappeared by 2:00 P.M.[36]

Ayatollah So!

A number of newspapers and radio and television stations began promoting letter-writing and petition-signing campaigns in protest of the taking of American hostages in the U.S. Embassy in Iran. Perhaps the peak was reached during the Christmas flood that hit the regional processing center at Chicago's O'Hare airport. The mail was a mixture of Christmas cards to the hostages and letters to the Ayatollah Khomeini demanding that he let the prisoners go. Four upper-Midwestern radio stations solicited and obtained more than 20,000 signatures on a letter to the Iranian U.N. mission, starting Nov. 29, 1979, and ending Dec. 5, when the letter and signatures were turned over to President Carter. Postal authorities estimated that more than a million letters were forwarded to Iran during this period.[37] The mobilizing information provided by newspapers, news magazines, and radio and television stations was tactical, identificational and locational.

Clip-'em-out-Polls and the Firing of Cox

Following Richard Nixon's firing of Special Prosecutor Archibald Cox, several news agencies ran mobilizing messages in the form of clip-out questionnaires and asked readers to send them in to a designated address. The *Chicago Sun-Times* reportedly printed the questionnaires for three days, then tallied responses on the fourth day.[38] In this extraordinarily short period of time, 8,390 replies were received (overwhelmingly in favor of impeachment).

The *Eugene Register-Guard*'s questionnaire received 10,424 responses slightly less than a week after running two days in the newspaper. Since the questionnaire was designed to minimize multiple returns by the same reader, it is interesting to note that the response represented about a fifth of the newspaper's total circulation. The newspaper noted that its response total was more than twice that of any of its previous polls.[39] The now defunct

National Observer was an inveterate printer of "plebiscite" ballots on Watergate during this period. Responses ranged from a low of 17,000 for an August 1973 poll on whether the tapes should be turned over, to a record 71,777 in the period following the Cox. firing.[40] The editors said the 71,777 response surprised and impressed them, since it exceeded the previous record by more than 18,000. The *National Observer*'s circulation was 517,319 at the time of the record response.[41] On the perhaps unlikely assumption that each subscriber family sent in only a single response, that would be a ratio of 1 return for every 7.2 possible returns.

The Speaker Is Not Amused

In June of 1978, cartoonist Garry Trudeau's "Doonesbury" strip carried a mobilizing message with a list of questions to be asked House Speaker Thomas P. (Tip) O'Neill concerning the lagging investigation of payoffs to House of Representatives members by South Koreans. The strip carried O'Neill's address and readers were invited to check a series of boxes to ask for information from O'Neill on payments to specific congressmen. The last box on the coupon concerned "$6,000 in parties" thrown for O'Neill. The first day's wave of mail containing the coupon produced two hundred of them, according to O'Neill's office. O'Neill's press aide said that Rep. O'Neill had vowed not to read or respond to the coupons and that they would no longer count them.[42]

The Truly "Hot" Line

Early in 1978, congressional committee hearings revealed that the leukemia rate was unusually high among U.S. soldiers who had participated in Nevada nuclear test maneuvers more than twenty years before. Shortly after, the Department of Defense set up a special toll-free telephone number in order to get reports from participants. This number was widely publicized, in both electronic and print media. Within two weeks ten thousand calls had been received from participants and the department had added ten more lines to handle the calls.[43]

AN EMERGING GENERALIZATION

In Chapter 5, I hypothesized that participation among Sequence 1 people (those with issue attitudes and with both skills and efficacy) will tend to increase with the salience or intensity of issue attitudes. The examples of the impact of MI cited throughout this chapter have all tended to have one or two things in common:

1. *The issue was salient* and/or *issue attitudes were intense* for large numbers of persons (meat prices and the run on horsemeat, the asbestos threat and the chance to get "pure" water, the environment and the SST, the Nevada atomic tests and health fears, the flow of mail to Iran, the war in Southeast Asia and Dow Chemical as a manufacturer of napalm), and

2. *Issue attitudes were temporarily made more salient and/or intense* by a precipitating event (Nixon and the Cox firing, House "Koreagate" hearings and Garry Trudeau's cartoon series, the preservation of traditional morality codes and the retired couple who refused to "live in sin," and feelings of economic or political deprivation and D. B. Cooper's dramatic Boeing 727 heist).

Using additional anecdotal evidence, it is relatively easy to argue that intensity of issue attitudes makes a difference in how many participants are mobilized by MI. We can take the first five years of public television's "The Advocates," a quasi-judicial series of issue programs, as a case study. This allows us to hold the amount of MI constant and note the sensitivity of the amount of participation to the issue being discussed. The program, which has returned to the air, usually was an hour-long, pro-and-con presentation of two sides of an issue. At the end of each program, viewers were invited to cast their "ballots" on the question of the week, the responses to be sent to an address superimposed on the screen.

Over a five-year period, 166 different programs appeared. The range of participation was from a low of 615 to a high of 177,342 (see Table 6.3).

According to Molly Geraghty, producer of "The Advocates," during its first incarnation, the largest spontaneous response to an issue was the third-ranking 52,148 who "voted" on whether President Nixon should be impeached.[44] This program also followed the Cox firing, though the delay after the firing was somewhat greater than for the newspaper polls. Nevertheless, it is noteworthy that "The Advocates" had aired another Watergate program two months before this one receiving "only" 11,082 replies (October 4: "Should the Senate Watergate Hearings Stop Now?") Again, the Cox firing seems to have been a precipitating event that reinforced the attitudes of Nixon opponents. As in most of the clip-out newspaper polls following the Cox firing, a substantial majority (61.7 percent) of the respondents to "The Advocates" wanted to see the president out of office. These high percentages contrasted somewhat with poll results at the time.

Although Table 6.3 cannot list all 166 programs on "The Advocates," it appears that, among issues that did not generate mail stimulated by special interests, emotional issues prompted more participation than technical ones. Undoubtedly, certain other variables—including time of year and whether it was early or late in the show's career—had some impact, but it would be a safe bet that the emotional-technical variable accounted for more variance in the participation figures. Ranking just below the top ten were further emotional topics: abortion on demand, the legalization of

Table 6.3
Highest and Lowest Participation
Topic on "The Advocates"**

I. The 10 Highest Participation Programs (Topice Question)	Air Date	Total Participating
"Should You Support the National Lettuce Boycott?"	3-8-73	117,342[a]
"The Middle East: Where Do We Go from Here?" (two-part show)	6-14-70 6-21-70	70,686[a]
"Should the President Be Impeached?"	12-6-73	52,148
"Should Congress Ban Private Ownership of Handguns?"	11-16-71	31,000
'Should We Grant Amnesty to Those Who Have Evaded Military Service?"	2-22-73	25,751
"Should J. Edgar Hoover Be Replaced?"	5-25-71	25,315
"Should Congress Approve Import Quotas on Shoes and Textiles?"	11-10-70	25,053[a]
"Should You Support the President's Policy in Indochina?"	10-19-72	22,618
"Should Congress Force Withdrawal of All U.S. Troops from Indochina by December 31, 1971?"	6-22-71	19,146
"Should Congress Appropriate Funds to Develop the Space Shuttle?"	4-11-72	16,971[a]

Table 6.3, continued.

II. The 10 Lowest Participation Programs (Topic Question)	Air Date	Total Participating
"So Women May Work and Men Share in Family Tasks, Should Unions Demand Everyone Be Given the Option to Work Full- or Half-Time?"	6-28-70	615
"Should We End All Wage and Price Controls Now?"	11-8-73	647
"Should Defenses Based on Pleas of Insanity Be Abolished?"	5-9-74	738
"Should We Limit the Size of Investments by . . . Large Institutions in the Stock Market?"	5-23-74	772
"Should Plea Bargaining Be Abolished?"	10-18-73	853
"Should Our President Be Limited to a Single Six-Year Term?"	12-21-71	876
"Should the News Media Refuse to Publish Candidate Preference Polls?"	11-16-72	952
"Should the Police Be Relieved of Responsibility for Social Problems to Concentrate on Major Crime?"	12-7-69	982
"Should the California Legislature Adopt the Petris Bill to Ban Sale of the Internal Combustion Engine by 1975?"	10-5-69	985
"Should We Require Each Ninth-grade Student to Take a Course in Afro-American Culture and History?"	12-14-69	1,035

aAccording to a telephone conversation of July 16, 1974, with Molly Geraghty, the program's producer, many of these letters/telegrams seemed "organized" by interest groups.

Sources: "The Nation Responds to 'The Advocates' " (mimeographed, WGBH-TV, Boston, no date). The mimeographed report, however, covers only the first version of this program: 160 programs, running from the 1969–70 season through the 1973–74 season. After several years off the air, the program returned.

prostitution, the unification of Ireland, and three more programs about the Southeast Asian conflict. Ranking just above the bottom ten were relatively technical programs about legalizing gambling on pro football, automatic probation for nonviolent crimes, and the efficacy of methadone treatments for drug addiction.

This anecdotal evidence supports the hypothesis that MI will be effective when the population already has issue attitudes it strongly wishes to express. Since "The Advocates" always provided the relevant MI, differences in participation probably have to be attributed to differences in audience size for each program and differences in issue attitude intensity/salience. Things are simplified even more when we remember that audience size, too, is hardly independent of intensity/salience.

So the extent of participation produced by MI depends on issue attitudes, but there is another side to the coin. In the influence framework, the extent of participation will be greatly diminished when MI is not provided by the mass media—no matter how intense issue attitudes are. *MI in the mass media facilitates linkage between large segments of the population and decision-makers.* In Schattschneider's terms, MI in the media enlarges the "scope" of an issue and thereby may very well change the outcome of the influence process.[45]

Without MI in the media, participation still will vary with attitude intensity and salience. But it will tend to be limited to persons who either already have the MI or can get it on their own. With MI publicly available in the mass media, the number and variety of participants is likely to increase markedly when the issue is important to media audiences. Once again, though, we must recall that, when journalists cover the more controversial issues, they screen out the MI. The effect of this, then, is to limit the scope of issue participation, giving more weight (by default) to the attitudes of participants who already have access to the political process.

SOME CAUTIONS

Mobilizing information probably is not a panacea for the failure of the American political system to live up to what has been called the classical democratic ideal, in which citizens have access, are informed, and participate consistently. Sequence 3 people lack issue attitudes and would have no reason to participate. In the short run, it is obvious that massive increases in political MI would by no means create universal participation in the influence framework, just as giving the vote to women, eighteen-year-olds, and people who don't own property has not created universal voting participation.

If some MI is good, does it follow that all MI is? For example, what about criminal MI, which journalists routinely provide in crime stories? Even if the criminal *modus operandi* provides interesting and newsworthy detail to crime stories, did we need the 727 hijackings following the D. B. Cooper episode? Do we want or need the names, photos, and addresses of undercover drug agents to be published in underground newspapers? Do we need tactical MI on how to build an H-bomb? If more than half the crime news stories contain the *modus operandi,* does providing the MI give advance warning to potential victims, or does it provide tactical MI for criminals? It has been argued by journalists that forewarning victims offsets the tactical help given criminals. But presumably there are many thousands of potential victims—all of whom, ultimately, would need to be forewarned—while we need to have only *one* criminal willing to act on the tactical MI.

Suppose we conclude only that MI is "good" when it concerns public opinion issues? If we do this, it only brings up another problem: whether widespread political participation is "good."

Even if universal participation could be produced, we would need to consider seriously whether universal participation in the influence framework is in the best interests of society. Indeed, a consensus seems to be lacking even on whether universal *voting* participation is in the best interests of society. Bachrach and other writers feel that political science generally has come to the conclusion that universal participation would be harmful, and they attempt to argue with this "theory of democratic elitism."[46] The issue is not settled. Often the debate proceeds on normative grounds, *rather than grounds where it is possible to test predicted consequences,* and this is one reason that the issue shows no signs of being settled.

It *is* possible to test some consequences of political MI in the mass media, and the next section of this chapter is devoted to this and related matters.

UNTESTED QUESTIONS ABOUT MI

Following are some untested questions regarding mobilizing information.

▶ If political MI increases the amount of short-run participation, does it also increase the diversity of attitudes expressed? And does it change the percentages received for each issue stand, whether or not it increases the diversity of policy preferences?

Important questions also remain about the long-run consequences of MI in the mass media.

▶ If political MI were provided, would it gradually force decision-makers to systematize their procedures for listening to the "voice of the people" in the influence framework?

Political actors normally do not have the capacity now to cope with, synthesize, and analyze large volumes of input from citizens. But Franklin D. Roosevelt regularly received enormous numbers of letters and telegrams. He was willing and able to set up staff and procedures to digest, synthesize, and sample his mail for him.[47] At present, legislators, editors, and others vary a great deal in the attention they pay to messages from constituents, let alone in the amount of staff effort they allocate to digesting and handling such messages.

If participation increased as a result of MI, we might expect these these decision-makers in the long run would begin to systematize their procedures for handling this information. (It is interesting that legislators always seem to be portrayed as receiving an "avalanche" or a "deluge" of messages in a high-participation incident—as if the response were an Act of God and nobody should be expected to cope with the flood of mail and telephone calls.)

▶ If political MI were provided by journalists, what would be the effect on efficacy feelings among citizens who are now "turned off" by politics?

We are not considering only the effects of participation on efficacy feelings, though that is important. We are also considering whether, in Downs' terms, it is indeed "rational" now for a citizen to ignore news of government.[48] Would some of these Sequence 3 people gradually begin to show more interest in political issues as MI began to build efficacy feelings? Ironically, *issue-centered journalists might find that the way to educate audiences about issues is to build more MI into their coverage of political issues, not to expand their issue coverage.*

The questions raised so far are similar to issues raised by a democratic elitism that seems to assume that political ignorance and apathy are fixed properties of the great mass of our citizenry, not byproducts of the current political and mass media systems. The point is that these questions can be tested and need not depend on normative images of human beings.

What would it take to test these several questions? First, the news media—or at least some of them—must be induced to provide more MI in political contexts.

The short-run impact of MI could be tested in a number of ways. One way could be to introduce MI in the media serving one of two matched communities. In one community the news media would carry MI on an issue, and in the other community they would not. We could then compare participation rates as well as the distribution of attitudes expressed on that issue to decision-makers.

A similar procedure could be used to study the several longer-range effects, but it is necessary to persuade journalists to provide political MI.

▶ But how do you get journalists to provide MI in political contexts?

It may be that the question of the effects of MI cannot be settled until after this question is settled. We need to know more about the obstacles placed in the way of MI by the craft of journalism.

(Ultimately, of course, we may need to seek an explanation beyond the attitudes of journalists. Screening out MI from the mass media may very well be a form of control over political participation in the influence framework, and Power Elite theorists might wish to forget about the working journalists and *Get to the Real Cause*. For my part, I'd first like to see what would happen if journalists could be persuaded to provide political MI.)

We need to know whether political journalists themselves intend to interfere with political participation, despite their own frequent invocation of the people's right to know and to participate in government. If screening out political MI turns out to be an unintended consequence of current craft practices, then we need to know whether these practices can be changed. If the craft practices instead serve as a means of cloaking and rationalizing "nondecisions" because of pressures on journalists, then we need to find out the source and form of these pressures.[49]

▶ How did journalists come to feel that MI is not objective? Was it, for example, the results of the transition from partisan to mass circulation newspapers in the nineteenth century? Was it, in addition, a byproduct of the growth of advertising as an important income-producer during roughly the same time period? In either case, historical comparisons might show that the MI rate for political items in newspapers gradually declined during the nineteenth century. A study of changes in front page content of the *New York Times* from 1852 through 1969 revealed what the researcher called "supraindividualization" of actors and "abstraction and anonymization" of targets in news stories over these years.[50] In other words, individual actors were replaced by groups, and the objects of actions became more abstract or were otherwise unidentified. It is forcing things a little to treat these trends as evidence that identificational MI declined, but it is suggestive enough to encourage historical study. Another suggestion is provided by journalism historian Edwin Emery:

> Some of the most popular items in the [Revolutionary] war newspapers were columns of names the Sons and Daughters of the American Revolution might find it embarrassing to read today. These items were lists of deserters and "bounty jumpers". . . . The papers were full of such information.[51]

▶ If not an accident of history, is the confusion of MI with partisan mobilizing messages the result of such things as the kind of political leaflet reprinted earlier in this chapter? Or if an accident of history, is the confusion reinforced by such leaflets? In this connection, does (or did) the underground press contain more MI than the mainstream press? Does (did) the underground press have *political* MI more often?

Preliminary work at Oregon suggests a much higher MI rate in most underground media, but not necessarily in all of them. It may be that the range of MI in the underground press is much more extended than in the mainstream press. If the range of MI rates is far more extended in underground newspapers/magazines/ radio, would this be because expressive needs led to issue-centered-ness in those few underground media with extremely low MI rates?

Obviously, both content analysis and structured interviews with writers/editors could help answer these questions.

▶ Does the elitist kind of issue-centeredness coexist with the expressive, mistaking-words-for-deeds kind? Or does the elitist never make the mistake of being "impractical"? Do journalists who treat MI as dull detail also tend to be issue-centered?

▶ What kinds of MI—if any—would audience members regard as most helpful to them?

When asked in a study about identificational, locational, and tactical MI, students were most likely to think tactical MI the least appropriate for journalists to provide.[52]

Could we predict that Sequence 3 and 2 people would be more likely than Sequence 1 people to prefer consumer MI over political MI? The reasoning behind the three sequences (Chapter 5) would probably also lead us to expect that persons with intense issue attitudes concerning a topic would be far more likely than those without them to prefer a story on that topic with MI. (Again, there is some preliminary evidence that this may be so.)

▶ If consumer "Action Line" columns represent an effort to provide consumer MI, do journalists regard such services as not their function? If a news medium has an "Action Line" feature, was the feature staffed with a regular public affairs reporter, or did the news medium bring in somebody from outside? When are "Action Line" writers isolated and excluded from the city room beat structure of newspapers? How much help and cooperation do public affairs reporters give "Action Line" journalists? (We have some limited evidence, from our interviews with journalists, that they dismiss consumer product MI as "not our job." For an interesting and somewhat related review of consumer protection coverage in the news media, see Pollock.[53])

CONCLUSION

Perhaps careful studies of such questions as these will provide a common factual basis for the neo-populists in political sociology to debate the merits of democratic elitism with those political scientists who seem now to have given up on the capacity of non-elites to do anything to contribute to a stable democratic order, other than, perhaps, to vote.

Control of participation obviously figures prominently in a discussion of what has been termed "power." The next chapter takes up this and other questions.

7

Journalists and Power Discrepancies among Participants

> *. . . The concept of power, while indispensable as an abbreviation of complex phenomena, does not unambiguously refer to anything, and therefore is not likely to play a major part in any useful theory. On the other hand, genuine nonsense is very rare. . . . People who have concentrated on power have usually meant something, however obscurely.*
>
> R. Harrison Wagner[1]

It is in a similar spirit that the word *power* is used in this book —that is, as a label for a number of complex relationships. As Bierstedt said long ago about sociology and the concept of power, "We all know perfectly well what it is—until someone asks us."[2]

Our interest will be in the things subsumed under the label, not in the label itself. In the case of this book, *power* refers to a number of relationships among actual or potential participants in the public opinion process. The emphasis on relationships also makes it easier to think of power as often changeable, not always the fixed characteristic of individuals. This in turn may make it easier to see how journalists affect these relationships, *by either action or inaction.*

This is not the place to examine all the reasons why some writers feel that decades of research into power haven't gotten us very far. Nevertheless, three reasons sometimes mentioned are worth noting because they tie in especially well with the approach of this book.

First, much research into power has used reputational methods. People who supposedly have the most power are designated by others who supposedly are in a position to know, and so on. Dependence on reputational techniques may confound visibility and other factors with what we call power. One solution to the problem has been recommended by Nelson Polsby, who suggests that we should study the way decision-makers make actual decisions, rather than depending on reputational methods.[3] This is consistent with the approach to public opinion recommended in Chapter 2— we should study the perceptions of decision-makers with regard to specific issues. But one may have to define "actual decisions" more broadly than Polsby, as we shall see later.

The second problem was already mentioned in Chapter 2: Power involves more than the question of whether, in a clash of policy preferences, one's own views carry the most weight with a decision-maker. For example, if one can control the kinds of information reaching decision-makers (about citizen attitudes, or about how a problem is defined), it appears the decision may also be affected.

Third, various competing ideological camps have viewed power through the prisms supplied by their own ideologies, and this has not been particularly helpful. In the case of the study of public opinion, one camp tends to view power as competing *against* public opinion, and has gathered data in a format assuring that either one or the other "wins," but not both.[4] (Journalists are likely to share this view.) Another group of researchers tends to feel that interest groups may themselves effectively represent public opinion, so power and public opinion do not necessarily clash.[5]

As far as possible, we should remain noncommittal, regarding this as an empirical question best settled in linkage research. In a useful, concise book, Nagel has suggested the application of path analytic techniques to the study of power.[6] There is no reason why we couldn't use path analysis to sort out, simultaneously, the linkage of public opinion and interest groups with legislative voting behavior. Miller and Stokes' often-cited study of constituency influence[7] may have begged the question whether legislators were responding to public opinion as well as, or instead of, some other influence because it failed to take into account such things as the civil rights preferences of key interest groups in each congressional constituency. And, of course, it may have been that the legislators' perceptions of public opinion correlated even more strongly with the views of the interest groups than they did with survey measures of constituency attitudes.

KEY ADVANTAGES OF POWER

In Chapter 2, power was defined, tentatively, as the relative ability of political actors to block or initiate public discussion of potential issues, to influence perceptions of public opinion held by key decision-makers once an issue "goes public," to define issues and options under discussion, to influence participation by others, and to induce decision-makers to adopt the desired policy.

We now need to expand this definition of power to nine key advantages: (1) greater access to initiating sources, (2) greater access to the mass media, (3) greater control of participation by other groups, (4) greater ability to reach support "privately," (5) greater skill, energy, and ability to concentrate, (6) greater access to decision-makers, (7) greater access to "experts," (8) greater access to money, and (9) a greater reputation for power.

Greater Access to Initiating Sources

Initiating sources are persons or groups with the capacity to call public attention to the existence of an issue. Obviously, greater access to these sources means a chance to suppress, release, and define the information that is made available to the citizenry. Coleman and many other writers agree that knowledge control—rather than knowledge itself—is an important basis of social power.[8]

The U.S. Food and Drug Administration and many other government regulatory agencies have the capacity to be initiating sources. In August 1974 a number of medical professionals employed by the FDA testified to a joint meeting of Senate Judiciary and Labor-Welfare subcommittees that the FDA frequently suppressed unfavorable reports on new drugs and disciplined those who drafted the reports. They testified that unfavorable aspects of their draft reports were changed and that they were transferred to other responsibilities after being reprimanded. A Dr. B. L. Appleton testified, "My superior at that time was going behind my back and giving my findings to the [drug company] sponsor" of the drug being reviewed.[9]

We have no independent way now of checking whether anybody was going behind anybody's back in this particular case. But we do know of another incident in which the Food and Drug Administration clearly and publicly provided access to drug companies before an issue was made known to the public. On April 27, 1968, *The Lancet,* a British medical journal, published the first documented evidence of a correlation between birth control pills and deaths from blood clots in women. Word of this finding received scant attention in American news media until *after* the FDA had called a meeting of American makers of the pill. The upshot of this meeting was the announcement of a joint agreement to put a cautionary insert in pill containers warning of a possible "increase in . . . morbidity due to thromboembolic diseases in women taking oral contraceptives. . . ." The insert appeared in pill containers starting July 1, 1968.

The Food and Drug Administration then announced the agreement to the press, long before there was any widespread popular awareness that the pill might have dangerous side effects.

It is rare that lobbyists themselves publicly assert that they have had access to initiating sources, but in the spring of 1978 the quarterly report of the American Petroleum Institute claimed that the U.S. Department of Energy had given API lobbyists advance notice of at least six of its pending regulations, before notice of the regulations was published in the Federal Register. (The Federal Register itself, of course, is much more available in the District of Columbia than out in the hinterlands.) The API report also claimed that API was able to take advantage of its access to do such things as successfully changing the Department of Energy's gasoline monitoring system "before the system was released for public comment."[10]

Although government regulatory agencies have the capacity to be initiating sources, Rubin and Sachs argue that greater access to them by special interest groups makes these agencies rather unreliable and tardy initiators, frequently resulting in the postponement of public consideration until the social costs are so high that solutions are hard to find.[11]

In the case of legislators and elected government officials, those who recruited them and helped organize and finance their campaigns may very well have greater access to them than anybody else. At the local level, Prewitt argues that what he terms "volunteerism" (the recruitment of people to run for office as a matter of *noblesse oblige*) works against access to elected initiating sources by the general public and in favor of access to them by their like-minded upper-status peers. He also argues that volunteerism is widespread in county, city, and school council rooms, and is starting to show up among state legislators.[12]

Early in President Carter's administration, news stories reported the gathering of many large campaign donors for a special session with the president. Interviewed before and after the meeting, many of these persons frankly stated that they gave campaign money in order to assure access should they need it.

Access to initiating sources helps determine (1) what matters are on the informal and formal political agenda,[13] (2) the way an issue is defined, and (3) whether the issue is placed in the election or the influence framework.

Greater Access to the Mass Media

There seems little question that not all potential initiating sources have equal access to the news. Journalists' objectivity norms make them rather dependent on "official" sources—largely government or previously legitimized sources—to initiate controversial issues in public affairs news.[14]

As for nongovernmental initiating sources, it is fairly difficult (though by no means impossible for those with requisite skills) to create and initiate issues through the press.

By the time even rudimentary news values have been taught to journalism students, it is apparent that they will not provide equal access to the news columns for sources who have essentially the same message. A thesis by Schwantes reported a marked bias in coverage against speakers at a public meeting who were representing only themselves as compared to speakers representing organized groups.[15] The subjects of the study were student reporters, but observation of behavior by professionals confirms the same kinds of inequalities of access to news coverage.[16]

As Roshco put it in his analysis of access to the press, "For the creation of a 'new' public issue, a basic requisite is either a source who is 'authoritative' . . . or a situation that has become obtrusive."[17] Authoritative sources have status, are frequently (but not always) thought by journalists to be knowledgeable, and often have *previously* received news coverage.

It is possible to gain access to broadcast and print news if one lacks status, but the cost often is prohibitively high. In effect, Vietnam protesters gained news attention by creating obtrusive situations that themselves captured the lion's share of the news coverage. Journalists covered these events as disturbances, paying little or no attention to the substantive issue that presumably motivated the demonstrations in the first place.

Given the dependence of journalism on "official" sources, access to initiating sources is likely also to mean access to the news media, with all the attendant advantages that such access gives. Sen. William Proxmire's "Golden Fleece Awards," for example, now routinely receive widespread coverage when they are announced. The "Awards" single out allegedly useless research projects funded by government money. According to Proxmire, more than two-thirds of the research programs thus identified "have been eliminated or reduced."[18] Given the perception that public opinion is against government waste, the publicity exerts considerable pressure, much in the way publicity enforces social norms.[19] One can't help but wonder whether the Golden Fleece Awards would receive as much publicity had they been the brainchild of even a quasi-official source such as Common Cause or Ralph Nader. Beyond that, one worries about the media resources available to the "winners" of the Golden Fleece.

An additional advantage also results from media access. Once an issue reaches the point at which decision-makers are interested in finding out the status of public opinion on it, the news media will also very likely act as one of several intermediary agencies that transmit versions of public opinion to decision-makers. In this sense, some prominent polling organizations have considerably more "power" than the rest of us.

Greater Control of Participation by Other Groups

An advantage that is indirectly related to the preceding ones is the ability to inhibit or stimulate the participation of others outside the groups to which you have direct access.

Inhibiting Participation. The last two chapters were concerned with ways in which journalists help inhibit or minimize participation whether they intend to or not. Krieghbaum, in his *Pressures on the Press,* has gathered a number of anecdotes suggesting that if and when journalists withhold information from potential participants, they do it more often because they anticipate pressure than because they have experienced it.[20] In this sense at least, journalists' actions strongly resemble what Bachrach and Baratz term *nondecisions.*[21]

Summarizing the results of a number of sociological studies of power, Lane concluded that in communities where power was more concentrated, widespread political participation was discouraged.[22] There is general agreement that one way to win political disputes is to restrict the scope of the conflict, leaving out the people who would oppose you.[23]

Although this book concentrates on media aspects of the public opinion process, it is worth reemphasizing occasionally that the mass media are not the only restricting influence. Participation also may be restricted in other ways. In May 1974, for example, the Supreme Court made it much more difficult for class action antitrust suits to be brought on behalf of large, dispersed populations. This decision added further restrictions to those imposed by a 1969 decision that claimants could not pool their claims in order to gain access to federal courts.

Also, Milbrath concluded that lobbyists have most influence when legislators are considering narrow, specialized matters (in which participation is restricted to those immediately affected).[24]

Another kind of evidence comes from an overview of the influence of the John Birch Society and three other conservative pressure groups on sex education programs. These groups were said to be generally far more successful in local influence and election frameworks than at state and national levels.[25] Similarly, Lane reported that local participation levels fall further behind participation concerning national issues as the concentration of community power increases.[26]

Stimulating Participation

Stimulating Participation. Individuals or groups who have the skills (or status) to gain access to the news columns can also raise issues in ways that will stimulate participation by persons unknown to them. For example, redefining the mine safety issue and causing it to be regarded as an issue about black lung disease had the effect of gaining more news attention. Likewise, Cesar Chavez' fast on behalf of the United Farm Workers' cause placed the UFW movement higher on media agendas. Both cases eventually stimulated widespread participation, drawing into the conflict persons who had not previously identified strongly with the issue.[27]

Of course, participation can be stimulated in ways other than through what we usually think of as the mass media. One of these ways is inherent in the next major advantage.

Greater Ability to Reach Support "Privately"

Exclusive dependence on the mass media to reach people who agree with you generally is a sign of weakness. Even if you gain access to media, legal and craft restrictions inevitably screen out some of the content you intended to reach your supporters.

It is tempting to try to persuade people, rather than to mobilize them, especially when you are trying to reach an unknown, heterogeneous audience through the mass media. A group that already has identified many of its supporters can energize them more efficiently through its own newsletters, phone trees, and mailings. People who depend too much on the media may in effect be conceding that they don't know who their supporters are and hope to pull them out of the woodwork through such unselective means of communication. Opponents are in the woodwork, too.

An example of the advantage inherent in alternative lines of communication occurred when police and other law enforcement personnel managed to put a death penalty initiative on a California ballot in an amazingly short period of time and at extremely low cost, considering the many hundreds of thousands of signatures they obtained. Though police officers and other law enforcement personnel presumably were operating on their own off-work time, it is obvious that the campaign was organized and coordinated through preexisting lines of communication.[28]

Computerized mailing lists of people who have already shown they support you are as good as gold—and worth about as much as gold in modern interest group politics. Rep. Charles Rose of North Carolina summarized the new era of mail generated by computerized mailing lists with words that recall for us with remarkable irony what was said in Chapter 2 about Franklin Delano Roosevelt's primitive letter-writing operation in the innocent 1930s. Rose said: "Any special-interest group that has a better mailing list than you, owns you. It can reach your constituents better than you can."[29] The result will be mail pressure from the constituency.

In addition to computerized mailouts, other means of quickly reaching supporters include telephone trees and Mailgrams to regional dispersal centers.

As long as your communications remain private among supporters, your message probably will not provoke the opposition. It would be interesting to see why journalists so often fail to cover—as legitimate political news—the contents of newsletters sent out to members of political interest groups. Certainly, interest group newsletters are at least as significant—and legitimate—an object of news coverage as many other things that do receive coverage.

In any event, present press practice gives very wide leeway to private communications sent by interest groups to many thousands of people.

Greater Skill, Energy, and Ability to Concentrate

Perhaps the most obvious difference among participants is talent. If we regard talent as more-or-less fixed or constant, what is *not* fixed is whether that talent can be used fully and whether the way journalists cover controversies allows full use of those talents. The relative quality of one's participation depends in large part on one's skill *and on one's ability to concentrate those skills* on an issue. Neither talent nor commitment—the latter is sometimes called the "intensity problem" by political scientists[30]—is equally distributed.

Anything that interferes with the ability to concentrate resources and energy weakens one's ability to influence public opinion, as it is defined in this book. In the short run, at least, political talent is not susceptible to media influence. Therefore, the aspect of difference among talents that is most susceptible to media influence and to the influence of other actors is ability (and willingness) to concentrate energies.

The National Rifle Association consistently has been portrayed by political journalists as a very potent one-issue cluster of potential voters, willing to forgive all flaws in candidates save a pro-gun-control ideology. While he was not writing about the NRA in particular, a banker put this special interest theory of voting very well: ". . . In dealing with the electorate, minorities punish but majorities seldom protect."[31]

On the other side of the coin, much material is now available on how political actors can be diverted from Taking Their Best Shot. Most of this anecdotal material, however, is concerned with the impact of published polls on the efforts of candidates who are behind. According to an analytical piece in the *Los Angeles Times,* when published polls show a candidate behind and not seeming to make headway, the candidate is forced to spend too much time whipping up staff morale, raising campaign money (promised money tends to dry up and not arrive as scheduled), and persuading journalists to cover him.[32] As Jesse Unruh put it in this same piece, "By the time he [the candidate] gets to the people he should be talking to—the voters—he's exhausted." Readers will recall from Chapter 4 that the only time Birch Bayh came close to getting the same amount of coverage as Morris Udall (who got far less than Carter) was, ironically, when Bayh was rumored to be withdrawing.

Greater Access to Decision-Makers

Obviously the advantage of greater access to decision-makers overlaps access to initiating sources to a certain extent, especially when we are considering decision-makers in government. Therefore, some of the support cited here could as well have been cited earlier, and vice versa.

Boynton, Patterson, and Hedlund concluded that the "missing links" between legislators and their constituencies were elite "attentive constituents," most of whom had frequently tried to influence decisions by the state legislature.[33] Nearly 60 percent of these elites said they talked "quite often" with local, state, and national officials. Many of these attentive constituents themselves had had experience as government officials. Importantly, they appeared to have been active in recruiting for office some of the people they talked with.

The gradual decline of the political parties should not be taken to mean that political party personnel no longer have advantages of access. Key felt that pressure groups gained power by forming coalitions with the parties,[34] but it is now an open empirical question whether parties or pressure groups have greater access to decision-makers and under what conditions. Another open question is whether the practice of personnel exchanges between industry and regulatory agencies was more commonplace in the recent past than, say, during the Truman administration.

Very often, political scientists studying influence can come up with nothing more than the statement from legislators that lobbyists are valued for their information or expertise rather than for their advice. Even if we assume this is all lobbyists have going for them, it is apparent that their information opens doors.

Staff clearly have great access to decision-makers at all levels of government. It is likely that as local government continues to get more complex, staff advice will continue to grow in influence, especially when decision-makers are unpaid, or underpaid, part-timers.

Nord suggests that one way to influence decision-makers at a federal regulatory agency is to define an issue for them in terms favorable to an interest group. In an historical study of a policy change toward educational broadcasting, Nord argued that the Federal Communications Commission first had to be convinced that the issue was not the quality of educational programming on the air (carried by commercial broadcasters) but instead was the reserving of frequencies for educational stations. He concluded, in effect, that educational interests had few advantages available to them *except* access and the ability to keep offering their definition of the issues to the FCC until events led the FCC to conceptualize the issue in the same way.[35]

Access to decision-makers, however, varies in important respects as the level of office increases, since it is likely that both the size of staff and the size of the decision-maker's reference public increase. Thus more intermediaries screen incoming information as the level of office and size of constituency go up. Also, the sheer volume of participation received is likely to increase with office level, other things being equal. Because many decision-makers are not, by habit and inclination, well equipped systematically to count, simplify, and carefully interpret the information they receive from citizens in the influence framework, they are likely to rely increasingly on staff and other agencies, such as the polls and the mass media, to provide simplified versions of public opinion for them.

Greater Access to "Experts"

This advantage also overlaps with some of the preceding ones. But assuming that an issue has been initiated publicly, having expert help obviously is an advantage in defining issues, defending positions, and getting certain options either considered or eliminated.

The problem of lacking access to expertise was illustrated somewhat ironically and unusually during the 1973 Arab oil embargo. This time it seemed to be the government that lacked accurate figures. The international oil corporations controlled the information on oil reserves, imports, and so on, thus heavily influencing the options available to policymakers in meeting the crisis and considering future policy. Efforts to set up an independent data source so far have been defeated in Congress.

A national study of testimony and other presentations made to local school boards showed a fairly clear tendency toward domination by experts (usually staff).[36] Experts dominated the oral introduction of new topics of discussion and shared dominance with board members of the actual discussions. Testimony by "the public" ranked very far down the list.

Greater Access to Money

Greater access to money probably is the element of power that occurs most often to everybody. It is true that money makes some participants more visible and important than others. And, as previously mentioned, it gives some people greater access to decision-makers.

One irony of this is the fact that as money became increasingly important in financing election campaigns, its influence occurred elsewhere—in the influence framework.

In this connection, a study by Jacobson[37] suggests that campaign money spent for broadcast political ads delivers more of an election edge at congressional and statewide levels than at the presidential level. (This analysis was done prior to public funding of presidential campaigns, however, and covered only the 1956 race.) In a later analysis of 1972 and 1974 House and Senate campaign spending, Jacobson concluded that spending by challengers has a much greater impact on the election outcome than does spending by an incumbent. Challengers need to get as much name recognition as the incumbent. Since the incumbent has already had much greater access to the news columns, challengers in effect have to buy their access to the media.[38] (Media advertising costs consistently represent the single largest share of campaign expenses in national and state elections.)

There is some debate about how decisive campaign money is in election outcomes, but it is easy to find examples suggesting its importance. In the 1978 California election, Proposition 5, a measure which would have prohibited smoking in public places, was defeated handily at the polls. A $5.5 million campaign against Proposition 5 was mounted by tobacco interests. A *Los Angeles Times* survey before the campaign started showed 53 percent in favor of Proposition 5; another *Times* poll just before the election showed only 40 percent favoring it.[39]

In a 1972 book, Dunn concludes that "candidates' increasing use of high-cost modern technology inevitably will make money more decisive in the future in determining election results."[40]

It is important also to realize that it is the *perception* by political actors that money makes an electoral difference that gives donors influence. Whether the actual difference is as large as it is thought to be is beside the point, at least in the short run.

Pàrtly as a result of several federal campaign finance reforms and some U.S. Supreme Court decisions, some extremely important (and often unanticipated) changes have taken place in where that money is coming from.

Even before the consequences of these laws and court decisions became clear, Adamany had argued that the increasing costs of statewide election campaigns gradually had forced the two parties to align their programs to appeal to potential interest group donors.[41] If so, this alone would imply that V. O. Key's interest group "tail" would now be wagging the dog. That is, political parties would be seeking out alliances with interest groups, rather than the reverse, as Key had argued in his book.[42]

Public financing of campaigns and a number of other factors have combined further to weaken political parties so much that now the *candidate* is the one who may be most actively seeking alliances with interest groups. Money from interest groups now flows from more than seventeen hundred "Political Action Committees" which have in effect been virtually freed from spending limitations. By just after the traditional Labor Day start of the campaigns in 1978, for example, PACs had donated five times as much money to fall campaigns as had both political parties combined.[43] By the time the election was over, PACs had spent $32 million on congressional races alone, most of this money going to incumbents.[44]

One side effect of the public funding of presidential campaigns probably has been to encourage the flow of special interest money into other races. According to former Iowa Sen. Dick Clark, special interest campaign contributions to congressional and senatorial campaigns increased by 60 percent from 1974 to 1976.[45] Ironically, Clark himself was defeated in his 1978 bid for reelection by a conservative Republican given heavy support by many PACs.

Reviewing the evidence on campaign money through the 1976 election, Adamany concluded that "the time is ripe to ask whether the new campaign finance laws are effective." He suggested that the new reform laws, in combination with U.S. Supreme Court decisions, may even have become counterproductive.[46]

The Reputation for Power

The reputation for power *is* power. When other actors believe a person has inside information, a large and dedicated following, and so on, this reputation can be translated into influence over others.

Journalists often play a large role in creating (and tearing down) such reputations (for example, the National Rifle Association example cited earlier in this chapter and the 1976 New Hampshire/ Massachusetts example cited in Chapter 4).

Journalists also are affected by others' reputation for power. Previous chapters provide many examples of information that was withheld from audiences by journalists. It certainly can be argued, as Krieghbaum does, that the information often is withheld because of anticipated, rather than exercised, power.[47]

And journalists themselves benefit from the reputation for power, as do the mass media institutions they work for. The idea that news reports (and editorial opinions) influence public opinion is, at base, a crucial reason why reluctant sources try to answer journalists' questions. And it is why vigorous and influential editor-publishers like William Loeb of the *Manchester Union-Leader* seem able to recruit, and discourage, potential candidates for office.[48]

RESEARCH PROSPECTS

We started this chapter by noting the disarray in power theory and research. Perhaps one underlying reason why empirical research is hard to do well in this area is that people with power are understandably reluctant to be studied. And, Power Elite theorists would probably say, people with power have the means to avoid being studied. Nevertheless, with a little imagination it is possible to investigate power relationships, as a Common Cause research project demonstrates. Common Cause investigators looked at the appointment calendars of thirty-nine members of various federal regulatory commissions and found that representatives of the regulated industries were ten times as likely to be on the commissioners' appointment calendars as were consumers of regulated products.[49]

The appointment calendar example is reminiscent of the earlier discussion about access to decision-makers. Probably, therefore, it will come as no surprise to find far better research prospects under each of the nine advantages listed in this chapter than under the aegis of the power concept itself.

If you have a background in the social sciences, but none in journalism, you *may* be surprised by the following statement: Most of the best journalists and journalism students I have known are absolutely convinced that good reporters and editors do *not* help maintain or enhance the nine advantages mentioned in this chapter. (The same is true of journalism professors, too!)

However, this chapter has repeatedly made the point that journalistic practices generally and systematically tend to support existing power discrepancies, whether or not journalists realize it. Many of these practices would be (and are) vigorously defended as being in the public interest by these good journalists.

To be sure, we can find derelictions by individual journalists that aid the powerful, and these derelictions would be condemned as well by good journalists. And to be sure, we can also find examples of such things as access to decision-makers being disrupted by elegant and widely admired journalistic endeavors. Remember the Associated Press stake-out of the Washington airport during the Watergate period, when reporters tallied the names of government officials being flown back to Washington in corporate jets?

But the problem is that such things as the journalistic craving for official sources stems from quite reasonable and plausible premises, when these premises are considered in isolation.[50] So, to a large extent, does the avoidance of mobilizing information in news of controversy (see Chapter 6), to cite another example.

It appears that "nondecision" theory and research ought to be applied to analysis of journalists and power. In fact, journalists' writing behavior may provide an unusually good chance to add to the extremely scanty empirical literature on nondecisions. The bane of nondecision theory appears to be the researchability of events that don't occur.[51] Critical research on journalists by Breed, Paletz et al., Hungerford and Lemert, and many others suggests that this is not nearly as great a problem with journalistic nondecisions.[52]

It is unfortunate that critical research in journalism and nondecision theory in political science have coexisted so far without mutual awareness. Each can benefit from the other.

8
Linkage I: Public Opinion, Decision-Makers, and Journalists

We have practically no systematic information about what goes on in the minds of public men as they ruminate about the weight to be given the public opinion in governmental decision.

V. O. Key, Jr., 1961[1]

Complete understanding of the frequency or infrequency of linkage between public opinion and policy is beyond the present knowledge of political scientists.

Robert Erikson and Norman Luttbeg, 1973[2]

We still can't say much to update either the 1961 or the 1973 evaluation of what is known about linkage of public opinion with public policy.

The present chapter, therefore, will deal more with problems related to the basic information available on linkage and less with trying to adapt and extend this knowledge to journalists and the mass media. Nevertheless, later in this chapter we shall consider journalists' role in the linkage of public opinion with public policy.

Both this and the next chapter will discuss linkage. Chapter 9 will be concerned almost exclusively with the assets and liabilities of polls as a linkage device. The present chapter will emphasize other linkage problems.

Chapter 2 defined public opinion as a perception imposed on information about citizen attitudes by the perceiver. It also emphasized that public opinion was more a subjective than an idiosyncratic phenomenon, especially when we look at perceptions held by the key decision-makers who provide (or might provide) the link between public opinion and policy decisions. These perceptions were less idiosyncratic than subjective largely because political pressures placed constraints on the variance decision-makers could have in their perceptions. We also saw in Chapter 2 that this definition of public opinion facilitated research; in fact, I provided several examples of previous research that might almost have been done with this conception of public opinion in mind.

Nevertheless, it is still true that there is a very lengthy list of problems, only some of which are covered in the following brief review.

PROBLEMS IN EXISTING
LINKAGE RESEARCH

▶ Linkage researchers have been preoccupied with whether public opinion has been followed, not with the means by which decision-makers discovered what "it" was. Far too little attention has been paid to the information-processing and assessment techniques involved when decision-makers try to form conclusions about public opinion. Scant as the existing research on linkage is, it is safe to say that the research has more often than not begged several questions about what led decision-makers to their perceptions of public opinion.[3]

To my knowledge only a handful of studies has touched on even the limited question of which form of attitude information decision-makers said they perferred. And these studies all have tended to ask about forms of information in the abstract. Of this handful, studies of Oregon legislators in 1971, 1972, and 1975 lead to the conclusion that, while their use of polls has increased somewhat since 1971, state legislators still feel that personal contacts (including letters and telephone calls) provide the most reliable information about their constituency's views on issues.[4]

▶ Increasing use of polls, without a similar increase in reliance, also appears to have occurred with members of the House of Representatives.[5] Since many members of Congress admit that they use mail-out polls for public relations purposes, it appears essential for researchers to begin to separate legislators' evaluation of their own polls from their evaluation of other polls that might come to their attention. Perhaps the professionally done polls wouldn't have fared as badly in their evaluations. (Already, there is evidence that some candidates for Congress view professional polling as an integral part of their election campaigns.[6]) At the moment, though, it does look as if more personal and more intuitive forms of information are preferred, especially in the noncampaign parts of the influence framework.

Another group of questions about information-gathering practices has to do with what "public" the decision-maker is thinking of when trying to determine public opinion. In other words, *if* we assume the decision-maker is a legislator, what is his or her constituency? Wilkins found that, on a high-visibility issue that had polarized sections of the state, many Oregon legislators made clear distinctions between mail from inside and outside their own districts.[7] During the televised impeachment hearings, at least two members of the House Judiciary Committee also clearly kept separate records of communications from inside and outside their congressional districts.[8]

Davidson found that congressmen from electorally "riskier" districts were more likely to conceptualize the public as their own voting constituency.[9] On the other side, it appears likely that aspirations for higher office tend to cause elected officials to think of a public that is larger than their own present constituency.[10] But none of these questions has really been thoroughly answered. (An amazingly uniform preoccupation with legislators as decision-makers is evident in linkage studies. Only occasionally has linkage been examined with government administrators' decisions in mind.[11] And only recently have linkage studies been extended to middle-level bureaucrats[12] or to employees of businesses.[13] Almost totally untouched is linkage between public opinion and executives in businesses, in the mass media, and in institutions such as Common Cause. But all this is another story.)

Following is a sample of the numerous other unresolved questions about how decision-makers process attitude information:

▶ Because they have larger staffs than most representatives, do U.S. senators devote more hours of staff time to processing information about citizen attitudes? (But even if they did, it does not necessarily follow that they would be more likely to follow "public opinion.")

▶ Does the fact that mail to decision-makers seems to have increased markedly from the 1930s on imply that decision-makers allocate more personal and/or staff time to processing this information? If it does, has this increased time been devoted more to "public opinion" mail or to the servicing of particularized constituent complaints about problems with government bureaucracy? Fiorina suggests the extra time (if any) now definitely goes to "service" problems. As he put it in a subhead to his article, "Better to be Reelected as an Errand Boy than Not to Be Reelected at All."[14]

▶ In the influence framework, do elected decision-makers devote more of their personal/staff time to processing information about citizen attitudes as elections draw near? Kuklinski feels that legislators' roll call *voting* corresponds more closely to public opinion in their constituencies as elections draw near.[15] But voting behavior is not the same thing as information processing behavior, a point worth stating and restating. The difference between these two kinds of behavior is especially clear in the case of Kuklinski's data, since he used past election results as his indicator of constituency opinion. It would take little effort for a legislator to note how his constituency voted on past referenda. On the other hand, Declercq's data could be interpreted as suggesting expenditures for polling are a function of perceived electoral risk.[16]

▶ So let us suppose decision-markers *do* increase their efforts to process information about citizen attitudes as they get closer to their next election. If so, would high-participation incidents increase or lower the amount of time devoted to the information at other times in the influence framework? We've seen repeatedly that rare high-participation incidents tend to be characterized as "floods" of messages *that cannot be handled by staff*— a kind of "Act of God" for which no change in staffing assignments is required. (Because Jimmy Carter appears deliberately to have tried to stimulate messages to him—in ways somewhat similar to those used by Franklin Roosevelt—it is not surprising to find that he was required to continue his large "temporary" White House staff to handle the messages. Incidentally, a National Public Radio report suggests that the first five hundred reactions to President Carter's first "Fireside Chat" were very quickly processed and characterized as highly favorable.[17])

▶ Has the role of keeping in touch with public input gradually shifted from decision-makers to staff over the years? If so, why?

▶ Under what conditions do decision-makers distort their perceptions of public opinion to suit their own attitudes? When are they least likely to "perceive selectively?"

▶ Under what conditions are elected decision-makers sure that the last election was a clear mandate endorsing a number of their own issue positions, thus minimizing the perceived need to monitor citizen attitudes in the influence framework?

▶ Under what conditions are decision-makers most likely to rely on low-effort means of monitoring public opinion, such as news media accounts, published polls, and elections results elsewhere?

▶ What criteria do decision-makers use to decide that an election result somewhere else is relevant to themselves?

▶ Given the enormous recent emphasis on single-issue voters (anti-gun-control, anti-abortion, etc.), do elected decision-makers even process information any more toward the goal of conceptualizing what *"the"* public opinion is? In other words, pressure has markedly increased on elected decision-makers to conceptualize their constituency as an aggregation of *separate* publics, each with its own "litmus test" that it applies at the next election. If this felt pressure (underscored by numerous recent news accounts of the "single issue" phenomenon) has increased, who has changed the way they conceptualize public opinion, and who hasn't? For example, would members of a lower house be more likely to have changed to multiple publics than members of an upper house (assuming lower house members face elections more often)?

▶ When are representatives of organized groups regarded as reflecting public opinion? (Evidence indicates that school board members tend to heed such representatives as districts become more heterogeneous and larger. On the other hand, anecdotal evidence suggests that city councils may not do the same in diverse, rapidly growing cities where neighborhood associations purport to represent neighborhood opinion.)

▶ In the private sector, the great bulk of polling is done for businesses. "United States campanies may spend as much as half a billion dollars a year, perhaps more, for outside market research and attitudinal studies," according to Wheeler.[18] Whether this spending estimate is correct or not, it does suggest that efforts to discern public opinion may be widespread among private sector decision-makers. But do these people make a distinction between what we would call market surveys and public opinion surveys? Assuming that they make this distinction, under what conditions are they likely to hire survey agencies to do "public opinion" work for them? And are they more likely than legislators to prefer polls over more personal communications? If so, why?

Even this list of questions doesn't come close to exhausting the single area of how decision-makers process information about citizen attitudes. But it is time to move to another area.

Miller and Stokes' classic study of linkage[19] provided a data set that has exceeded its twentieth year of existence. The same data have been reanalyzed at least three times by other researchers.[20] Even a Mother Lode must eventually run out.

Either elections or their surrogates—polls—have consistently been used in linkage research as the ultimate validity check against which public opinion perceptions are compared.

To be sure, some fairly persuasive arguments can be mounted on behalf of elections as validity check, especially given the fact that not everybody voted. And similarly persuasive arguments can be found on behalf of polls (see next chapter, however).

But the failure to consider the whole process of validating such perceptions stacks the deck against getting the most out of those few studies that have examined decision-makers' perceptions. For example, a comparison of perceptions against whatever decision-makers say they *use* as their information about citizen attitudes itself can be used to test accuracy or validity. In other words, perceptual distortions can be checked in ways that do not require validation against criteria which are not available to the decision-maker.

Perhaps the most severe conceptual problems of using polls as validity check can be found in some otherwise quite valuable co-orientational research efforts.[21] The coorientation approach stresses the *joint* consideration of some common object by actors *A* and *B*. As it evolved, coorientation research was applied to what I would call the decision-maker (*A*) and his or her perception of *B* (the public opinion of some aggregate of people). For instance, Hesse found that Wisconsin state senators' accuracy of public opinion perception was *higher* among rural senators and *lower* among those whose communications with their constituents were of the "all mouth, and no ears" variety.[22] The latter finding, especially, has a certain plausibility. But in what sense did the people who were polled *jointly* orient themselves, along with their senator, toward a common object? Strictly from the point of view of appearing to be consistent with its own original assumptions, coorientation research would seem to be required to consider the attitudes of people who *contacted* (that is, tried to *co*orient with) the decision-maker as the validity check against which to compare the perception.

In some ways, research has far too narrowly defined and measured decision-makers' responsiveness to public opinion.

For instance, what about the selection of candidates? The growth of presidential primaries certainly has not removed the selection of the eventual nominees from the influence framework. Some writers feel that the pre-primary-season polls rather than the primaries, have been the decisive factor in presidential candidate selection,[23] but in any case the final selection is made by conventions in the influence framework. Do previously uncommitted delegates "bow" in their choice to public opinion, as they understand it? Or are other criteria—such as ideology—at work?

When decision-makers try to duck some issues, is it because they are afraid of public reactions to their own policy preferences? Suppose former Arkansas Sen. William Fulbright were absent more often than others on civil rights votes (I have no idea whether he was). Would Sen. Fulbright have been absent because his own attitudes conflicted with constituency preferences as he perceived them? Would constituency opinion therefore have *prevented* the casting of a pro-civil-rights vote? If this indeed happened, conventional measures of roll-call responsiveness would not have caught it.

And when decision-makers are encouraged and emboldened by public reactions to strengthen a position they have already stated, aren't they also responding to public opinion? According to his son, Sen. Arthur Vandenberg's first, carefully offered Senate speech in support of a bipartisan foreign policy produced such favorable public reactions that the senator became much more active, and visible, in support of bipartisanship:

> The Senator *had* kept open an avenue of political retreat . . . and, certainly, it was the unexpected public enthusiasm for his speech that irrevocably confirmed his new course. Still more important, it was this public support that in one great surge gave him the political stature and the strength necessary to carry on his unique role in the following critical years. . . ."[24]

And what about the desire to avoid being recorded on roll-calls when the legislator is voting against perceived constituency opinion? And, in deference to The Folks Back Home, the introduction of bills that the legislator realizes haven't got a chance? Or, as another alternative measure of responsiveness, the speed of replies to questions raised by journalists and others about a decision-maker's record? Or even how fast the decision-maker agrees to hold a press conference or an interview under such circumstances?

All these questions fall within the so-called demand-response approach to representation, and thus do not depart from the prevailing approach, at least in that sense. The term demand-response refers to policy demands by constituencies and the ways the representative responds to those specific demands.

Other writers, however, question whether the demand-response approach is even an appropriate way of conceptualizing linkage.[25] While their argument is complex, and raises many issues that might lead far from the purposes of this discussion, one of their points is worth stating here: Whether or not decision-makers are responsive to perceived demands may be less important than whether or not decision-makers' actions are intended to create the perception *by constituents* that the decision-maker is responsive to them. Attention, in other words, needs to be directed to precisely such things as ducking of issues, the defensively motivated introduction of doomed bills, and the haste with which possible constituency problems are diverted.

Many of the questions asked above thus would be regarded as useful and appropriate by political scientists of either the demand-response or the opposing school. Perhaps their appeal to both schools will make it more tempting for political scientists to begin to get answers.

▶ Linkage researchers have had real trouble unequivocally identifying public opinion—and not something else—as the "cause" of decision-makers' behavior.

For instance, even Miller and Stoke's elegant multivariate analysis entered only three factors as potential independent variables —constituency attitudes, perceived constituency attitudes, and the decision-makers' own attitudes.[26] And, ultimately, only the last two were considered as competitive explanations of roll-call voting.

If we take the view that the wishes of important pressure groups cannot be viewed as part of "real" public opinion, then we clearly could have a problem with Miller and Stokes's conclusion that perceived public opinion was influential on civil rights votes. Suppose the wishes of important pressure groups arranged the congressional districts at least as well as did perceived constituency opinion. If we had entered this into the equation, could we then conclude that legislators were responsive to pressure groups rather than to public opinion?

Of course, *if* pressure groups' views were part of the data taken into account by the legislators in forming their perceptions of public opinion, we might not have a problem with a competitive pressure group's explanation. No data are provided in this study to allow us to tell whether these legislators isolated such group expressions in a category separate from data about public opinion expressions. (The literature in political science and sociology, by the way, is ambivalent about whether to include interest group expressions as part of the information about citizen attitudes. Perhaps we should rely on how decision-makers say *they* classify such expressions—another argument for the need to study the information-processing practices of decision-makers.)

The literature also shows a great deal of confusion as to whether (1) the political parties link constituency opinion to policy through elections (the "Political Parties Model" of linkage[27]) or (2) the parties' policy preferences *compete with* constituency preferences.[28] In studies of roll-call voting, these rather opposed ways of thinking of the parties will obviously lead to considerably opposed methods of calculating whether legislators are responsive to public opinion in their districts.

We turn now to mass media aspects of the linkage process.

MEDIA DECISION-MAKERS AS A FOCUS OF LINKAGE RESEARCH

Do public opinion perceptions play a role in decisions by journalists to provide or withhold mobilizing information? Is a context safe or noncontroversial because of perceived audience reactions? In what other kinds of day-to-day writing/editing decisions may public opinion perceptions play a role in the newsroom?

Earlier we saw that linkage research has concentrated heavily on government decision-makers—especially elected ones and even more especially legislators. And it was suggested briefly that there clearly were opportunities for public opinion to influence decisions made by corporate decision-makers.

In an interesting decision of why the networks have reduced the amount of violence on television, five TV show producers vehemently claimed that it was pressure groups, not public opinion, that had influenced the networks to cut back on violence in entertainment programming.[29] From their point of view, neither the evidence of polls (which showed a substantial majority deploring the amount of televised violence) nor the positions of such widely dispersed national groups as the Parent-Teachers Association should be regarded as information about public opinion. The evidence they felt best reflected public opinion was the Nielson ratings for "Starsky and Hutch" and other cop shows: The polls were misleading, and the PTA was just a special-interest pressure group.

The journalists participating in the discussion didn't seem to share the producers' disdain for these forms of information, but everyone agreed that the networks *had been influenced* to cut back on violence—that corporations had responded in the influence framework. (It would have been even more interesting to have had some network decision-makers there and to have heard from them about whether it was "public opinion" they were responding to—or even whether they had responded, for that matter.)

As a subset of American corporations, the mass media can be compared with other corporations in their linkage activities. If it is true that American corporations are actively trying to keep in touch with public opinion concerning them, can the same be said of similar-size news media corporations? If we were to match media and nonmedia corporations on one or more other characteristics, such as gross sales, one working hypothesis might be that media corporations generally try less actively to learn about public reactions to them as institutions.

Another working prediction might be that media corporations devote proportionately more of their research budgets to readership, viewership, and other kinds of *marketing* studies than do other corporations. In other words, other corporations might be more interested in themselves—as potential issues—than would mass media corporations.

You may recall an apparent exception to this predicted pattern —namely, the polls underwritten by television networks in the aftermath of the Agnew attack on the media. Clearly, in this case, the networks were trying to find out the extent of support for Agnew. And in this case they did seem to have conceptualized attitudes toward the media as a public opinion issue, not a market research question.

However, this also brings up another point made earlier in this chapter about linkage: Responsiveness to perceived public opinion has been defined far too narrowly. I would argue that the decisions to pay for these national surveys represented a real response to the telegrams, mail, and telephone calls that came to the networks after Agnew's Des Moines speech. Obviously, the networks' response was to spend money for surveys that they hoped would show support for them out there in the country. Unfortunately, the results were not entirely reassuring, so the polls were not widely released as part of the network counterattack. But it is hard to believe that all the surveys would have been authorized had Agnew's attack not been followed by mail, telegrams, and phone calls that were perceived as extremely hostile to the networks.

Some anecdotal evidence indicates that, at the decision-making level, the mass media ordinarily don't make much of an effort to have themselves conceptualized as an issue. For example, newspapers nationally have expressed relatively little enthusiasm for the Community Press Council movement. Community Press Councils have been advocated as a way of helping newspapers understand community feelings about them better. Probably it is no accident that the few attempts at press councils so far have been at least partly organized by journalism academicians and funded by outside grant money.

JOURNALISTS AS A LINK BETWEEN PUBLIC OPINION AND DECISION-MAKERS

Much of the information about citizen attitudes gets to decision-makers directly or through their staff or trusted informants. Some, however, comes through media reports and/or outside "experts" (such as advisors, pollsters, or colleagues).

In this section we shall be concerned with how journalists relay information about citizen attitudes to decision-makers. We saw in Chapter 3 that the press acts as one of several "institutionalized aggregation and transmittal agencies."[30] That's a rather formal way of saying that public affairs journalists collect, report, and interpret information about citizen attitudes as a traditional part of their ongoing activities.

For example, they report and interpret election results by grouping some of them together and excluding others. They report on polls and carry Harris or Gallup Poll releases. They provide footage of crowd reactions. When Ronald Reagan speaks in town, they show and tell us how big the crowd was and how much each person paid to have dinner. They routinely do man-on-the-street reaction stories to breaking events. They print letters to the editor. They carry stories from one politician, reporting on the kind of letters he or she is receiving, to a mass audience that includes other politicians. They carry other kinds of reaction stories, reporting, for example, on the reactions of environmentalist leaders to the Carter administration's enforcement of the new strip mining bill. And on and on.

Such activities are deeply embedded in craft practices. Journalists have a vested interest in public opinion as symbol. The symbol gives journalists leverage, presumably making public officials and others more willing to answer questions. If there were no such thing as public opinion, then the "people's right to know" wouldn't be one of those unanswerable challenges to officialdom. Besides this quite pragmatic advantage as symbol, we can speculate that public opinion also provides valuable psychological satisfactions to journalists, giving their work social value and providing a vicarious sense of potential.

Making Information "Exist"

The decision to report or not to report a given bit of information about citizen attitudes has clear implications for changing the kind of information that reaches decision-makers. We can assume that the odds are very high that information about citizen attitudes will get to decision-makers when it appears in print or on the air, especially when there is a possibility the decision-maker will later be asked for reactions to that information.

Defining the Information

Further, the way information about citizen attitudes is defined and organized can more subtly alter the kinds of information decision-makers think they have. Six elections were held in the late winter and spring of 1974 to fill traditionally Republican House seats that had been left vacant by death or resignation. The first of these, in western Pennsylvania, was won by Democrat John Murtha in early February. Murtha had predicted a win by 6,000 votes but won by only 220.

Journalists often would have treated such ill-advised predictions by converting Murtha's win into a disappointing showing. Instead, *Newsweek* treated the election result as a "riddle" with no particular meaning as a test of voters' Watergate sentiment, as did Associated Press.[31] Little attention was paid to Murtha's prediction and the narrowness of the win, except in reference to the lack of clarity the narrow win gave the result.

Two weeks later, however, when Democrat Richard Vander-Veen took Gerald Ford's old House seat, the Pennsylvania result began to be included in stories as part of a Watergate rebellion by voters. The *St. Louis Post-Dispatch,* for example, concluded editorially that the Michigan result had clarified the previous election result by showing that there was no longer room for argument about a voter revolt on Watergate.[32] ABC's Howard K. Smith concluded that his analysis of the Michigan results showed that "Watergate is a gut voting issue" that had "rubbed off" on all Republican candidates for the House.[33] Later, the Pennsylvania result was simply included on the list of other "Watergate" elections, without qualification. Perhaps *Newsweek*'s change was especially noteworthy in this regard, because of its earlier caution.[34]

About midway through this series of elections, there were already plenty of signs that Republican decision-makers felt they knew what the voters were saying. Oregon Republican Senator Bob Packwood said in late March that more than half the Republican representatives who were facing November election fights wanted Nixon to resign: "Most people would now regard close association with the administration as the kiss of death."[35] Earlier, Barry Goldwater had estimated that Watergate would be costing Republicans 10 percent at the polls. Thus began a kind of circular linkage process with journalists, pollsters, election winners, and other politicians reciprocally defining and reinforcing the meanings and portents of these elections.

The point of this example is that when electoral survival becomes intertwined with salient matters such as Watergate, there may emerge a peculiar kind of circular linkage process in which journalists play a crucial role. Sens. Packwood and Goldwater were not immediately threatened by the congressional races, but they were using the press to send other dicision-makers (including Nixon) a message. In the process, they reinforced a single set of situation definitions that then fed back into the kinds of postelection questions that were asked by pollsters in the Michigan and Ohio congressional elections. And, starting with VanderVeen in Michigan, every winning Democratic candidate—and some losing Republicans—declared that Watergate made the decisive difference. (This despite the fact that postelection polls in Ohio and Michigan suggested that inflation and energy shortages ranked higher than Watergate on a list of voter concerns.[36])

So what journalists write is only part of the story. The questions they ask news sources often are based on assumptions about public opinion.

The Press Itself As Indicator

A third way in which the press provides information to decision-makers about public reactions involves feedback that journalists themselves provide. For instance, one sure sign of whether a candidate is regarded as up-and-coming during the presidential primary season is whether or not the candidate attracts enough reporters to require a full-fledged press bus. According to Jules Witcover, a full bus seems to boost candidate/staff morale and to impress other political figures.[37]

In the preceding chapter, we saw that one facet of power is access to the press. People who have acquired the reputation for public support also find they have greater access to the news.

Additional Research Suggestions

At least two coorientation studies have produced some results that seem to lead to the startling hypothesis that distorted news portrayals of decision-makers' policy positions result in *greater* "accuracy" of public opinion perceptions by these decision-makers.[38] (Remember, however, that accuracy is validated by poll data.) This finding was at best a peripheral one in these two coorientation studies and definitely needs to be tested in a study that focuses more closely on media portrayals of decision-makers' policy preferences. But this bizarre finding, if reliable, might be consistent with a scattered literature in political science that in effect suggests that accurate perceptions *by the public* of decision-makers' policy positions heavily distorts the kind of letters sent to each decision-maker: Decision-makers who are known to prefer a policy position tend to hear only from people who agree with them.[39] So media distortions of their policy positions presumably would diversify the "public opinion" input to these decision-makers. This should be tested.

Earlier, in Chapter 3, we saw that newspapers varied considerably in their estimates of crowd size. In the study by Mann, it turned out that the newspapers' position on the Vietnam war predicted the newspapers' estimated size of antiwar protest demonstrations.[40] If this finding is reliable, would we expect the biasing of information about citizen attitudes to be (1) restricted to certain "subjective" kinds of information (such as crowd estimates) and (2) restricted to certain salient (to the newspaper) policy areas? And under what conditions would we expect decision-makers to be influenced by the distorted information?

Do the needs of television news inevitably call for inflation of the estimated numbers of people participating in crowds (for example, the Langs' analysis of MacArthur Day in Chicago[41]) and the perceived extent of participation in deviant social movements?[42]

Is it harder for decision-makers to avoid being aware of information about citizen attitudes when the information is reported in the news?

Is it harder for decision-makers to avoid having at least to give the appearance of responsiveness if they are asked about public opinion on an issue by reporters at press conferences? When decision-makers feel public opinion is not on their side, what kinds of verbal circumlocutions would analysis of press conference transcripts reveal? Could we use such circumlocutions later as an index of decision-maker perceptions of public opinion?

Who tends to bring up the matter of public opinion first in such press conferences? A possible pattern would be this: Decision-makers bring public opinion up first when they think "it" is on their side; reporters bring "it" up first when they think public opinion is against the decision-maker or when there is doubt about "it." (I put "it" in quotes because some decision-makers may not think of public opinion as a single, unitary concept. It may very well be, for example, that they think of various contending publics, each with its own central tendency.[43])

Journalists also may provide cues to decision-makers about whether they (journalists) think public opinion should be followed. If we could index such cues (and I think we can—see next paragraph below) in a press conference situation, would we then expect to find the type and extent of circumlocutions varying with such cues?

Journalists themselves probably vary in the respect they accord public opinion. A good working hypothesis would be that, in writing about public opinion, U.S. journalists would fall into at least four conceptually distinguishable schools of thought about public opinion, ordered from most to least elitist.

1. *Elitists*—public opinion is foolish, short-sighted, and ignorant of the consequences of preferred policies. Civil liberties and free speech are maintained despite, and not because of, public opinion. Elites preserve civil liberties and maintain relatively impartial administration of law because they believe in them and because operating this way helps talented newcomers to be recruited and identified early.

2. *Semielitists*—public opinion is foolish, short-sighted, and ignorant of the consequences of policies. Civil liberties and free speech are maintained partly despite public opinion, but a number of institutional and political pressures partly force maintenance of civil liberties, the impartial administration of law, and some

occasional responsiveness to public opinion. These pressures include periodic elections and the presence of competing elites, including journalists.

3. *The "folk-magic" school*—the people generally are foolish and ignorant, but when it really counts they make the right decision—at least in the election framework at crucial times. They may make these electoral choices for all the wrong reasons, but they make them. Therefore, one must always maintain the free flow of information (and other civil liberties) because one can never be sure when or why people make up their minds to vote a certain way.

4. *The "simple-democratic" school*—the people are informed, interested, and altruistic. While they may not always participate, they follow public affairs closely and one must always maintain the free flow of information to them and otherwise maintain the people's access to government.

These four schools of thought are ideal types, of course, but a good working hypothesis would be that editorial writers and Washington political columnists would be more likely than other political journalists to fall into the relatively elitist schools of thought.

We turn now to Chapter 9, which concentrates on the polls as a linkage device.

9
Linkage II:
The Polls as
Public Opinion

More than thirty years have passed since Herbert Blumer's famous attack on the polls as information about what we think of as public opinion.[1] Blumer's attack was not without influence, but it seems clear that the field was not convinced. This chapter will first consider Blumer's position because it appears that he created unnecessary difficulties for himself in the course of making his argument. Then I will develop my own position on the polls as a set of information about citizen attitudes.

BLUMER'S ARGUMENT

Blumer argued that polls measured what he might term "mass attitudes" instead of public opinion, and were better suited to the study of consumer behavior. He criticized polls for sampling the citizenery as a whole, thereby including both the people whose attitudes counted and those whose attitudes did not. The argument that polls had proven themselves by successfully predicting elections he dismissed by stating that elections were a kind of mass behavior —people cast equally important ballots, much as people engaged in consumer behaviors. Elections did not constitute a measure of public opinion. In effect, Blumer regarded public opinion as a phenomenon taking place only in what I call the influence framework.

Flaws in Blumer's Argument

Encountering Blumer's argument in the literature when I was a graduate student partly inspired the eventual writing of this book. His argument marked a radical departure from the kind of simple reductionism that prevailed when I read it. And there are reasons for skepticism concerning the rebuttals then made to Blumer's argument by Theodore Newcomb and Julian Woodward.[2]

Nevertheless, Blumer's argument is seriously flawed and cannot be accepted—even on its own terms.

1. For one thing, Blumer suggested that the most appropriate way to study public opinion would be to start with the decision-maker and work backwards:

> ... We ought to begin with those who have to act on public opinion and move backwards along the lines of the various expressions of public opinion that come to their [decision-makers'] attention. ...[3]

But if decision-makers treat polls as if they index public opinion, Blumer would appear to have us ignore his own advice to deal with the expressions that public opinion decision-makers are attending to. To the extent that decision-makers attend to polls as "expressions of public opinion," Blumer wouldn't have us follow his own recommended procedure. And the evidence is that some decision-makers *do* treat poll data as expressions of public opinion (see Chapter 8).

For essentially the same reason, if decision-makers treat previous election results as a form of information about citizen attitudes—and, manifestly, they do—Blumer again would have us ignore his own advice.

2. An even more fundamental problem is created by Blumer when he in effect excludes elections because they don't reflect power discrepancies. It appears to me the only way he can argue that power is equalized in elections is to assume that nothing hap-

pening before election day makes a difference in terms of how those equal votes are cast. When stated this way, the flaw is evident. What has happened is that, while he imposes no time constraint on public opinion processes (as he thinks of them), he has imposed a one-day time frame on elections. Since everybody's ballot counts more or less the same *on election day,* elections supposedly equalize power. As soon as this implicit time frame is removed, it quickly becomes apparent that power discrepancies affect balloting in many ways: selection of candidates, whether or not a proposition gets on the ballot, how the ballot measure is worded and entitled, funds for campaigns, and on and on.

(The astute reader may by now have noticed what appears to be a contradiction in my own position. Earlier, in Chapter 2, the influence framework was defined as including, among other things, all information about citizen attitudes during election campaigns; only the election result and its immediate aftermath were part of the election framework. How can I argue that Blumer wrongly imposed a time constraint on elections while I seem to be imposing the same constraint? The answer requires a distinction between [1] information about citizen attitudes and [2] factors affecting the outcome of an election. My distinction between the two frameworks has to do with the former, not the latter. But Blumer's distinction has to do with the latter, not the former.)

3. Probably Blumer felt it necessary to exclude elections partly because he felt the polls had solved the problem of predicting them. So by excluding elections, the polls' successes could be ignored. The problem is that polls are relatively successful at predicting elections only under certain favorable conditions. When historic conditions remain the same, the best polls seem to do well in predicting election outcomes. But when new factors enter the picture, the *ad hoc* adjustments pollsters have made will not work because they were based on previous experience.

It isn't necessary to go back to Dewey-Truman in 1948 to find examples of the historic blind spot in polling. In 1970, the British held the first national parliamentary election they had ever held during the summer. A Labor victory was predicted by all the major polls, based on usual estimates of turnout. The Conservatives won in what was considered a stunning upset. Apparently it didn't occur to the pollsters to worry about the effects of holding an election during workers' summer vacations.[4] They simply applied the turnout estimates that had always worked before.

Nor did the polls do at all well in the 1974 Canadian election, predicting a Trudeau plurality when his party's candidates won a clear majority of seats. To my knowledge the Canadian poll fiasco hasn't been subjected to the same careful analysis as the election in Britain, but it is noteworthy that the Trudeau majority occurred in only the third summer Canadian national election in this century. Turnout was unusually low.[5]

Turnout also was extremely low in the November 1978 elections and several polling organizations produced embarrassingly large errors in a few of these races. For example, Iowa's Senator Dick Clark was given a 30 percent lead by Peter D. Hart in early October, a lead of more than 10 percent in late October by the Iowa Poll—yet he lost by 4 percent in an election where there was an unusually low turnout *and* a large amount of undervoting. The undervoting occurred when more than twenty thousand people voted for other offices in that election but did not cast a ballot on the Senate race.[6]

Burns Roper put the problem fairly well during a discussion of election predictions on Public Television's MacNeil-Lehrer Report just before the 1976 presidential election:

> Polling uses scientific methods, and it also uses art, and the art is to decide which scientific method to use, and what the results mean when you get them back. I think the difference, for example, between our four-point lead for Carter and Gallup's one-point lead for Ford—it may be sampling error; certainly it is within the range of sampling error—I doubt if that's the reason. *I think it's difference in judgments as to how to determine who the likely voters are....*[7] (Emphasis added.)

Polls have never been very successful in predicting whether a specific person will vote. But they have been somewhat successful in predicting turnout by *groups* of voters, as long as historic conditions continued as before. As many readers of this chapter undoubtedly know, the poll responses obtained from groups of potential voters are usually weighted by some actuarial estimate of probable turnout—an estimate based on what seemed to work in the past.

Turnout, of course, is only one factor that may change when past history doesn't repeat itself. Apportionment of the "undecided" vote is another example of past experience guiding present practices. The American Gallup organization is still using some techniques that were introduced in 1950—one wonders whether the same methods were being used by Gallup in Britain's 1970 election.

In brief, then, Blumer correctly emphasized the importance of what I'm calling the influence framework, but his attack on elections and their surrogate, the polls, created as many problems as it solved.

POLLS AS PUBLIC OPINION: ASSETS AND LIMITATIONS

Polls are no better—and probably no worse—than the many other kinds of information about citizen attitudes that reach decision-makers. All have distinct handicaps. But polls do differ from the other kinds, so their assets and limits tend not to be like those of the others. However, because polls seem to be dominant in both popular and social scientific conceptions of public opinion, it appears necessary to spend somewhat more time on their limitations than on their obvious assets as conveyors of information.

With the exception of polls that must be mailed back, polls as a form of information about attitudes require less of the citizen than any other form of information, including elections. This is because all other forms ultimately involve some act of participation. The contrast is so clear that Bogart has even coined the term "Silent Politics" to refer to poll information.[8] Since other kinds of information involve participation, it should not be surprising to find that often both the demographic characteristics and the policy preferences of participants may differ from those who are polled.[9]

It should be made clear, before we begin, that our consideration of both the limitations and the assets of polls *assumes "good"* polling *techniques:* adequate sample size, adequate completion rate, adequate questions, and so on. In other words, this is *not* going to be a recital of what makes a "good" or a "bad" poll. Therefore, the following limitations of polls most likely cannot be overcome by improvements in polling methodology.

Limitations of Polls

▶ Political polling legitimized itself by its successes in predicting election results. Given "normal" historical conditions, the reason a well conducted poll can predict elections is that an election boils down complicated issues into choices on which people vote, so it is rather easy to write poll questions that closely resemble ballot choices.

The fact that polls have been validated fairly often with elections hardly implies validity when an election is not available to provide both the criterion language for the poll question and a relatively clear-cut validity test.

In periods between elections, people often disagree on what the issue is, let alone what options should be considered regarding it. Issues are much more complicated and open-ended—and there is less certainty as to question wording—than are ballot measures. Under such conditions, polls designed to measure public opinion have been notoriously vulnerable to discrepancies in question wording.

Given the absence of criterion language for poll questions and the absence of an electoral validity test, there remains only the slim hope that some other poll might have worded a "similar" question about the "same" issue as a kind of quasi-validity test.

An example of such a test was provided by the way the Gallup organization asked about the issue of impeaching President Nixon. From June 1973 to February 1974, the question was worded as follows: "Do you think President Nixon should be impeached and compelled to leave the Presidency, or not?" The number saying yes to this question gradually increased but never exceeded 38 percent. However, critics began to note that the question should have separated the issue of a House impeachment from the question of whether Nixon should have been found guilty and "compelled to leave" by the Senate. No doubt acutely embarrassing for Gallup was the fact that other major polls showed much higher percentages for House impeachment when compared with Gallup's results. This discrepancy was important, because Rep. Peter Rodino's Judiciary Committee was still many months away from making its impeachment recommendations and, of course, a possible Senate trail would have been even further in the future.

Finally, Gallup did separate the two issues in the April 1974 poll. Immediately the "yes" responses went up over 50 percent to a question about House indictment of Nixon. To the best of my knowledge, the Gallup organization never explicitly conceded that its earlier wording had underestimated pro-impeachment feelings.

If other polls helped "correct" Gallup's in this instance, why is a check against other polls such a slim hope? In the first place, only *very* rarely will such a long-term, extremely salient issue arise and be asked about uniformly by several reputable polling organizations. In the second place, how often does one polling organization concede that it obviously worded its question badly and proclaim to the world that another poll's question was better? And who says that the polls will always come up with differing questions about the "same" issue? Pollsters do follow each other, after all, and we might more often come up with a reliability check of pollsters' question-writing habits instead of a quasi-validity check of the effects of question wording. Finally, given the relatively small number of polling agencies with assured access to news coverage, there is no guarantee that when different percentages result from different polls' questions, both polls have an equal chance of reaching decision-makers. Once again, the Gallups, Ropers, Harrises have much greater access to coverage than would many other polls.

(Before we move on to the next limitation of polls, it might be worth restating and elaborating here a point originally made in Chapter 2. Even preelection polls occur in the influence framework. So the distinction between preelection polls and polls that lack the chance of an electoral validity check is not based on the distinction between influence and election frameworks. The only polls that fall into the election framework are, ironically, *post*-election polls. We'll consider them later in this chapter.)

▶ Closely related to the preceding problem of the absence of criterion language is the problem of attitude object change. We've seen in Chapter 3 and elsewhere that the percentages obtained can be changed radically when an apparently minor change is made in the way a question is worded.

Because polls obviously include people who fall into Sequence 2 and 3 types, there doesn't seem to be any way of avoiding this problem in well-conducted polls. Even a question worded by the Patron Saint of Polling could have been worded another way. And, even if the miracle were performed and the question worded The Right Way, by the time an issue reaches a political decision in the influence framework, that issue may well have undergone considerable mutation.

This brings up another limitation of polls (and elections, too.)

▶ Generally speaking, influence framework poll questions hardly ever correspond to the choices decision-makers eventually have to make. And even a once-a-month Gallup Poll doesn't occur often enough for both the question and the percentages to correspond to the judgment situation. Too many decisions have to be made too fast between polls (and elections). Therefore, if the decision-maker tries to take poll results into account he or she will generally have to read things into the results that may or may not have been there. This problem leads directly to the next limitation.

▶ Polls are notoriously bad indicators of how people might react to things that haven't occurred yet. For instance, a large number of polls during the Vietnam war repeatedly showed a majority opposing such things as mining Haiphong Harbor—until after it was done, when suddenly a majority supported it. Phillip Converse and Howard Schuman concluded after looking at a number of such polls: "Support of the president seems to rise after every new initiative, whether it is in the direction of escalation or a reduction of commitment."[10] Given this problem, what is "real" public opinion? The percentage before the action was taken or the percentage afterward?

Chapter 4 provided data that get us to this same point about polls, but by a somewhat different route. Candidate preference questions can be quite misleading when, early in the primary season, the contenders are not equally well known.

▶ In an interesting review of "mass society" literature, Siune and Kline point out that

> ... The organizers of opinion polls are rarely if ever representative of the whole population, nor are the concerns that they organize questions around necessarily everyone's concerns. Where the poll questions and issues become centralized and allied with elite strata we do not really have feedback [from mass to elite decision-makers].[11]

There is little doubt that a relatively small circle of polling organizations provides most of the nationally recognized experts who are called on to do such things as testify before Congress on American public opinion.

But perhaps pollsters can try to avoid being allied with elite strata, even if they themselves have centralized the national circle of poll resources. So let's suppose that every effort is made *not* to have an elite bias in issue selection: How or where would the issues be selected? One source of issues probably would be the agenda implicit in the news, but even that ultimately reduces itself to another possible elite bias in issue selection.

So we may be left with relatively few other ways of selecting issues. And these other ways come very close to selecting issues by means of perceptions imposed on all the forms of information about citizen attitudes *except* polls. In other words, an honest effort to select issues might at times result in reliance on all the kinds of *non*-poll data about citizen concerns that extreme advocates of poll superiority would regard as unacceptable. Such extremists would then be left, ultimately, with the choice between (1) having a weak link in their chain of information about the citizenry and (2) becoming elitists and deciding for themselves what it was best to ask citizens about.

Polls have as other limitations information about citizen attitudes. They are perhaps more obvious than some mentioned already, so little time will be spent on them.

▶ It is quite possible to answer a fixed-response question without ever having thought about the issue before. Generally, no distinction is made between thoughtful and "top-of-the-head" respondents when percentages are aggregated.

▶ Poll respondents are also notorious for a tendency toward response unreliability.

▶ Words to interviewers, spoken while seated on the living room couch, are not the same thing as political deeds. The difference in political weight between the two was put somewhat melodramatically by Leo Bogart:

> A 1964 NORC survey . . . found that 7 percent of U.S. adults agreed that Hitler was right to try to kill all the Jews. We attribute no particular importance to this 7 percent, which projects to some 8 million individuals, because the sentiments they express to an interviewer are made individually without awareness of their collective strength. By contrast, we may feel enormous concern about the similarly small percentage of people who now vote for the neo-Nazi party in Germany. . . .[12]

Assets of Polls

Polls are uniquely suited to do some things, at least one of which is only now becoming fashionable: the postelection poll.

Postelection polls can do a great deal to clarify the meaning of election outcomes. When conducted immediately after an election —preferably using techniques that produce a high completion rate and focus on citizens leaving the voting booth—much of the residual ambiguity of election results can be resolved. When done in this way, such polls should be regarded as part of the information available in the election framework. It is not altogether surprising to find that postelection surveys have been a relatively recent phenomenon, at least in terms of media visibility. Commercial polling organizations learned that using polls to predict elections appealed to journalists much more than would polls done after elections. Even now, there seems to be high visibility given to postelection polls primarily when the news agencies themselves commission or otherwise participate in them. One could speculate and suggest that one of the factors which may have influenced the networks and prestige newspapers to commission such polls was the publication in 1970 of Scammon and Wattenberg's influential *The Real Majority,*[13] a book which leaned heavily on some postelection polls to clarify and correct certain misinterpretations of various elections.

We turn now to other things polls can do.

As a set of information about citizen attitudes, polls may increase the diversity and variety of information available to decision-makers in the influence framework.

Polls can also provide politically important information about relative size and availability of pools of potential participants.

Apart from election results, information produced by descriptive polls is perhaps the most easily processed and absorbed by decision-makers.

RESEARCH PROSPECTS

● We saw in the last chapter that legislators were using polls more than before but still didn't seem to be depending on them very much. How much of this low reliance results from the methods legislators use in their own polls? If poll data were available, timely, and produced by more reputable methods, would legislators still rank polls lower than some other, more personal forms of information? One way to approach this possibility by standard questionnaire techniques would be to ask a portion of the sample of legislators in the usual way about polls versus other kinds of information and to ask the remaining subsamples in a way that allowed them to distinguish between their own constituency polls, as they did them, and more reputable polling methods. One would have to be careful about stacking the deck, however, and it might be necessary to have one questionnaire version pitting the best polling information against the best of the other kinds of information.

● Of course, the problem as stated above assumes that legislators *know* they don't use the best polling techniques. Are legislators and other decision-makers all that sophisticated about what makes a good poll? How much do they know about polling? Does their knowledge level predict their preferences for types of information?

● Given the increasing frequency and visibility of postelection polls, would we expect elected decision-makers to be more influenced by them than by other polls, done later during their terms of office? Certainly we could expect that simple curiosity would prompt recently elected decision-makers to give the results of post-election polls close scrutiny. But would their later decisions be influenced by these polls? If so, under what conditions? How would the existence of a postelection poll interact with Kingdon's proposed "congratulation-rationalization effect"?[14]

● Lucy has concluded that, from 1936 to 1972, a very strong relationship occurred between candidates' standings in the polls and their chances of nomination at party conventions.

> Yet little is known about the extent to which delegates are aware of poll results, or about conflicting poll information—if any—much less how they are influenced by information they [do] perceive.[15]

● Considerable anecdotal evidence indicates that polls affect candidate and staff morale, campaign money, and the amount of news media coverage.[16]

It would seem that an indirect consequence of this effect would be to make the leader in early polls hard to beat. Hadley has even argued that the primaries have in effect been replaced by the polls as a selection mechanism.[17] However, in the 1972 and 1976 Democratic races, the early-season leader did *not* get the nomination.

One way of resolving the apparent contradiction would be to say that candidates who are behind in early polls will have no viable alternative except to invest almost all their available resources in their earliest primaries, in the hope that a win will increase their name familiarity (hence, their standing in the polls) and access to the media. Many writers have observed that this was Jimmy Carter's strategy in 1976.[18]

A testable hypothesis would be that the proportion of available funds spent on the nonincumbent candidate's first presidential primary will increase as the candidate's standing in the polls decreases. Assuming data were available, we might also expect that this inverse relationship has become stronger in successive presidential years.

Further questions suggest themselves.

● When and why did political journalists shift to polls as the best kind of information about citizen attitudes? Did the shift occur before or after the 1948 Truman-Dewey polls' fiasco? One way to approach these questions would be through content analysis of newspapers back to about 1932—that is, before the 1936 *Literary Digest* polling disaster.

● Finally, do reporters know as much as the politicians they are covering about what makes a good or a bad poll? What predicts sophistication about polls (and the lack of it) among journalists?

10
Conclusions

The best we can say for ourselves right now is that we are still so busy identifying and naming the things in which we should be interested that we haven't gotten much beyond that stage.

REDUCTIONISM

None of simple reductionism's three correspondence rules stands up to scrutiny. Chapter 5 made it clear that attitude change is neither necessary nor sufficient for public opinion change. As for the third correspondence rule, of all the many forms of information about citizen attitudes, only the polls give even the appearance of plausibility to it. And even in this case the most superficial examination shows that some people's attitudes count more than do others'. For one thing, even in polls some attitudes are weighted more than others—remember the discussion of correcting pre-election percentages by the actuarial likelihood that a given group of respondents will turn out to vote? It is *not* true that everybody is equal—not even in preelection polls, and certainly not in the election framework.

Simple reductionism led social science prematurely to give up on mass communication as a cause of changes in public opinion. While once again we are identifying and naming mass communication factors as important, the field has tended to do so for the wrong reasons and in ways that may again prove prematurely discouraging. As waves of second thoughts wash over mass communication scholars, most of the revisions they offer merely add to a list of individual-level effects, rather than raising questions about the correspondence rules that govern the uses made of that list. While it is true that the present book also adds some hypothesized individual-level attitude effects, the approach taken here would still allow me to talk about changes in public opinion even if nothing but issue attitude reinforcement were taking place.

In the last analysis, the essential weakness of our field is that each new school of thought about the media ultimately depends on showing that an individual-level mental change of some sort takes place. So if we can't demonstrate media agenda-setting—or whatever—we are out of business. The reason for this state of affairs is that the fundamental assumptions of simple reductionism have not been examined and discarded.

It is simple reductionism, not reductionism, that is at issue. In the approach suggested here, linkage research may be more central than it appears to have been to mainstream political science. Why? Because many of the correspondence rules we will need must come from future linkage research. For example, a kind of hidden correspondence rule has been embedded in my statements about changes in participation and power producing changes in public opinion. That hidden "rule" is that decision-makers make a good-faith effort to discern what public opinion is, *based on the information that comes to them*. If they made no such effort, changes in the information arriving might make no difference in conclusions reached about public opinion. As we've seen, linkage researchers have barely begun to look at the information-processing habits of decision-makers. We need to know far more than we do now about whether, and under what conditions, such a hidden correspondence rule works.

In addition to research at the decision-maker end, one or more new correspondence rules probably will have to come from the media end. For instance, if future research does support the ideas presented in Chapter 5 about Sequences 1, 2, and 3, we will have started constructing some of the new correspondence rules about how mass communication changes information concerning citizen attitudes.

Even at this primitive, early stage it seems clear that an adequate reductionism will be much more complex—and will require specifying a greater number of interrelations among more variables—than was the case with the reductionism we have been living with for the past thirty to forty years.

So this book at least picks out for us the variables—and the areas of study—that seem most promising. Participation and power clearly are among these variables.

PARTICIPATION AND POWER

There are grounds for believing that the mass media may produce changes in participation and in power. Changing either, of course, would result in changes in the information going to decision-makers.

In reviewing the existing literature and offering some original new evidence, I have tried to show that the media role in affecting participation probably has been greatly underestimated because of the way political science has studied participation.

As for power, the nondecision approach seems unusually well suited to media applications, so well suited that nondecision researchers would be well advised to treat mass media situations as a golden opportunity to show that they can, indeed, generate a larger number of testable propositions.

THE INFLUENCE FRAMEWORK

This book has pointed out that, in addition to participation and power, the influence framework is of crucial importance to understanding a number of things about public opinion, including:

—why existing studies of participation have been very misleading concerning the impact of mass media,

—why even the best polls have major weaknesses when they lack elections to provide a validity check and criterion wording for their questions,

—why political mobilizing messages in the news media mostly concern either elections or meetings,

—how Sequence 2 and 3 people differ from Sequence 1 people,

—how the scope of an issue can be reduced by putting it in the influence framework, and

—where the linkage between public opinion and public policy occurs most often.

The News Media
As Collectors of
Attitude Information

Obviously, the news media can and do change information about citizen attitudes merely through their decisions to cover (or not to cover) this information.

The situation definitions imposed on this information often indirectly affect the power of political actors, making it harder or easier for them to concentrate their resources.

And the decision to collect and interpret a set of information probably makes it harder for a decision-maker to avoid being made aware of that information. We might also predict that reports of citizen attitudes may affect the tactics being used by lobbies in the influence framework.[1]

Attitude Formation and Change

The Langs' argument about attitude change taking place before the fall election campaigns[2] did receive some support in a study reported here.

So even attitude change and attitude formation may be found under some conditions. One of the most interesting findings from the New Hampshire/Massachusetts results, however, was the short-term discrepancy between news media definitions of who was gaining the most in these primaries and the gains made by Udall among Oregonians. Over the long run, however, the news media definitions may have become self-fulfilling prophecies.

Attitude Object Change

Attitude object change is another variable that has been singled out as potentially very important.

Two conceptual issues concerning object change—whether objects or attributes are changed and whether there is any need to worry about object change, since supposedly it always occurs when attitude change occurs—cannot be solved without the development of attitude measuring devices that allow the separation of object change from affect change.

Object change can account for increases and decreases in participation and is useful in analyzing the extraordinary efforts political actors sometimes strain to make so that an issue is defined a certain way. Theoretically, at least, nonelites are much more vulnerable to object change than are elites.

MOBILIZING INFORMATION

A combination of journalistic craft practices leads systematically —but probably not deliberately—to the exclusion of mobilizing information in the influence framework. The fact that MI is withheld precisely when citizens most need it makes this area potentially a fruitful one for nondecision research.

The lack of MI in the mass media probably helps make the influence framework what it is. For instance, low participation allows decision-makers to devote very limited resources to processing information about citizen attitudes. And large numbers of citizens keep getting implicit messages in the media about their chances of coping whenever they attend to public affairs content.

If and when MI is provided, dramatic short-term increases in participation occur when issue attitudes are intense. The fact that issue attitudes are intense often means that the matter is controversial—and that's precisely when MI is rare. Since we suspect strongly that MI packs a wallop under such conditions, the failure of journalists to provide MI in these cases also means that their nondecision probably changed participation.

The absence of MI in news of politics also probably helps maintain a large population of Sequence 3 people. Emphasizing issue content in public affairs news may have the ironic long-term effect of dampening the level of public affairs knowledge in the population—a result that surely would be an unintended one among journalists. Newspapers have become increasingly worried about circulation and readership losses. There is some evidence that potential readers are now looking at newspapers from an increasingly self-interested point of view. If the newspaper doesn't provide an answer to "What's in it for me?" those readers may be lost. Mobilizing information may be one of the services readers would appreciate. Readers' narcissism was a constant theme at the 1978 proceedings of the American Association of Newspaper Editors. According to a research manager for the *Chicago Tribune:*

> ... The biggest value that emerged [from a study of actual and potential subscribers in the Chicago area was] the fact that people are placing the chief emphasis on self, the home and the family and how these worldwide or global incidents would affect their lives. ...[3]

A RESEARCH AGENDA

One of the major reasons for the failure of efforts to persuade the field against simple reductionism was the inability of the resistance to provide as tempting a set of research prospects as was seemingly offered by simple reductionism. But there is no logical necessity for empirical research on public opinion to be available only under simple reductionism.

I hope this book shows that empirical research *can* be done without operating on simple reductionist correspondence rules. After we got past the vocabulary and definitions, much of this book was composed of testable problem statements and hypotheses. After reading this manuscript, one person told me that it contained enough research ideas for four or five lifetimes. That may be a little too kind, but I will count this book a success if it does stimulate the kind of research outlined in these pages.

Some of these research suggestions appear to be directed at basic areas that, on the surface at least, have little or nothing to do with mass communication. Other suggestions appear to be mixed—of interest to researchers in either mainstream political sociology or mass communications. And, finally, some are directed at my colleagues in mass comunication. A rough measure of the weakness of our basic knowledge in a given area would be to compare the ratios of suggestions, per chapter, for (1) basic mainstream versus (2) mixed versus (3) mass communication research. Obviously, the higher the ratio of basic to other suggestions per chapter, the weaker our knowledge of that area appears to be. But the reverse is *not* true. That is, a lower ratio of media research suggestions implies nothing about the strength of our media-related knowledge in that area.

Implicit in this book, then, is an appeal to mainstream scholars in the other social sciences to follow up some of the ideas suggested here. Though this book is concerned with the mass media, it is clear that we cannot understand the role of the media by ourselves. Basic research is needed by persons who are not, themselves, interested in the mass media.

Let's get on with it.

Notes

PREFACE

1. Perhaps the best example is an article by Otto N. Larsen, "Social Effects of Mass Communication," in *Handbook of Modern Sociology*, ed. Robert E. L. Faris (Chicago: Rand McNally, 1964), pp. 348–381. Larsen had effectively dismantled some simple reductionist assumptions more than a decade before this book was written. I did not encounter Larsen's argument until after Chapters 1 and 5 were written, and both of them virtually echo some of the points made earlier.

CHAPTER 1

1. Milton Rokeach, *Beliefs, Attitudes, and Values* (San Francisco: Jossey-Bass, 1968), pp. 156–59.
2. Robert A. Dahl, "The Behavioral Approach in Political Science: Epitaph for a Monument to a Successful Protest," *American Political Science Review* 55 (December 1961): 763–72.
3. Joseph T. Klapper, *The Effects of Mass Communication* (New York: Free Press, 1960), p. 8.
4. A good illustration of both the nature of the issue and an apparent reluctance to bring it up may be found in *Behavior Today*, 23 April 1973, pp. 1–3, including a note and a reprint of parts of a National Institute of Mental Health staff report. *Behavior Today* said the report "may never see the light of day," so reprinted excerpts of it. The report criticized NIMH funding of attempts to account for social problems by means of individual-level variables.

5. Angus Campbell, Philip E. Converse, Warren E. Miller, and Donald E. Stokes, *Elections and the Political Order* (New York: Wiley, 1966).

6. Quoted in Angus Campbell, "Voters and Elections: Past and Present," in *Political Opinion and Electoral Behavior*, ed. Edward C. Dreyer and Walter A. Rosenbaum (Belmont, Calif.: Wadsworth, 1966), p. 364.

7. Ernest Nagel, *The Structure of Science: Problems in the Logic of Scientific Explanation* (New York: Harcourt, Brace & World, 1961), p. 542.

8. Notably by Herbert Blumer, whose 1947 argument will be considered at length in Chapter 9.

9. Leo Bogart, *Silent Politics: Polls and the Awareness of Public Opinion* (New York: Wiley-Interscience, 1972), p. 152.

10. Herbert Blumer, "Public Opinion and Public Opinion Polling," *American Sociological Review* 13 (October 1948): 542–49. The article was prepared from his 1947 presentation to a group of public opinion scholars.

11. Floyd H. Allport, "Toward a Science of Public Opinion," *Public Opinion Quarterly* 1 (Spring 1937): 7–23.

12. Warren E. Miller and Donald E. Stokes, "Constituency Influence in Congress," *American Political Science Review* 57 (March 1963): 45–56; Charles F. Cnudde and Donald J. McCrone, "The Linkage Between Constituency Attitudes and Congressional Voting Behavior: A Causal Model," *American Political Science Review* 60 (March 1966): 66–72.

13. Dan Nimmo, *The Political Persuaders: The Techniques of Modern Election Campaigns* (Englewood Cliffs, N. J.: Prestice-Hall, 1970), pp. 180–81.

14. Jay G. Blumler and Jack M. McLeod, "Communication and Voter Turnout in Britain" (paper presented at the annual meeting of the Association for Education in Journalism, Ft. Collins, Colo., August 1973).

15. Maxwell E. McCombs and Donald L. Shaw, "The Agenda-Setting Function of Mass Media," *Public Opinion Quarterly* 36 (Summer 1972): 176–87.

16. Jack M. McLeod, Lee B. Becker, and James E. Byrnes, "Another Look at the Agenda Setting Function of the Press" (paper presented at the annual meeting of the Association for Education in Journalism, Ft. Collins, Colo., August 1973).

17. Walter Lippmann, *Public Opinion* (New York: Macmillan, 1922).

18. Thomas E. Patterson and Robert D. McClure, *The Unseeing Eye: The Myth of Television Power in National Elections* (New York: Putman's, 1976).

19. Arthur H. Miller, Edie N. Goldenberg, and Lutz Erbring, "Type-Set Politics: Impact of Newspapers on Public Confidence," *American Political Science Review* 73 (March 1979): 67–84.

20. Blumler and McLeod, "Communication and Voter Turnout"; Steven H. Chaffee and Sun Yuel Choe, "Time of Decision and Media Use During the Ford-Carter Campaign," *Public Opinion Quarterly* 44 (Spring 1980): 53–69.

21. For example, Steven H. Chaffee, L. Scott Ward, and Leonard P. Tipton, "Mass Communication and Political Socialization," *Journalism Quarterly* 47 (Winter 1970): 647–59.

22. John C. Wahlke, "Pre-Behavioralism in Political Science," *American Political Science Review* 73 (March 1979): 9–31.

23. Maxwell E. McCombs, "Mass Communication in Political Campaigns: Information, Gratification, and Persuasion," in *Current Perspectives in Mass Communication Research,* ed. F. Gerald Kline and Phillip J. Tichenor (Beverly Hills: Sage, 1972), pp. 187–88.

24. Colin Seymour-Ure, *The Political Impact of Mass Media* (London: Constable; Beverly Hills: Sage, 1974), p. 47.

25. Keith R. Stamm and John E. Bowes, both of the University of Washington, have perhaps been more active than most other co-orientation researchers in this area. I thank Keith Stamm for his helpful and open-minded consideration of some of the ideas expressed in this book.

26. Thomas J. Scheff, "Toward a Sociological Model of Consensus," *American Sociological Review* 32 (February 1967): 32–46; Jack M. McLeod and Steven H. Chaffee, "The Construction of Social Reality," *The Social Influence Process,* ed. James T. Tedeschi (Chicago: Aldine-Atherton, 1972).

CHAPTER 2

1. Ralph H. Turner, "Collective Behavior," in *Handbook of Modern Sociology,* ed. Robert E. L. Faris (Chicago: Rand McNally, 1964), p. 415.

2. Leila A. Sussmann, *Dear FDR: A Study of Political Letter-Writing* (Totowa, N. J.: Bedminster Press, 1963), p. 79. Perhaps because it was done under the auspices of Columbia University's Bureau of Applied Social Research, this book shares with Joseph Klapper's book (*The Effects of Mass Communication*) a simple reductionist view of public opinion. Nevertheless, the research methodology used seemed less affected by this reductionist conception than did the conclusions drawn by its author about the superiority of "scientific" polls over other forms of information about citizen attitudes.

3. Ibid., pp. 75–76.

4. Philip E. Converse, Aage R. Clausen, and Warren E. Miller, "Electoral Myth and Reality: The 1964 Election," in *Political Opinion*

and Electoral Behavior: Essays and Studies, ed. Edward C. Dreyer and Walter A. Rosenbaum (Belmont, Calif.: Wadsworth, 1966), p. 24.

5. For example, James M. Fields and Howard Schuman, "Public Beliefs about the Beliefs of the Public," *Public Opinion Quarterly* 40 (Winter 1976-77): 427–48; Hubert O'Gorman with Stephen L. Garry, "Pluralistic Ignorance—A Replication and Extension," *Public Opinion Quarterly* 40 (Winter 1976-77): 449–58; Elizabeth Noelle-Neumann, "Pluralistic Ignorance and the Spiral of Silence," *Public Opinion Quarterly* 41 (Summer 1977): 143–58.

6. This unpublished study was done by the author, his graduate assistant, Eric Belden, and members of his undergraduate public opinion class.

7. James E. Grunig and Keith R. Stamm, "Communication and Co-orientation of Collectivities," *American Behavioral Scientist* 16 (March-April 1973): 567–91.

8. Ralph K. Martin, Garrett J. O'Keefe, and Oguz B. Nayman, "Opinion, Agreement and Accuracy Between Editors and Their Readers," *Journalism Quarterly* 49 (Autumn 1972): 460–68.

9. Bruce H. Westley, "Part II: Communication Settings," *Human Communication Research* 1 (Winter 1975): 186–89.

10. Roger W. Cobb and Charles D. Elder, *Participation in American Politics: The Dynamics of Agenda-Building* (Boston: Allyn and Bacon, 1972).

11. Gerald M. Pomper, "Controls and Influence in American Elections (Even 1968)," *American Behavioral Scientist* 13 (November-December 1969): 216.

12. Paul Burstein and William Freudenberg, "Changing Public Policy: The Impact of Public Opinion, Antiwar Demonstrations, and War Costs on Senate Voting on Vietnam War Motions," *American Journal of Sociology* 84 (July 1978): 99–122.

13. James N. Rosenau has used a technique that is ideally suited to certain research purposes in the study of the influence framework: He drew large samples of actual participants rather than trying to sort out participants from general samples (see Chapter 5). However, the title of his work, *Citizenship Between Elections: An Inquiry Into the Mobilizable American* (New York: Free Press, 1974), may affirm the need to keep reminding people that the influence framework also includes campaigns. Nevertheless, Rosenau's book stands apart from most others in political science for its concern with participation in the influence framework.

14. E.g., Richard F. Carter, "Communication and Affective Relations," *Journalism Quarterly* 42 (Spring 1965): 203–12.

15. Samuel A. Stouffer, *Communism, Conformity and Civil Liberties* (New York: Doubleday, 1955).

16. See especially David Easton's work and that by Fred Greenstein. E.g., David Easten and Robert D. Hess, "The Child's Political

World," and Fred I. Greenstein, "The Significance of Party Identification," both in *Psychology and Politics,* ed. Leroy N. Rieselbach and George I. Balch. (New York: Holt, Rinehart & Winston, 1969), pp. 89–106, and p. 190, respectively.

17. See Jack M. McLeod and Garrett J. O'Keefe, "The Socialization Perspective and Communication Behavior," in *Current Perspectives in Mass Communication Research,* ed. F. Gerald Kline and Phillip J. Tichenor. (Beverly Hills: Sage, 1972), pp. 121–58.

18. Theodore M. Newcomb, Ralph H. Turner, and Philip E. Converse, *Social Psychology: The Study of Human Interaction* (New York: Holt, Rinehart & Winston, 1965), p. 54.

19. Leo Bogart, "No Opinion, Don't Know, and Maybe No Answer,"*Public Opinion Quarterly* 31 (Fall 1967): 344.

20. Newcomb, Turner, and Converse, *Social Psychology,* pp. 82–88.

21. José L. Guerrero and G. David Hughes, "An Empirical Test of the Fishbein Model," *Journalism Quarterly* 49 (Winter 1972): 684–91.

22. Milton Rokeach, "Attitude Change and Behavioral Change," *Public Opinion Quarterly* 30 (Winter 1966–67): 529–50. In Rokeach's vocabulary, an attitude toward the situation has been aroused and is being expressed, rather than the attitude toward the intended attitude object.

23. Alex S. Edelstein, "A Fresh Look at Some Stale Canards about Mass Communication" (paper presented at the annual convention of the Pacific chapter, American Association for Public Opinion Research, Asilomar, Calif., 4 March 1972).

24. Peter Grothe, "Attitude Change of American Tourists in the Soviet Union" (paper presented at the annual convention of the Pacific chapter, American Association for Public Opinion Research, Asilomar, Calif., 4 March 1972).

25. Probably the best-known evidence for this view may be found in Philip E. Converse, "The Nature of Belief Systems in Mass Publics," a 1964 report that was slightly edited and then reprinted in *Public Opinion and Politics: A Reader,* ed. William T. Crotty (New York: Holt, Rinehart & Winston, 1970), pp. 129–55.

26. For an insightful review of the debate, see W. Lance Bennett, "The Growth of Knowledge in Mass Belief Studies: An Epistemological Critique," *American Journal of Political Science* 21 (August 1977): 465–500.

27. Herbert McClosky, Paul J. Hoffmann, and Rosemary O'Hara, "Issue Conflict and Consensus among Party Leaders and Followers," *Public Opinion and Public Policy,* ed. Norman R. Luttbeg, rev. ed. (Homewood, Ill.: Dorsey Press, 1974), p. 367.

28. See, for example, an early review of the history of social psychology by Gordon W. Allport, "The Historical Background of Modern Social Psychology," in *Handbook of Social Psychology, Vol.*

1: Theory and Method, ed. Gardner Lindzey (Cambridge, Mass.: Addison-Wesley, 1954), pp. 3–54.

29. Rokeach, "Attitude Change," p. 531.

30. Allan W. Wicker, "Attitudes versus Actions: The Relationship of Verbal and Overt Behavioral Responses to Attitude Objects," *Journal of Social Issues* 25 (Autumn 1969): 75.

31. Wilbur Schramm, *Men, Messages and Media: A Look at Human Communication* (New York: Harper & Row, 1973), pp. 215–20.

32. E.g., Steven H. Chaffee and Joseph W. Lindner, "Three Processes of Value Change Without Behavioral Change," *Journal of Communication* 19 (March 1969): 30–40.

33. Rokeach, "Attitude Change," p. 533.

34. Martin Fishbein, "Attitude and the Prediction of Behavior," in *Readings in Attitude Theory and Measurement,* ed. Martin Fishbein (New York: Wiley, 1967).

35. Icek Ajzen, "Attitudinal vs. Normative Messages: An Investigation of the Differential Effects of Persuasive Communications on Behavior," *Sociometry* 34 (June 1971): 263–80.

36. On changes concerning efficacy, compare Lester W. Milbrath and M. L. Goel, *Political Participation: How and Why Do People Get Involved in Politics?* (Chicago: Rand McNally, 1977), pp. 57–61.

37. Sidney Verba, Norman H. Nie, and Jae-on Kim, *The Modes of Democratic Participation: A Cross-National Comparison* (Beverly Hills, Calif.: Sage, 1971); and Sidney Verba and Norman H. Nie, *Participation in America: Political Democracy and Social Equality* (New York: Harper & Row, 1972).

38. Sidney Verba and Norman H. Nie, "Political Participation," in Fred I. Greenstein and Nelson W. Polsby, eds., *Handbook of Political Science* (Reading, Mass.: Addison-Wesley, 1975), as cited in Milbrath and Goel, *Political Participation,* pp. 22–23.

39. Verba, Nie, and Kim, *Modes of Democratic Participation;* Milbrath and Goel, *Political Participation.*

40. Sidney Verba and Richard Brody, "Participation, Policy Preferences, and the War in Vietnam," *Public Opinion Quarterly* 34 (Fall 1970): 325–32.

41. Projected figure was adapted from data provided in the *Gallup Opinion Index,* December 1973, p. 5.

42. For $2.00, anyone can send a one-hundred word "Public-Opinion Mailgram" to a public official. A combination of telegraph with mail delivery, the service began in 1971. Western Union reported that the 450,000 messages easily set a record in their history for a single event. The service now is used extensively for lobbying purposes; source is a report by Paul E. Hood, "Dial-a-Lobby . . . Buttonholing Congress pays off for Western Union," *National Observer,* 11 May 1974, p. 8.

43. Edward C. Dreyer and Walter A. Rosenbaum, *Political Opinions and Electoral Behavior: Essays and Studies* (Belmont, Calif.: Wadsworth, 1966), pp. 382–83.

44. Norman R. Luttbeg, ed., *Public Opinion and Public Policy,* rev. ed. (Homewood, Ill.: Dorsey Press, 1974), pp. 1–10.

45. E.g., Roger Cobb, Jennie Keith Ross, and Marc Howard Ross, "Agenda Building as a Comparative Political Process," *American Political Science Review* 70 (March 1976): 126–38.

46. Peter Bachrach and Morton S. Baratz, "Decisions and Nondecisions: An Analytical Framework," *American Political Science Review* 57 (September 1963): 632–42.

CHAPTER 3

1. Walter Lippmann, *Public Opinion* (New York: MacMillan, 1922; Free Press, 1965).

2. W. I. Thomas, *The Child in America* (New York: Knopf, 1928), p. 584.

3. See, for example, Jack M. McLeod and Steven R. Chaffee, "The Construction of Social Reality," in *The Social Influence Processes,* ed. James T. Tedeschi (Chicago: Aldine-Atherton, 1972), pp. 50–99; Peter McHugh, *Defining the Situation: The Organization of Meaning in Social Interaction* (Indianapolis: Bobbs-Merrill, 1968); Edward L. Fink and Nadyne G. Edison, "Definition of the Situation and Interactional Continuity: An Experimental Analysis" (paper presented at the meeting of the International Communication Association, Portland, Ore., April 1976); Raymond L. Gordon, "Interaction Between Attitude and the Definition of the Situation in the Expression of Opinion," *American Sociological Review* 17 (February 1952): 50–58; Thomas J. Scheff, "Negotiating Reality: Notes on Power in the Assessment of Responsibility," *Social Problems* 16 (Summer 1968): 3–17.

4. Herbert Blumer, "Social Problems as Collective Behavior," *Social Problems* 18 (Winter 1971): 298–306; Ralph H. Turner, "Collective Behavior," in *Handbook of Modern Sociology,* ed. Robert E. L. Faris (Chicago: Rand McNally, 1964), pp. 397–422.

5. Monica B. Morris, "The Public Definition of a Social Movement: Women's Liberation," *Sociology and Social Research* 57 (July 1973): 526–43.

6. Murray Edelman, "Language, Myths and Rhetoric," *Society* 12, no. 5 (July/August 1975): 14–21.

7. Lippmann, *Public Opinion,* p. 12.

8. McLeod and Chaffee, "Construction of Social Reality," p. 57.

9. Kurt Lang and Gladys Engel Lang, *Collective Dynamics* (New York: Crowell, 1961), pp. 390–91.

10. Maxwell McCombs and Donald L. Shaw, "A Progress Report

on Agenda-Setting Research" (paper presented at the meeting of the Association for Education in Journalism, San Diego, Calif., August 1974), pp. 37–38.

11. NBC "Radio News," 23 October 1973.

12. Douglas A. Kneeland, *New York Times* syndicated article in the *Eugene* (Ore.) *Register-Guard,* 21 October 1973.

13. Timotsu Shibutani, *Improvised News: A Sociological Study of Rumor* (Indianapolis: Bobbs-Merrill, 1966).

14. Leon Mann, "Counting the Crowd: Effects of Editorial Policy on Estimates," *Journalism Quarterly* 51 (Summer 1974): 278–285.

15. Susan L. Johnson, "Press Interpretation of the 1968 New Hampshire Democratic Primary" (M. A. project, School of Journalism, University of Oregon, March 1972).

16. Richard M. Scammon and Ben J. Wattenberg, *The Real Majority* (New York: Coward-McCann, 1970).

17. The article appeared in the *New Yorker* and is reprinted with a new title. "The Panthers and the Press," in Edward J. Epstein, *Between Fact and Fiction: The Problem of Journalism* (New York: Random House, 1975), pp. 33–77.

18. McCombs and Shaw, "Progress Report."

19. Edelman, "Language, Myths and Rhetoric."

20. Warren Breed, "Mass Communication and Sociocultural Integration," *Social Forces* 37 (December 1958): 109–16.

21. E.g., Hillier Krieghbaum, *Pressures on the Press* (New York: Crowell, 1973).

22. Steven E. Hungerford and James B. Lemert, "Covering the Environment: A New 'Afghanistanism'?" *Journalism Quarterly* 50 (Autumn 1973): 475–81, 508.

23. David Mark Rubin and David Peter Sachs, *The Environmental Information Explosion: The Press Discovers the Environment,* vol. 2 of *Mass Media and the Environment,* 3 vols. (Stanford, Calif.: Stanford University Medical Center, 1971).

24. James B. Lemert, "Two Studies of Status Conferral," *Journalism Quarterly* 43 (Spring 1966): 25–33; idem, "Status Conferral and Topic Scope," *Journal of Communication* 19 (March 1969): 4–13; idem and Karl J. Nestvold, "Television News and Status Conferral," *Journal of Broadcasting* 14 (Fall 1970): 491–97.

25. Ellen Goodman newspaper column, "TV advertisers court government control," *Eugene* (Ore.) *Register-Guard,* 6 December 1978, p. 17A.

26. Philip Converse, "The Nature of Belief Systems in Mass Publics," in *Public Opinion and Public Policy,* ed. Norman R. Luttbeg, rev. ed. (Homewood, Ill.: Dorsey Press, 1974), pp. 300–334.

27. W. Lance Bennett, "The Growth of Knowledge in Mass Belief Studies: An Epistemological Critique," *American Journal of Political Science* 21 (August 1977): 465–500.

28. Lang and Lang, *Collective Dynamics*, p. 391.
29. David K. Berlo, James B. Lemert, and Robert J. Mertz, "Dimensions for Evaluating the Acceptability of Message Sources," *Public Opinion Quarterly* 33 (Winter 1969-70): 563–76.
30. For a lengthier expression of this argument, see James B. Lemert, "Dimensions of Source Credibility" (paper presented at the meeting of the Association for Education in Journalism, Lincoln, Neb., August 1963).
31. "A Question of Race: How Have Americans Changed?" *Gallup Opinion Index* 160 (November 1978).
32. Scammon and Wattenberg, *Real Majority*.
33. Richard L. Maullin, "Los Angeles Liberalism," *Transaction: Social Science and Modern Society* 6 (May 1971): 40–48.
34. Ibid., p. 48.
35. William J. Crotty, ed., *Public Opinion and Politics: A Reader* (New York: Holt, Rinehart & Winston, 1970), pp. 4–5.
36. I. A. Lewis, a vice president of The Roper Organization, Inc., was especially skeptical of media definitions of a widespread "Tax Revolt." See his "Tax Revolt: the California Data" (paper presented to the 34th Annual Conference of the American Association for Public Opinion Research, Buck Hill Falls, Pa., May 31-June 3, 1979). Lewis warned politicians not to base their election strategies upon the belief there is a Tax Revolt. Similar feelings were voiced by Warren Mitofsky of CBS News at the same AAPOR convention in a paper entitled, "The Tax Revolt and the 1978 Election." My own study of Oregon's November 1978 tax election showed that many votes in favor of the more moderate of two tax cut measures were cast because voters feared that, otherwise, the more severe measure would pass.
37. James McCartney, "Must the Media Be 'Used'?" *Columbia Journalism Review* 8 (Winter 1969–70): 36–41.
38. David L. Altheide and Robert P. Snow argue that media situation definitions gain their power because *other* institutions and elites have been led to "follow a media logic in the definition and solution of problems." See their *Media Logic* (Beverly Hills: Sage, 1979). This quotation is from page 236.
39. Hans Mathias Kepplinger and Herbert Roth, "Creating a Crisis: German Mass Media and Oil Supply in 1973-4," *Public Opinion Quarterly* 43 (Fall 1979): 285–96. The quoted passage is from page 295.

CHAPTER 4

1. Carl Hovland, "Reconciling Conflicting Results Derived from Experimental and Survey Studies of Attitude Change," *American Psychologist* 14 (January 1959): 8–17.
2. For example, Bernard Roshco, *Newsmaking* (Chicago: University of Chicago Press, 1975); James B. Lemert, "Craft Attitudes,

the Craft of Journalism and Spiro Agnew" (paper presented to the Western Speech Association, Portland, Ore., November 1970).

3. See especially Michael J. Robinson, "American Political Legitimacy in an Era of Electronic Journalism: Reflections on the Evening News," in *Television as a Social Force,* ed. Richard Adler (New York: Praeger/Aspen, 1975), pp. 97–139.

4. Lee Becker and Charles Whitney, "The Effects of Media Dependencies on Audience Assessment of Government" (paper presented to the Association for Education in Journalism, Seattle, Wash., August 1978); Garrett J. O'Keefe and Harold Mendelsohn, "Nonvoting: The Media's [sic] Role," in *Deviance and Mass Media,* vol. 2, ed. Charles Winick (Beverly Hills, Calif.: Sage, 1978), pp. 263–86; Garrett J. O'Keefe, "Newspaper versus Television Reliance and Political Disaffection" (paper presented to the Association for Education in Journalism, Seattle, Wash., August 1978); Jack M. McLeod, Carl R. Bybee, William D. Luetscher, and Gina M. Garramone, "Mass Communication and Voter Volatility" (paper presented to the Association for Education in Journalism, Seattle, Wash., August 1978).

5. Kurt Lang and Gladys Engel Lang, "The Mass Media and Voting," in *Reader in Public Opinion and Communication,* ed. Bernard Berelson and Morris Janowitz, 2d ed. (New York: Free Press, 1966), pp. 455–72.

6. In addition to the author, interviewers were Alan Abbey, Tony Dirksen, Scott Fitch, Glen Gibbons, Barry Hood, David Lawrence, Ronald Selin, and Ralph Thrift, graduate and undergraduate students in journalism at the University of Oregon.

7. These percentages, before New Hampshire, generally are fairly similar to those obtained nationally in a CBS/*New York Times* poll, released February 13, 1976. Their nationwide telephone survey (N of more than 1,400) obtained name recognition figures of 35 percent for Shriver, 30 percent for Jackson, 28 percent for Carter, and 16 percent for Bayh. Udall and four other Democratic contenders all were known to less than 10 percent of the sample. Their method of determining recognition of candidates was not reported, but it appears their results were obtained at roughly the same time as our pre-New Hampshire results.

8. Some 14 of the 57 Democratic Central Committee members showed positive shifts in ratings of Udall, compared to only 4 negative shifts ($p<.05$). Carter had 6 positive and 10 negative changes.

9. An essentially similar kind of argument is made at several points in James David Barber, ed., *Race for the Presidency: The Media and the Nominating Process* (Englewood Cliffs, N.J.: Prentice-Hall, 1978).

10. Committee for the Study of the American Electorate, 421 New Jersey Avenue S. E., Washington, D.C. 20003, release dated 5 September 1976.

11. Committee for the Study of the American Electorate, release dated 17 November 1976.

12. Thomas E. Patterson and Robert D. McClure, *The Unseeing Eye* (New York: Putnam's, 1976).

13. Ronald Gene Humke, Raymond L. Schmitt, and Stanley E. Grupp, "Candidates, Issues and Party in Newspaper Political Advertisements," *Journalism Quarterly* 52 (Autumn 1975): 499–504.

CHAPTER 5

1. In political science: Michael J. Robinson, "Public Affairs Television and the Growth of Political Malaise: The Case of 'The Selling of the Pentagon,'" *American Political Science Review* 70 (June 1976): 409–432; idem, "American Political Legitimacy in an Era of Electronic Journalism: Reflections on the Evening News," in *Television as a Social Force: New Approaches to TV Criticism*, ed. Richard Adler (New York: Praeger, 1975), pp. 97–139; in sociology: Herbert J. Gans, "The Famine in American Mass Communication Research: Comments on Hirsch, Tuchman and Gecas," *American Journal of Sociology* 77 (January 1972): 697–705.

2. Angus Campbell, "Has Television Reshaped Politics?" *Columbia Journalism Review* 1 (Fall 1962): 10–13; William A. Glaser, "Television and Voting Turnout," *Public Opinion Quarterly* 29 (Spring 1965): 71–86; Herbert A. Simon and Frederick Stern, "The Effect of Television upon Voting Behavior in Iowa in the 1952 Presidential Election," *American Political Science Review* 49 (June 1955): 470–77.

3. See Lester W. Milbrath, *Political Participation: How and Why Do People Get Involved in Politics?* (Chicago: Rand McNally, 1965), p. 18.

4. In fact, Milbrath's 1965 book mentions the mass media only twice in its index. Many conceptual problems in the book were corrected in Sidney Verba and Norman H. Nie, *Participation in America: Political Democracy and Social Equality* (New York: Harper & Row, 1972). However, Verba and Nie rarely treated the media as predictors of participation. The one time they did (pp. 244–47), the media served only as a surrogate of another factor termed "community identity."

5. Lester W. Milbrath and M. L. Goel, *Political Participation: How and Why Do People Get Involved in Politics?* (Chicago: Rand McNally, 1977), pp. 5–34.

6. E.g., Glaser, "Television and Voting," p. 72.

7. Carl I. Hovland, "Reconciling Conflicting Results Derived from Experimental and Survey Studies of Attitude Change," *American Psychologist* 14 (January 1959): 8–17.

8. "Germans view 'Holocaust,'" *Eugene* (Ore.) *Register-Guard*, Jan. 27, 1979, sec. A, p. 3. Rewritten by unidentifed local staff from

wire service accounts. Also see " 'Holocaust' hits home," *Broadcasting Magazine* 48, 4, p. 56.

9. Associated Press, " 'Holocaust' TV show brings in most calls," *Eugene* (Ore.) *Register-Guard,* March 2, 1979, sec. A, p. 3.

10. Charles McDowell, a reporter for the Richmond *Times Dispatch,* interviewed on National Public Radio's "All Things Considered," Jan. 19, 1980, on KLCC-FM, Eugene, Oregon.

11. The study with voters was by Jay G. Blumler and Jack M. McLeod, "Communication and Voter Turnout in Britain," (paper presented at the annual convention of the Association for Education in Journalism, Ft. Collins, Colo., August 1973. The study with television news effects on "malaise" was by political scientist Michael J. Robinson, "Public Affairs Television" and "American Political Legitimacy."

12. In fairness to these authors, I should point out that there was a brief, if somewhat vague, mention of black "organizational development" as the presumed underlying mechanism, and Salamon has written extensively elsewhere about such organizations in the South. Lester M. Salamon and Stephen Van Evera, "Fear, Apathy, and Discrimination: A Test of Three Explanations of Political Participation," *American Political Science Review* 67 (December 1973): 1288–306.

13. For example, one article formally and carefully defines all key concepts *except* "mobilization of citizen political action": Louis A. Zurcher and J. Kenneth Monts, "Political Efficacy, Political Trust, and Anti-Pornography Crusading: A Research Note," *Sociology and Social Research* 56 (January 1972): 211–20. Also see J. P. Nettl, *Political Mobilization: A Sociological Analysis of Methods and Concepts* (New York: Basic Books, 1967).

14. W. S. Robinson, "The Motivational Structure of Political Participation," *American Sociological Review* 17 (April 1972): 151–56.

15. Lester W. Milbrath, *Political Participation.* Milbrath's position was based on the findings of many other authors, including especially Donald R. Mathews and James W. Prothro, *Negroes and the New Southern Politics* (New York: Harcourt, 1962).

16. Milbrath and Goel, *Political Participation,* 2d ed.

17. Verba and Nie, *Participation in America.*

18. In fact, the two media variables—"density" of external media and "density" of media located in the community—were used as surrogates for community identity. There appeared to be little interest in the media for their own sake. See Verba and Nie, *Participation in America,* pp. 244–47.

19. Ibid., p. 126.

20. David L. Sallach, Nicholas Babchuk, and Alan Booth, "Social Involvement and Political Activity: Another View," *Social Science Quarterly* 52 (March 1972): 879–92.

21. Robert Dahl, *Who Governs? Democracy and Power in an American City* (New Haven: Yale University Press, 1961).

22. Michael Robinson, "Public Affairs Television" and "American Political Legitimacy."

23. Kurt Lang and Gladys Engel Lang, "The Mass Media and Voting," in *Reader in Public Opinion and Communication,* ed. Bernard Berelson and Morris Janowitz, 2nd ed. (New York: Free Press, 1966), pp. 455–72.

24. See, for example, Verba and Nie, *Participation in America;* Sidney Verba and Richard Brody, "Participation, Policy Preferences, and the War in Vietnam," *Public Opinion Quarterly* 34 (Fall 1970): 325–32.

25. Sidney Kraus, Dennis Davis, Gladys Engel Lang, and Kurt Lang, "Critical Events Analysis," in *Political Communication: Issues and Strategies for Research,* ed. Steven H. Chaffee, (Beverly Hills: Sage, 1975), pp. 195–216.

26. James B. Lemert and Jerome P. Larkin, "Some Reasons Why Mobilizing Information Fails to Be in Letters to the Editor," *Journalism Quarterly* 56 (Autumn 1979): 504–12.

27. Norris R. Johnson, "Television and Politicization: A Test of Competing Models," *Journalism Quarterly* 50 (Autumn 1973): 447–55, 474.

28. Blumler and McLeod, "Communication and Voter Turnout."

29. Verba and Brody, "Participation, Policy Preferences, and the War."

30. Verba and Nie, *Participation in America,* pp. 267–98.

31. Paul Perry, "A Comparison of the Voting Preferences of Likely Voters and Likely Nonvoters," *Public Opinion Quarterly* 37 (Spring 1973): 99–109.

32. Raymond E. Wolfinger, Barbara K. Wolfinger, Kenneth Prewitt, and Sheilah Rosenhack, "America's Radical Right: Politics and Ideology," in *Ideology and Discontent,* ed. David E. Apter (Glencoe, Ill.: Free Press, 1964), pp. 262–93.

33. Robert A. Stallings, "Patterns of Belief in Social Movements: Clarifications from an Analysis of Environmental Groups," *Sociological Quarterly* 14 (Autumn 1973): 465–80.

34. Bernard R. Berelson, Paul F. Lazarsfeld, and William N. McPhee, *Voting: A Study of Opinion Formation in a Presidential Campaign* (Chicago: University of Chicago Press, 1954).

35. The exception might be the special case of a poll that happened to ask the right question and happened to be brought to the attention of decision-makers. Strictly speaking, even this would not be enough, if *change* were to show: The relevant question would have had to be asked in two different surveys at two different times. And even in this

case, ordinary change would be more likely to show than minor change because only ordinary change involves a shift in sign.

36. For example, the outcome can be changed if there is a larger "pool" of former inactives on one side than the other, especially if the other had more members participating already. Another possibility is polarization and stalemate when all sides have roughly equal numbers.

37. Elihu Katz and Jacob J. Feldman, "The Debates in the Light of Research: A Survey of Surveys," in *The Process and Effects of Mass Communication,* ed. Wilbur Schramm and Donald F. Roberts, rev. ed. (Urbana: University of Illinois Press, 1974), pp. 701–53.

38. Leon Festinger, "Behavioral Support for Opinion Change," *Public Opinion Quarterly* 28 (Fall 1964): 404–17. Festinger appeared not to have been aware of some sociological and political panel studies that might have expanded his list of three. For a list of them, see Harlan Hahn, "The Political Impact of Shifting Attitudes," *Social Science Quarterly* 51 (December 1970): 730–42.

39. Festinger, "Behavioral Support," p. 414.

40. David R. Seibold, "The Attitude-Verbal Report—Overt Behavior Relationship in Communication Research: A Critique and Theoretic Reformulation" (paper presented at the annual convention of the Association for Education in Journalism, San Diego, Calif., August 1974).

41. H. Lever, "Factors Underlying Change in the South African General Election of 1970," *British Journal of Sociology* 23 (June 1972): 242.

42. Hahn, "Political Impact."

43. John Holm, Sidney Kraus, and Arthur P. Bochner, "Communication and Opinion Formation: Issues Generated by the Watergate Hearings," *Communication Research* 1 (October 1974): 373.

44. Michael J. Robinson, "The Impact of the Televised Watergate Hearings," *Journal of Communication* 24 (Spring 1974): 25.

45. *Gallup Opinion Index,* December 1973.

46. Many writers suggest that political party identification is a stronger factor in off-year congressional voting than it is in presidential elections. Republican turnout percentages historically are higher than Democratic voter turnout, especially in off-year elections. "GOP's income less than Demos' in scandal year," *Eugene* (Ore.) *Register-Guard,* 7 February 1974, sec. A, p. 7.

47. Verba and Nie, *Participation in America.*

48. A review of many of these studies may be found in Martin Fishbein and Icek Ajzen, *Belief, Attitude, Intention and Behavior: An Introduction to Theory and Research* (Reading, Mass.: Addison-Wesley, 1975).

49. Alan G. Weinstein, "Predicting Behavior from Attitudes," *Public Opinion Quarterly* 36 (Fall 1972): 355–60.

50. Jeffery Paige, "Political Orientation and Riot Participation," *American Sociological Review* 36 (October 1971): 810–20.

51. Joel D. Aberbach, "Alienation and Political Behavior," *American Political Science Review* (March 1969): 86–99.

52. Zurcher and Monts, "Political Efficacy."

53. Herbert Hyman and Paul Sheatsley, "Why Information Campaigns Fail," in *The Process and Effects of Mass Communication,* ed. Wilbur Schramm and Donald F. Roberts (Urbana; University of Illinois Press, 1971), pp. 448–65.

54. See, for example, Phillip J. Tichenor, George A. Donohue, and Clarice N. Olien, "Mass Media and Differential Growth in Knowledge," *Public Opinion Quarterly* 34 (Summer 1970): 158–70.

55. David L. Paletz, Peggy Reichert, and Barbara McIntyre, "How the Media Support Local Government Authority," *Public Opinion Quarterly* 35 (Spring 1971): 80–92.

56. Samuel J. Eldersveld, "Experimental Propaganda Techniques and Voting Behavior," *American Political Science Review* 50 (March 1956): 154–65.

57. Samuel H. Barnes, "Participation, Education, and Political Competence: Evidence from a Sample of Italian Socialists," *American Political Science Review* 60 (June 1966): 348–53.

58. Lester W. Milbrath and M. L. Goel, *Political Participation,* 2d ed.

59. Robert Dahl, *Who Governs? Democracy and Power in an American City.*

60. Arthur T. Hadley, *The Empty Polling Booth* (Englewood Cliffs, N.J.: Prentice-Hall, 1978).

61. James B. Lemert and Jerome P. Larkin, "Some Reasons Why Mobilizing Information Fails to Be in Letters to the Editor."

62. E.g., Edward N. Muller, "Cross-National Dimensions of Political Competence," *American Political Science Review* 64 (September 1970): 792–809.

63. James B. Lemert and Jerome P. Larkin, "Some Reasons Why Mobilizing Information Fails to Be in Letters to the Editor."

64. Edward N. Muller, "Cross-National Dimensions of Political Competence."

65. Kenneth M. Jackson, "Powerlessness Conceptualization for Political Knowledge Prediction," hectographed, Communication Research Center, University of Washington, March 1969.

66. The letters to the editor study with Larkin strongly showed a relation between efficacy and knowledge of influence strategies; a study in progress at this time shows strong relations between efficacy, knowledge of strategies, *and* knowledge of four public affairs information items: two local issues and two international issues.

67. Charles K. Atkin, John Galloway, and Oguz B. Nayman, "News

234 / NOTES

Media Exposure, Political Knowledge and Campaign Interest," *Journalism Quarterly* 53 (Summer 1976): 231–37.

68. B. K. L. Genova, "Testing an Interest Model of the Knowledge Gap Phenomena," (Ph.D. diss., Michigan State University, 1975).

69. E.g., Angus Campbell, Gerald Gurin, and Warren E. Miller, *The Voter Decides* (Evanston, Ill.: Row, Peterson, 1954); Angus Campbell, Philip E. Converse, Warren E. Miller, and Donald F. Stokes, *The American Voter* (New York: Wiley, 1960).

70. Phillip J. Tichenor, Jane M. Rodenkirchen, Clarice N. Olien, and George A. Donohue, "Community Issues, Conflict, and Public Affairs Knowledge," in *New Models for Mass Communication Research*, ed. Peter Clarke (Beverly Hills: Sage, 1973), pp. 45–79.

71. Peter Bachrach, *The Theory of Democratic Elitism: A Critique* (Boston: Little, Brown, 1967).

72. The Center for Policy Studies/Survey Research Center at the University of Michigan. This development roughly coincides with the strengthening of the center's cooperative ties with communication researchers at the University of Michigan.

73. Richard F. Carter et al., *The Structure and Process of School-Community Relations*, vols. 1–5 (Stanford, Calif.: School of Education, Stanford University, 1966).

74. Donald Kenny, "A Functional Analysis of Citizens' Committees During School Financial Elections" (Doctoral diss., Stanford University, School of Education, 1961).

75. For a list of their mass communication variables, see Richard F. Carter, Lee Ruggels, and Richard F. Olson, *The Structure and Process of School-Community Relations, vol. 3* (Stanford, Calif.: Stanford University, School of Education, 30 June 1966).

76. Ana Barbic, "Participation or Escape?" *Journal of Communication* 26 (Spring 1976): 36–42.

77. Paul F. Lazarsfeld and Robert K. Merton, "Mass Communication, Popular Taste, and Organized Social Action," in *The Process and Effects of Mass Communication*, ed. Wilbur Schramm and Donald F. Roberts, rev. ed., (Urbana: University of Illinois Press, 1971), pp. 554–78.

78. Paletz, Reichert, and McIntyre, "How the Media Support."

79. A test of newspaper effects on efficacy recently appeared in the *American Political Science Review*. Another improvement represented by this study was a long-overdue reconceptualization of the efficacy measure. Arthur H. Miller, Edie N. Goldenberg and Lutz Erbring, "Type-Set Politics: Impact of Newspapers on Public Confidence," *American Political Science Review* 73 (March 1979): 67–84.

CHAPTER 6

1. *The Collision of Mind with Mind: The Story of Bowman Retreats*

(Eugene: University of Oregon Office of Development, September 1974).

2. The mill is owned by Western Kraft Corporation of Portland, Oregon.

3. E.g., Joseph T. Klapper, *The Effects of Mass Communication* (New York: Free Press, 1960).

4. Freedom of Information Center, *Fairness in TV News*, report no. 235 (University of Missouri School of Journalism, January 1970), p. 1.

5. Dennis T. Lowry, "Agnew and the Network TV News: A Before/After Content Analysis" *Journalism Quarterly* 48 (Summer 1971): 205–10.

6. Subscription circular, *The Environmental Action Bulletin*, Emmaus, Pa. (n.d.). The chart was reprinted from the magazine and used in its subscription circular, from which it is reprinted again with the editors' permission.

7. "Oregon solons report ad campaign supporting SST backfired," *Eugene* (Ore.) *Register-Guard*, 25 March 1971, sec. C, p. 3.

8. Advertisement, *Eugene* (Ore.) *Register-Guard*, 10 March 1971, sec. B, p. 5. Permission to reprint this ad was refused by the Portland-area man who was listed as chairman of the Oregon Committee for an American SST. In his letter to me, he asked also that his name not be used, and claimed that he had had nothing to do with the preparation and placement of the ad, which was arranged from outside the state.

9. The Oregon Bend-in-the-River Council and the "Living Room Referendum," both partly the brain-children of author Ken Kesey.

10. Steven E. Hungerford and James B. Lemert, "Covering the Environment: A New 'Afghanistanism'?" *Journalism Quarterly* 50 (Autumn 1973): 475–481, 508.

11. James B. Lemert, Barry N. Mitzman, Michael A. Seither, Roxana H. Cook, and Regina M. O'Neil, "Journalists and Mobilizing Information," *Journalism Quarterly* 54 (Winter 1977): 721–26.

12. David M. Rubin and Stephen Landers, "National Exposure and Local Cover-up: A Case Study," *Columbia Journalism Review* 8 (Summer 1969): 17–23.

13. Information jointly gathered by the author and *Eugene* (Ore.) *Register-Guard*.

14. More than seven-hundred calls were "officially" recorded, since these callers fulfilled a requirement by giving both a name and an address. An estimated three-hundred additional calls were received but not tape-recorded, according to LRAPA spokesman David Gemma, who said many callers uttered a brief curse against "the people who allowed this to happen," and then hung up. They may have been operating on the mistaken assumption that LRAPA authorized that day's field burning.

15. The LRAPA office number was listed in the directory, but it

was no longer correct. If a person dialed that number, the new office number was provided, but this new number would *not* connect the caller with the "complaint" line.

16. James B. Lemert, "Craft Attitudes, the Craft of Journalism, and Spiro Agnew" (paper presented at the annual meeting of the Western Speech Association Convention, Portland, Ore., November 1970).

17. "No $90 wages of sin for these newlyweds," *Eugene* (Ore.) *Register-Guard,* 13 July 1974, sec. A, p. 1.

18. "Benefits were cut: Offers pour in to elderly pair," *Eugene* (Ore.) *Register-Guard,* 15 July 1974, sec. A, p. 1.

19. Hungerford and Lemert, "Covering the Environment: A New 'Afghanistanism'?"

20. Lemert, Mitzman, Seither, Cook, and O'Neil, "Journalists and Mobilizing Information."

21. The students involved with me in this research were Leo Mann, Michael L. Gaynes, and Gary L. Stigall. Each student did a separate paper on one aspect of the problem of MI in broadcasting as a term project in Journalism and Public Opinion. Their results are summarized in the next three paragraphs.

22. Ralph R. Thrift, Jr., "How Chain Ownership Affects Editorial Vigor of Newspapers," *Journalism Quarterly* 54 (Summer 1977): 327–31.

23. Interviews were done by Jackman Wilson as part of his under-graduate public opinion paper in May 1976 (editors' quotes are from Wilson's report).

24. "First things first," editorial, *Eugene* (Ore.) *Register-Guard,* 6 May 1976, sec. A, p. 14.

25. "Illegal Aliens," *The Oregonian* (Portland, Ore.), 3 May 1976, sec. A, p. 18.

26. Ben H. Bagdikian, "Oracles and Their Audiences," *Columbia Journalism Review* 5, no. 4 (Winter 1966/1967): 22–29; Bernard C. Cohen, *The Press and Foreign Policy* (Princeton: Princeton University Press, 1963).

27. James B. Lemert and Jerome P. Larkin, "Some Reasons Why Mobilizing Information Fails to Be in Letters to the Editor," *Journalism Quarterly* 56 (Autumn 1979): 504–12.

28. Roxana H. Cook, "Mobilizing Information and Free Speech Messages" (unpublished paper, School of Journalism, University of Oregon, August 1978).

29. Ed Jacobson, student paper in public opinion class, June 1977. Jacobson did this comparison of a week's political ads and commercial ads in a single newspaper. Obviously, like many of the small studies reported here, these results are suggestive but preliminary.

30. Frank Parkin, *Middle Class Radicalism* (Manchester, Eng.: University of Manchester Press, 1968).

31. Donald K. Coe to James B. Lemert, 5 April 1973. I thank Mr. Coe for permission to quote his letter and to reprint the editorial.

32. Dorwin Cartwright, "Some Principles of Mass Persuasion: Selected Findings of Research on the Sale of U.S. War Bonds," in *The Process and Effects of Mass Communication,* ed. Wilbur Schramm and Donald F. Roberts (Urbana: University of Illinois Press, 1971), pp. 426–47.

33. Ibid., pp. 443–44.

34. Paul F. Lazarsfeld and Robert K. Merton, "Mass Communication, Popular Taste, and Organized Social Action," in *The Process and Effects of Mass Communication,* ed. Wilbur Schramm and Donald F. Roberts (Urbana: University of Illinois Press, 1971), pp. 554–78.

35. James Wilson, "Water they drink hazardous to health," *Eugene* (Ore.) *Register-Guard,* 18 August 1974, sec. D, p. 15.

36. "Horsemeat market owner can't keep up with demand," *Eugene* (Ore.) *Register-Guard,* 27 March 1973, sec. A, p. 5.

37. "Mail Call for Teheran," *Newsweek,* December 24, 1979, p. 25.

38. "Chicago poll about 6 to 1 to impeach," *Eugene* (Ore.) *Register-Guard,* 29 October 1973, sec. A, p. 4.

39. Henny Willis, "Over 80% in poll favor impeachment or resignation," *Eugene* (Ore.) *Register-Guard,* 30 October 1973, sec. A, p. 1.

40. "Plebiscite Trend is Steady," *National Observer,* 8 December 1973, p. 2.

41. Total paid circulation at the end of 1973. Source was *Newspaper Rates and Data,* Standard Rate and Data Service, Inc., 12 April 1974.

42. Report on the CBS Morning News, 21 June 1978; Associated Press, "Speaker not amused by cartoon coupons," *Eugene* (Ore.) *Register-Guard,* 22 June 1978, sec. C, p. 6.

43. Report on the NBC Evening News, February 26, 1978; *New York Times* News Service, "10,000 phone nuclear agency over radiation," *Eugene* (Ore.) *Register-Guard,* 26 February 1978, sec. C, p. 3.

44. Telephone conversation with Molly Geraghty, Boston, 16 July 1974. I thank Ms. Geraghty for her informative discussion of the participation figures in this conversation.

45. E. E. Schattschneider, *The Semi-Sovereign People: A Realist's View of Democracy in America* (New York: Holt, Rinehart & Winston, 1960).

46. Peter Bachrach, *The Theory of Democratic Elitism: A Critique* (Boston: Little, Brown, 1967).

47. Leila A. Sussmann, *Dear FDR: A Study of Political Letter-Writing* (Totowa, N.J.: Bedminster Press, 1963).

48. Anthony Downs, *An Economic Theory of Democracy* (New York: Harper's, 1957).

49. Peter Bachrach and Morton S. Baratz, "Decisions and Nondecisions: An Analytical Framework," *American Political Science Review* 57 (September 1963): 632–42.

50. Siegwart Lindenberg, "The Cognitive Dimension of Depersonalization: A Content Analysis of *The New York Times*" (paper pre-

sented at the annual meeting of the American Sociological Association, New Orleans, 1972).

51. Edwin Emery, *The Press and America*, 2d ed. (Englewood Cliffs, N.J.: Prentice-Hall, 1962), p. 120.

52. Another student project, this one by Jim Russell.

53. Francis Pollock, "Towards Protecting Consumers," *Columbia Journalism Review* 12 (March-April 1974): 22–25.

CHAPTER 7

1. R. Harrison Wagner, "The Concept of Power and the Study of Politics," in *Political Power: A Reader in Theory and Research*, ed. Roderick Bell, David V. Edwards, and R. Harrison Wagner (New York: Free Press, 1969), p. 11.

2. Robert Bierstedt, "An Analysis of Social Power," *American Sociological Review* 15, no. 6 (December 1950): 730.

3. Nelson Polsby, "How to Study Community Power: The Pluralistic Alternative," in Bell, Edwards, and Wagner, *Political Power*, pp. 31–35.

4. E.g., David Kovenock, "Influence in the U.S. House of Representatives: A Statistical Analysis of Committees," *American Politics Quarterly* 1 (October 1973): 407–64.

5. E.g., Henry Teune, "Legislative Attitudes toward Interest Groups," *Midwest Journal of Political Science* 11 (1967): 489–504.

6. Jack H. Nagel, *The Descriptive Analysis of Power* (New Haven: Yale University Press, 1975).

7. Warren E. Miller and Donald E. Stokes, "Constituency Influence in Congress," *American Political Science Review* 67 (March 1963): 45–56.

8. See especially James S. Coleman, *Power and the Structure of Society* (New York: Norton, 1974), pp. 78–80; George A. Donohue, Philip J. Tichenor, and Clarice N. Olien, "Mass Media Functions, Knowledge and Social Control," *Journalism Quarterly* 50 (Winter 1973): 652–59.

9. "FDA staff charges suppression," *Eugene* (Ore.) *Register-Guard*, 16 August 1974, sec. A, p. 3.

10. Murray Kempton, "The Way Things Are," *The Progressive*, August 1978, p. 32; CBS News with Walter Cronkite, May 15, 1978.

11. David Mark Rubin and David Peter Sachs, *The Environmental Information Explosion: The Press Discovers the Environment*, vol. 2 of *Mass Media and the Environment*, 3 vols. (Stanford, Calif.: Stanford University Medical Center, 1971).

12. Kenneth Prewitt, "Political Ambitions, Volunteerism, and Electoral Accountability," *American Political Science Review* 64 (March 1970): 5–17.

13. Roger W. Cobb and Charles D. Elder, *Participation in American Politics: The Dynamics of Agenda Building* (Baltimore: Johns Hopkins Press, 1975).

14. James B. Lemert, "Craft Attitudes, the Craft of Journalism and Spiro Agnew" (paper presented at the Western Speech Association conference, Portland, Ore., November 1970).

15. David L. Schwantes, "Media Accessibility as a Function of Source Group Identity" (M.A. thesis, School of Journalism, University of Oregon, 1977); see also David L. Schwantes and James B. Lemert, "Media Access as a Function of Source-Group Identity," *Journalism Quarterly* 55 (Winter 1978): 722–55.

16. E.g., David L. Paletz, Peggy Reichert, and Barbara McIntyre, "How the Media Support Local Government Authority," *Public Opinion Quarterly* 35 (Spring 1971): 80–92; also see Jerome Barron, *Fredom of the Press for Whom? The Right of Access to Mass Media* (Bloomington: Indiana University Press, 1973).

17. Bernard Roshco, *Newsmaking* (Chicago: University of Chicago Press, 1975), p. 94.

18. Sen. William Proxmire, "The Donahue Program," March 1, 1979.

19. Paul F. Lazarsfeld and Robert K. Merton, "Mass Communication, Popular Taste, and Organized Social Action," in *The Process and Effects of Mass Communication,* ed. Wilbur Schramm and Donald F. Roberts, rev. ed. (Urbana: University of Illinois Press, 1974), pp. 562–64.

20. Hillier Krieghbaum, *Pressures on the Press* (New York: Crowell, 1973).

21. See especially Peter Bachrach and Morton S. Baratz, "Decisions and Nondecisions: An Analytical Framework," *American Political Science Review* 57 (September 1963): 632–42; and idem, *Power and Poverty: Theory and Practice* (New York: Oxford University Press, 1970).

22. Robert Lane, *Political Life* (New York: Free Press, 1959), p. 261.

23. E. E. Schattschneider, *The Semisovereign People* (New York: Holt, Rinehart & Winston, 1960).

24. Lester W. Milbrath, *The Washington Lobbyists* (Chicago: Rand McNally, 1963).

25. Mike Evers, "Pressure Groups and Sex Education" (Freedom of Information Center Report no. 241, School of Journalism, University of Missouri, May 1970).

26. Robert Lane, *Political Life.*

27. See especially Cobb and Elder, *Participation in American Politics.*

28. Everette E. Dennis and William L. Rivers, *Other Voices* (San Francisco: Canfield Press, 1974), pp. 70–80.

29. As quoted in "The New Machines," *Newsweek,* 6 November 1978, p. 53.

30. Willmoore Kendall and George W. Carey, "The 'Intensity' Problem and Democratic Theory," *American Political Science Review* 62 (March 1968): 5–24.

31. Gabriel Hauge, "Everybody's Special Interest," *Newsweek,* 15 December 1975, p. 19. Hauge, chairman of the board of Manufacturers Hanover Trust Co., was writing for *Newsweek's* "My Turn" column.

32. David Shaw, "Political Polls: How to Avoid the Distortions," *Los Angeles Times,* 3 January 1975, sec. 1, p. 1.

33. G. R. Boynton, Samuel C. Patterson, and Ronald D. Hedlund, "The Missing Links in Legislative Politics: Attentive Constituents," *Journal of Politics* 31 (August 1969): 700–721.

34. V. O. Key, Jr., *Public Opinion and American Democracy* (New York: Knopf, 1961), especially Chapter 20.

35. David Paul Nord, "The FCC, Educational Broadcasting, and Political Interest Group Activity," *Journal of Broadcasting* 22 (Summer 1978): 321–37.

36. Harmon Zeigler, Harvey J. Tucker, and L. A. Wilson II, *Communication and Decision-Making in American Public Education: A Longitudinal and Comparative Study* (Center for Educational Policy and Management, University of Oregon, June 1976).

37. Gary C. Jacobson, "The Impact of Broadcast Campaigning on Electoral Outcomes," *Journal of Politics* 37 (August 1975): 769–93.

38. Gary C. Jacobson, "The Effects of Campaign Spending in Congressional Elections," *American Political Science Review* 72 (June 1978): 469–91.

39. Report by Jack Perkins, NBC Evening News, November 2, 1978.

40. Delmer Dunn, *Financing Presidential Campaigns* (Washington: Brookings Institution, 1972).

41. David Adamany, *Financing Politics: Recent Wisconsin Elections* (Madison: University of Wisconsin Press, 1969).

42. V. O. Key, *Public Opinion and American Democracy,* especially Chapter 20.

43. Report by Bruce Morton, CBS Morning News, September 28, 1978. The figures at that time were $2.1 million given by the two political parties and $10.5 million contributed by PACs.

44. "AMA biggest spender on political scene," *Eugene* (Ore.) *Register-Guard,* 16 January 1976, sec. E, p. 11.

45. "Claims special interests gaining ground. Solons call for public

campaign financing," *Eugene* (Ore.) *Register-Guard* 16 December 1976, sec. A, p. 17.

46. David Adamany, "Money, Politics, and Democracy: A Review Essay," *American Political Science Review* 71 (March 1977): 289–304.

47. Krieghbaum, *Pressures on the Press.*

48. Eric Paul Veblen, "Newspaper Impact in Election Campaigns: The Case of Two New England States" (Ph.D. diss., Political Science, Yale University, 1969).

49. NBC "Radio News" report, 9:00 A.M. Pacific Daylight Time, 24 August 1977, KUGN Radio, Eugene, Ore.

50. See James B. Lemert, "Craft Attitudes."

51. See both Bachrach and Baratz, *Power and Poverty,* p. 46, and the productive methodological and conceptual suggestions for non-decision research in Chapter 5 of Andrew S. McFarland, *Power and Leadership in Pluralist Systems* (Stanford: Stanford University Press, 1969), pp. 70–92.

52. Warren Breed, "Mass Communication and Sociocultural Integration," *Social Forces* 37 (December 1958): 109–116; Paletz, Reichert, and McIntyre, "How the Media Support"; and Steven E. Hungerford and James B. Lemert, "Covering the Environment: A New 'Afghanistanism'?" *Journalism Quarterly* 50 (Autumn 1973): 475–81, 508.

CHAPTER 8

1. V. O. Key, Jr., "Public Opinion and the Decay of Democracy," *Virginia Quarterly Review* (Autumn 1961): 490.

2. Robert S. Erikson and Norman R. Luttbeg, *American Public Opinion: Its Origins, Content, and Impact* (New York: Wiley, 1973), p. 282.

3. Warren E. Miller and Donald E. Stokes, "Constituency Influence in Congress," *American Political Science Review* 67 (March 1963): 45–56.

4. The first was done in 1971 by members of one of my public opinion classes; the second, done in 1972, was reported in Donald T. Cundy, "Can Representatives Represent?" a Ph.D. prelim. paper for the Department of Political Science, University of Oregon, June 1973; the last was done in 1975 and is reported in Lillian Claire Wilkins, "The Missing Linkage: Public Opinion and the 1975 Oregon Legislature" (M.A. thesis, University of Oregon School of Journalism, December 1976).

5. Compare Martin Kriesberg, "What Congressmen and Administrators Think of the Polls," *Public Opinion Quarterly* 9 (Fall 1945):

333–37, with Erikson and Luttbeg, *American Public Opinion*, p. 268.

6. Eugene Declercq, "The Use of Polling in Congressional Campaigns," *Public Opinion Quarterly* 42 (Summer 1978): 247–58.

7. Wilkins, "The Missing Linkage," pp. 66–67.

8. Personal communication with William Cohen of Maine and a former member of the House of Representatives who did not wish to be identified.

9. Roger H. Davidson, *The Role of the Congressman* (New York: Pegasus, 1969), pp. 128–30.

10. E.g., Wilkins, "The Missing Linkage."

11. Exceptions would include two studies of U.S. presidents: Leila Sussmann, *Dear FDR: A Study of Political Letter-Writing* (Totowa, N.J.: Bedminster Press, 1963); and Doris A. Graber, *Public Opinion, the President, and Foreign Policy* (New York: Holt, Rinehart & Winston, 1968).

12. Bryan D. Jones, Saadia R. Greenberg, Clifford Kaufman, and Joseph Drew, "Bureaucratic Response to Citizen-Initiated Contacts: Environmental Enforcement in Detroit," *American Political Science Review* 71 (March 1977): 148–65. Some coorientation studies also could be included in this small group of "bureaucratic linkage" studies.

13. James E. Grunig, "Accuracy of Communication from an External Public to Employees in a Formal Organization," *Human Communication Research* 5 (Fall 1978): 40–53.

14. Morris B. Fiorina, "The Case of the Vanishing Marginals: The Bureaucracy Did It," *American Political Science Review* 71 (March 1977), especially pp. 179–81.

15. James H. Kuklinski, "Representativeness and Elections: A Policy Analysis," *American Political Science Review* 72 (March 1978): 165–77.

16. Eugene Declerq, "The Use of Polling in Congressional Campaigns."

17. NPR, "All Things Considered," 3 February 1977. Telegrams were about 240 to 3 favorable and telephone calls ran about 240 to 50 favorable. Not surprisingly, an unnamed spokesperson said this showed the "reaction of the American public" to be favorable.

18. Michael Wheeler, *Lies, Damn Lies, and Statistics* (New York: Liveright, 1976), p. 225.

19. Miller and Stokes, "Constituency Influence."

20. Helmut Norpoth, "Explaining Party Cohesion in Congress: The Case of Shared Policy Attitudes," *American Political Science Review* 70 (December 1976): 1156–71; David R. Segal and Thomas S. Smith, "Congressional Responsibility and the Organization of Constituency Attitudes," *Social Science Quarterly* 51 (December 1970): 743–49; and Charles F. Cnudde and Donald J. McCrone, "The Linkage Between Constituency Attitudes and Congressional Voting Behavior: A Causal Model," *American Political Science Review* 60 (March 1966): 66–72.

21. See especially James Grunig and Keith Stamm, "Communication and Coorientation of Collectivities," *American Behavioral Scientist* 16 (March–April 1973): 469–99.

22. Michael D. Hesse, "A Coorientation Study of Wisconsin State Senators," *Journalism Quarterly* 53 (Winter 1976): 626–33, 660.

23. In light of the 1972 and 1976 Democratic primary campaigns, this argument probably is no longer tenable. Nevertheless, the argument was made in 1976 by Arthur T. Hadley, *The Invisible Primary* (Englewood Cliffs, N.J.: Prentice-Hall, 1976).

24. Arthur H. Vandenberg, Jr., ed., *The Private Papers of Senator Vandenberg* (Boston: Houghton Mifflin, 1952), p. 139.

25. Edward N. Muller, "The Representation of Citizens by Political Authorities: Consequences for Regime Support," *American Political Science Review* 64 (December 1970): 1149–66.

26. Miller and Stokes, "Constituency Influence."

27. See Norman R. Luttbeg, ed., *Public Opinion and Public Policy* (Homewood, Ill.: Dorsey Press, 1974).

28. See Julius Turner and Edward V. Schneier, Jr., *Party and Constituency: Pressures on Congress* (Baltimore: Johns Hopkins Press, 1970).

29. "Sex and Violence: Hollywood Fights Back," *TV Guide* 27 August 1977.

30. William J. Crotty, ed., *Public Opinion and Politics: A Reader* (New York: Holt, Rinehart & Winston, 1970), pp. 4–5.

31. "Elections: A Riddle in Punxsutawney," *Newsweek*, 18 February 1974, pp. 30–31; and "Congressional election: Demo leads by 220 votes," *Eugene* (Ore.) *Register-Guard*, 6 February 1974, sec. A, p. 5. The articles did suggest that Watergate may have played a "shadowy role," but the vote margin was too close to tell whether it did.

32. "Blue Monday for the G.O.P.," editorial, *St Louis Post-Dispatch*, 20 February 1974.

33. ABC, "Evening News," 20 February 1974.

34. For example, see "Swing Vote: Bad News for the GOP." *Newsweek*, 29 April 1974, p. 29.

35. "Packwood statement: GOP candidates want Nixon to quit" (Associated Press, New York), *Eugene* (Ore.) *Register-Guard*, 27 March 1974, sec. A, p. 4.

36. Two polls were conducted in Cincinnati after Democrat Thomas Luken's March 5 election win there. One was done by Peter D. Hart Research Associates for the Democratic National Committee, the other by the *Cincinnati Enquirer*. The postelection Michigan poll was done by a Detroit newspaper, and a preelection poll also suggested that Watergate was not foremost on voters' minds.

37. Jules Witcover, *Marathon: The Pursuit of the Presidency, 1972–1976* (New York: Viking Press, 1977).

38. See both Hesse, "A Coorientation Study," and John E. Bowes

and Keith R. Stamm, "Evaluating Communication with Public Agencies," *Public Relations Review* 1 (Summer 1975): 23–37.

39. Sussmann, *Dear FDR*.

40. Leon Mann, "Counting the Crowd: Effects of Editorial Policy on Estimates," *Journalism Quarterly* 51 (Summer 1974): 278–85.

41. Kurt Lang and Gladys Engel Lang, "The Unique Perspective of Television and Its Effect: A Pilot Study," in *The Process and Effects of Mass Communication*, ed. Wilbur Schramm and Donald F. Roberts, rev. ed. (Urbana: University of Illinois Press, 1974), pp. 169–88.

42. Byron Shafer and Richard Larson, "Did TV Create the Social Issue?" *Columbia Journalism Review* 11 (September-October 1972): 10–17.

43. Public opinion scholar Doris A. Graber has argued that to assume a single public opinion begs too many questions (Graber to James B. Lemert, June 1975). And I myself know from interviews with local public officials that several of them conceptualize public opinion in multiple-public terms. To them, there is no such single thing as "public opinion." The single-public notion may be a more common conceptualization since the arrival of polls as an institution, however.

CHAPTER 9

1. Herbert Blumer, "Public Opinion and Public Opinion Polling" (paper presented at the annual meeting of the American Sociological Society, New York City, December 1947). This paper was later printed in the *American Sociological Review* 13 (1948): 542–54 and reprinted in Daniel Katz, *Public Opinion and Propaganda* (New York: Dryden Press, 1954), pp. 70–78.

2. Theodore M. Newcomb and Julian Woodward, "Discussion," pp. 78–83 in Katz, ibid.

3. Blumer, "Public Opinion," in Katz, ibid., p. 78.

4. Mark Abrams, "The Opinion Polls and the British Election of 1970," *Public Opinion Quarterly* 34 (Fall 1970): 317–24.

5. "Trudeau Victory Fooled Pollsters" (United Press International), *Eugene* (Ore.) *Register-Guard*, 9 July 1974, sec. A, p. 1.

6. See both "1978's Wobbly Polls," *Newsweek*, 27 November 1978, pp. 32–33, and the Mary McGrory column, "Senate Loses One of Its Best," *Eugene* (Ore.) *Register-Guard*, 15 November 1978, sec. A, p. 14.

7. "The MacNeil/Lehrer Report" ("Roper Poll"), 1 November 1976. The quotation is taken from page 9 of the transcript of the program, supplied by WNET, New York (library no. 285, show no. 2041).

8. Leo Bogart, *Silent Politics: Polls and the Awareness of Public Opinion* (New York: Wiley-Interscience, 1972).

9. See, as one example among many, Sidney Verba and Richard Brody, "Participation, Policy Preferences, and the War in Vietnam," *Public Opinion Quarterly* 34 (Fall 1970): 325–32.

10. As quoted in Michael Wheeler, *Lies, Damn Lies, and Statistics: The Manipulation of Public Opinion in America* (New York: Liveright, 1976), p. 145.

11. Karen Siune and F. Gerald Kline, "Communication, Mass Political Behavior, and Mass Society," in *Political Communication: Issues and Strategies for Research*, ed. Steven H. Chaffee (Beverly Hills: Sage, 1975), p. 74.

12. Leo Bogart, "No Opinion, Don't Know, and Maybe No Answer," *Public Opinion Quarterly* 31 (Fall 1967): 335–36.

13. Richard M. Scammon and Ben J. Wattenberg, *The Real Majority* (New York: Coward-McCann, 1970).

14. John W. Kingdon, *Candidates for Office: Beliefs and Strategies* (New York: Random House, 1966).

15. William H. Lucy, "Polls, Primaries, and Presidential Nominations," *Journal of Politics* 35 (November 1973): 847.

16. David Shaw, "Political Polls: How to Avoid the Distortions," *Los Angeles Times*, 3 January 1975 (as reprinted by *Los Angeles Times*, 1975); sec. 1, p. 1.

17. Arthur T. Hadley, *The Invisible Primary* (Englewood Cliffs, N. J.: Prentice-Hall, 1976).

18. E.g., Jules Witcover, *Marathon: The Pursuit of the Presidency, 1972–1976* (New York: Viking Press, 1977).

CHAPTER 10

1. This possibility is suggested by a recent study of congressional lobbyists. The researcher found that issues raised in presidential campaigns seem to affect lobbyists' tactics when the news media report these issues. Lobbyists said they had to expend more effort on influencing floor votes when this happened. See John M. Bacheller, "Lobbyists and the Legislative Process: The Impact of Environmental Constraints," *American Political Science Review* 71 (March 1977): 252–63.

2. Kurt Lang and Gladys Engel Lang, "The Mass Media and Voting," in *The Process and Effects of Mass Communication*, ed. Wilbur Schramm and Donald F. Roberts, rev. ed. (Urbana: University of Illinois Press, 1974), pp. 678–700.

3. John B. Timberlake, as quoted in *Problems of Journalism: Proceedings of the American Society of Newspaper Editors, 1978* (Washington: ASNE, 1978), pp. 142–43.

Index